Listening Prayer

"If you are serious about being a friend of Christ, get *[Listening Prayer]*. Read it slowly and repeatedly, putting what she says into practice step-by-step. Then you will certainly succeed in the spiritual aspirations that are at home in the New Testament, but that most Christians only verbalize occasionally.

Beyond this, the book is profound in its theological understanding and prophetically penetrates to the core of the current 'Christian situation.' In the current and coming battle over 'spirituality'—which the institutional church has lost or will certainly lose—the chapters on 'Neognostic Listening' are essential reading for all who want to walk Christ's way."

—Dallas Willard, author of *In Search of Guidance*

"A noted minister of grace and healing and an author who writes profoundly of the things of the soul, Leanne Payne has put us all in her debt once again. . . . Help is found here for both the beginner and the mature Christian. Notes of long experience, great insight, humility, and a desire to help pervade every page. This book . . . concerns itself with the one thing that matters, the one thing that abides, and the one thing most neglected in our activistic culture."

—John H. Rodgers Jr., Trinity Episcopal School for Ministry

"Leanne Payne has given us not only a book on prayer, but a compelling invitation to pray. This is a rare and wonderful book that shows, not just tells about, the various faces of prayer. Many will be led to healing and spiritual depth as they come to experience the embrace of God and genuinely meet the God of love, beauty, forgiveness and restoring strength shown in these pages."

—James C. Wilhoit, Wheaton College

Listening Prayer

Learning to Hear God's Voice and Keep a Prayer Journal

Leanne Payne

A Hamewith Book

 Baker Books

A Division of Baker Book House Co
Grand Rapids, Michigan 49516

© 1994 by Leanne Payne

Published by Hamewith Books
a division of Baker Book House Company
P.O. Box 6287, Grand Rapids, MI 49516-6287

Printed in the United States of America

Library of Congress Cataloging-in-Publication Data

Payne, Leanne.
    Listening prayer : learning to hear God's voice and keep a prayer journal /
Leanne Payne.
        p.   cm.
    Includes bibliographical references.
    ISBN 0-8010-7139-9
    1. Prayer. 2. Spiritual journals—Authorship. 3. Spiritual life—Christianity.
I. Title.
    BV215.L33   1994
    248.3—dc20   94-37753

To Sara

Courageous lover of truth,

Emboldened by Christ to pioneer
pathways to truth and freedom
for beloved others.

This is what the LORD says, he who made the earth, the LORD who formed it and established it—the LORD is his name: "Call to me and I will answer you and tell you great and unsearchable things you do not know."

—Jeremiah 33:2–3

My sheep listen to my voice; I know them, and they follow me. I give them eternal life, and they shall never perish; no one can snatch them out of my hand. My Father, who has given them to me, is greater than all; no one can snatch them out of my Father's hand. I and the Father are one.

—Jesus, John 10:27–30

The prayer preceding all prayers is "May it be the real I who speaks. May it be the real Thou that I speak to."

—C. S. Lewis,
Letters to Malcolm: Chiefly on Prayer

Contents

Acknowledgments

The first time I shared the form in which I keep a prayer journal was with my Milwaukee prayer partners: Lucy Smith, Connie Boerner, and Patsy Casey. Ever after, they encouraged me to write out the "How-to's" for others as well. Once the writing project was started, these incredible women faithfully prayed not only for the book as it was forming, but for the souls who would eventually read it! For these and reasons too many to count, I thank these precious ones.

During the writing of this book, the Revs. William and Anne Beasley, Mario Bergner, Rev. Conlee and Signa Bodishbaugh, John Fawcett, and Valerie McIntyre, besides praying for and with me, have lifted heavy loads from my shoulders and encouraged me in every conceivable way. Their vision and enthusiasm for this book on listening prayer, through its long inception, never ceased to strengthen and bless me. Dr. Jeffrey Burke Satinover has been a special blessing to me during this time as well, and the Christ-light shining through his loving mind and heart has encouraged me in ways that may be beyond his knowing.

In their own unique and diverse ways, the same is true for each individual member who makes up the Pastoral Care Ministries prayer team. Though scattered over the United States and now on most every continent abroad, we keep the fax and long distance phone lines alive with prayer and all manner of encouragement. I am so deeply grateful for each one.

My special thanks go to Stephen Griffith who first envisioned and then set up our new Hamewith Imprint with Baker Book House, and to Amy Boucher who has not only proven to be just the right editor but a delightful one who has fit right into the work of prayer to which God has called us.

Preface

I awakened early this Christmas morn, got my first cup of coffee, and came with great anticipation to prayer. Talking to God and listening to Him is the making of every day, but it is especially momentous on the great feast days such as Christmas, and at times of new beginnings such as New Year's Day, birthdays, and so on. Keeping a journal that gives shape and direction to this immensely important activity seems, if possible, even more rewarding at these holiday times.

A little before 5:00 A.M. I awakened ready to pray and praise God to the strains of some of the most glorious music ever written, the Christmas hymns that reflect the church in utter awe of the incarnation. This morning, however, I found myself dull and sluggish. The coffee did not help either.

This could have bothered me. I could have settled for a sluggish time, leaving my Christmas day a good deal less than it was meant to be. I could have been tempted to "misread" the situation, overspiritualize it, and feel guilty. Or I could have been tempted to ascribe it simply to getting older! Thankfully, I did none of this. Reflecting on the blessing of living in an airtight home built for a cold, wintry climate—capable of keeping out not only the polar winds but also blocking the fresh air—I bundled up in my warmest wraps and went skipping out, praising and thanking the Lord "with my spirit and . . . with my mind" (1 Corinthians 14:15) to the banks of Lake Michigan and back.

Outside in the early, dark Christmas morning, I had the frosty, tree-lined streets all to myself. The houses, their large windows boasting Christmas trees that blinked and twinkled, were nevertheless still snugly asleep. Not a single child had yet sounded an excited alarm. The avenue was a private and lovely out-of-doors prayer closet.

I returned full of energy. The first part of my prayers, giving praise and thanksgiving to God, were special indeed. Returning home and taking my prayer journal in hand, I was now eager to continue my early morning readings and meditations on the incredible mystery of Christ's incarnation—His descent into our flesh and world, His very own creation.

Then, in the middle of journaling my "listenings" to God there came the inspiration, full-blown and mightily insistent, to write this little tome. It is not usual to start such a project on Christmas, but because the book chose this day to start birthing itself it was the only thing to do.

It is therefore with an unusual joy, amplified to almost a wild abandon at times as I hear brass and organ playing all the "glorias" of Christmas and with my hope that this book will be a special gift to you, that I begin. This book is intended to be practical and easy to use. My hope is that it will quickly usher you into a fuller prayer life.

Introduction

And thou shalt remember all the way which the
LORD thy God led thee these forty years . . .
(Deuteronomy 8:2, KJV).

Because keeping a prayer journal is so helpful and
meaningful to me, I often refer to it when speaking
or writing. And in response, people ask me to share
just *how* it is I keep one and all that goes into it.

In the past, I have been slow to respond to these requests, partly
because my own journal, with its shape and content, simply
evolved. I expected the same to happen to others who took pen
and paper in hand while in a posture of prayer with the Scriptures
before them. But this does not always happen—except perhaps
with the "writerly" types. On my discovery that some of my own
prayer-team members have struggled to put one together to no
avail, I concluded that there is something of value I am to share.

There are other reasons I have lagged, however. Keeping a
prayer journal is one of the most personal things we can ever do.
Within it are love letters between the soul and her God. As the
soul seeks to hear and obey—fallen and needy as it is—it shares
the most intimate and profound things with God. Shameful ones
too. It names and confesses its sins, repenting of them. It begs for
grace and mercy to face all of life—its joys ("Lord, help me to
stand steady under joy!"), its dry periods ("Lord, send Your gentle rains, soften the ground of my heart, cause the seed of your
word planted there to sprout and grow"), its sorrows ("Lord,

somehow turn this anguish into healing power for others"). It asks the questions it may never have the courage to bring up in this finite world, which is filled with ambiguity and fear. Because a prayer journal is such a private matter, perhaps I have unconsciously guarded mine by not analyzing it too closely or talking about it in any detail. Then too, knowing that one's prayer journal reflects one's own particular and unique needs, I have hesitated to lay out mine as a model.

The largest reason for hesitancy, however, is that it seems risky to write on listening prayer itself. It is no small thing to teach modern people to come present to God and their own hearts in this way; it has large consequences. One priest summed up the riskiness by saying, "It is much easier to preside over a graveyard than a kindergarten!" And, alas, all too often we have opted for the graveyard of legalism—or just plain twentieth-century materialism—rather than the kindergarten of freedom through walking in the Spirit. This freedom is what maturity in Christ and listening prayer are all about.

Most of us can appreciate that prayer is truly a dialogue with God. We see it modeled in the Scriptures from Genesis through Revelation, and in the lives of the saints down through the ages. But the concept of listening and seeing with the ears and eyes of our hearts is alien to modern Christians. Indeed, our very hearts are foreign to us as we suffer ignorance of their true motions and the way our souls should interact with God.[1]

As I look back into all my teaching and writing, however, I see I have already taken the risk. Listening prayer is a theme that runs through all my work. It is key in bringing the wounded out of psychological and spiritual darkness. All who need restoration of the soul listen to the wrong voices and are under the law of those voices. In order to be healed they must identify, refute, and renounce them. Then, as importantly, with their faces lifted straight up to God, they must receive the healing word God is always speaking in the place of the misleading or lying words.

Once over this hurdle, I thought about keeping this book quite impersonal by writing out a few principles and a "how-to" on setting up a journal that incorporated these principles. But, alas, that seemed so abstract and cold. Besides, I seem incapable of writing in those "reasonable" kinds of ways. *Meaning*, the principles fleshed out into the *being* and *doing* of life, starts pouring out and overcomes the neat, rational little "how-to's." I find I am sharing from my own journals—which threatens any vestigial fear of exposure yet left in my life.

The only way for me to go about this, then, is to share simply and personally on how I keep a prayer journal and how I learned to listen to God. Prayer is the most important thing I do: praise, give thanks, intercede, make personal petitions, confess my sins, forgive others, set goals with God, and listen to His response. It is the most creative "work" I do, out of which any and all other "making" flows.

PART *1*

Keeping
a Listening
Prayer Journal

The Simple How-to's

Take words with you and return to the LORD
(Hosea 14:2).

Bring whatever you see during the day into relationship with God and immerse it in eternity.
Then you will find it again in eternity as a
blessing.[1] (Mother Basilea Schlink)

*A*lthough some of the most profound experiences and insights of life come out of keeping track of what we say to God and what we hear Him say, the procedure itself is simple. And it can be an easy "organizational" tool that brings shape and order to everything else we do. The divine order and blueprint lies like a mantle over the lives of those who learn to pray effectively. Because my gifts do not lie in the direction of organization, this ordering is a lifesaver for me in terms of keeping priorities straight and doing the necessary things.

To set up your listening prayer journal, start by filling a loose-leaf binder with good-grade paper and five or six dividers. Have a supply of good pens nearby—I like black, extra-fine point, using red pens to underline. Then order your dividers as follows: Word, Praise and Thanksgiving, Intercession, Petition, Forgiveness.

The bulk of loose-leaf paper is placed after the Word divider, for here we write down those salient points of our daily conversation with God. Prayer starts with and *remains deeply rooted* in the Scriptures; the revealed Word of God quickly discerns our hearts. If our hearts are anxious, fearful, unforgiving, or sinful then they are to be immediately set right in conversation with God. If they are thankful and rejoicing in the work of the day, we will be praising and blessing the Lord, spending more time in intercession for others and personal petition. Whether in joy or in crying out of deep need and utter wretchedness; whether in times of great clarity, the light shining all around; whether in times of confusion, the darkness so oppressive we can barely squeak out our questions before God: all is brought into conversation with Him. The Word section, therefore, is for our daily dialogue with God. This listening to Him "exercises" our spiritual ears to receive the word He sends throughout the day.

The other dividers grant us easy access to prayer lists and the Scriptures and insights that not only pertain to them, but boost our faith and spur us on to prayer. These lists evolve naturally out of our journaling as we receive insight on not only for whom and what to pray but *how* to pray. The Lord yearns to grant us "the Spirit of wisdom and revelation" (Ephesians 1:17) as we continue in prayer. We need only to ask for it. In this way He builds on the previous insights He has given us. These lists often turn into veritable treasure troves. Apart from journaling these insights and listing them for easy access, however, they can become buried treasure—neglected or forgotten altogether.

With dividers and paper in your binder, your pens and pencils at hand, gather up your favorite reference Bible and begin. I am currently enjoying the New International Version Study Bible with its easy-to-use reference helps, but always have several other translations and commentaries within arm's reach.

In order to neglect no part of the Scriptures, a sound plan for daily Scripture reading is needed. I am reminded of the plight of a congregation whose pastor was especially fond of the Scriptures on angels. He therefore fed his people a steady diet of sermons about them. He was obviously presenting an unbalanced and restricted gospel message to his flock! But this story speaks of something we are all prone to if not careful—that of valuing some part of the Scripture to the exclusion of other parts. Be careful to follow a plan that fully utilizes the Old Testament as well as the New.

The plan I have used the most is from *The Book of Common Prayer*. It follows the church year: Advent, Christmas, Epiphany, Lent and the Passion of our Lord, the Feasts of the Resurrection, of Ascension, of Pentecost, and then Trinity—the full celebration of God as Father, Son, and Holy Spirit. I prefer the Scripture listings from older versions of this great classic. It is also good to switch plans from time to time. At present, I am enjoying a thematic plan of Scripture reading, *Daily Light from the Bible*.[2] It employs the King James translation; I read the Scriptures in the NIV as well. This double reading of the same texts has proven to be a blessing, for I grew up with the King James and its archaic language. The comparison of words and passages yields wondrous insight and meaning.

Besides the Scripture readings, I keep several of the great devotional writers' books close at hand. Their meditations on the Scriptures are short and mostly topical, and rarely fail to stimulate. An ancient classic by Thomas à Kempis, *The Imitation of Christ*, and later ones by F. B. Meyer, *Our Daily Walk*, and Oswald Chambers, *My Utmost For His Highest*, are longtime favorites. There are other devotional classics, however, that I simply cannot imagine being without.

Daily Prayer Outline

As a guide for daily prayer, you may want to type the following out on strong, durable paper and place at the front of your journal:

Daily Prayer Outline

I. Meditation on the Scriptures (listening to God through His written word)

II. Praise and Thanksgiving: "Our Father, who art in heaven, hallowed be thy Name."

   III. Intercession: "Thy kingdom come, thy will be done, on earth as it is in heaven."

   IV. Personal Petitions: "Give us this day our daily bread."

   V. Repentance and Forgiveness Prayers: "And forgive us our trespasses, as we forgive those who trespass against us."

   VI. A full committal of ourselves and our day to God: "And lead us not into temptation, but deliver us from evil. For thine is the kingdom, and the power, and the glory, for ever and ever. Amen."

   VII. Listening Prayer

This format for daily prayer can fit into a half-hour prayer time or a full day of prayer. Although we do not need to pray *all* these parts of prayer *every* day, or necessarily in the order given here, they hold within them the principles of a well-rounded prayer-life. This is a way of always praying the prayer Christ taught us.

Guarding Your Prayer Journal

A prayer journal is not something for anyone else's eyes, and so the matter of guarding the privacy of one's journal must be considered before beginning it. Any "open" prayer journal is unlikely to be a *real* one. Even the fear that someone will invade the privacy of its pages can keep a soul from the searching kind of honesty that should go into it.

This does not mean that we will not share large parts of our journals. Much of the content of my books first formed in my journals. But the journals are private, and those people closest to me know that my prayer journals are not to survive me. Besides the fact that these are for God's and my eyes only, if I worried about others interpreting my scribblings, or misinterpreting the multitude of hastily written insertions that only I could ever either decipher or interpret, the journals would themselves become "self-conscious." They would lose their keenest edge and value.

This is not to say, of course, that we do not listen to God together with others. There is nothing more valuable to a married couple, ministry teams, or prayer partners than coming together in listening prayer. In fact, if we are not listening to God together with God's people, we endanger our private listening. When we come together as God's people, He inhabits our praises and prayers in a greater way. Our brothers and sisters are gifted by the Spirit in ways we are not. Their speaking and listening to God sharpens ours, adding dimensions of wisdom and knowledge we would not gain otherwise.

And besides, there is the matter of our blind spots. We all have them. I thank God for prayer partners who speak light and vision into my blind spots. In this way, our listening is enhanced and judged, our idiosyncrasies revealed. Our prayer journals therefore prepare us for the kind of honesty and openness that is required for listening to God with our spouses and prayer ministry partners. Open communication with God enables us to be open, in discerning wisdom and without fear, to our brothers and sisters in Christ. Individual and corporate listening prayer are complementary one to the other. Neither are to be neglected.

The keeping of a prayer journal is so important that I begin it anew each year with a *J.J.* penciled in at the top of the title page and an *S.D.G* at the bottom. These are Latin initials that stand for the prayer, "Jesus help me," and "*Soli Deo Gloria,*" which means "to the glory of God alone." I learned this from Johann Sebastian Bach, who started and ended his musical compositions in this way. This is how a man of great genius committed his day's work to God. The fact that he wrote, as some say, the equivalent of a masterpiece per day is undoubtedly due in great part to this committal.

A Scripture passage that reveals why such a practice is so rewarding, even when we are far from being geniuses, is one that I make a part of daily prayer:

> Commit thy works unto the LORD, and thy thoughts shall be established (Proverbs 16:3, KJV).

You may want to pause now to commit your work of journaling to the Lord in some such way. We next move on to consider meditation on the Scriptures as part of listening prayer.

2

The Word

Seek ye out of the book of the Lord, and read (Isaiah 34:16, KJV).

When your words came, I ate them; and they were my joy and my heart's delight (Jeremiah 15:16).

The sacred writings . . . have power to make you wise and lead you to salvation through faith in Christ Jesus (2 Timothy 3:15, NEB).

e can never finish plumbing the depths of the treasures God has given us in the sacred writings. These, the *lectio divina* (sacred texts), are inspired by God. They are variously called the Word, the Word of God, the Word of Christ, and the Word of Truth, as well as the Book of the Lord, the Book of the Law, the Sword of the Spirit, and the Oracles of God.

Because God "chose to give us birth through the word of truth" (James 1:18), it is extremely dangerous for anyone with a low view of Scripture—or any part of it—to keep a listening prayer journal. For example, the New Testament cannot be fully understood apart from the Old, especially when one has a *low view* of the Old

Testament. The Christian faith does not stand apart from her Judaic root, but is the full flower of it.

God speaks to us in what can only be described as supernatural ways when the "imperishable seed," the Word of God, is continually hidden away in our hearts. The Holy Spirit takes the truth of the gospel of Christ from both Testaments, anoints it and seals it on our minds and hearts. To the extent our hearts are bereft of the Holy Writ, our capacity to listen and discern aright is limited. Using terms from Peter's first epistle, the "perishable" is more apt to be mixed in with the "imperishable."

> For you have been born again, not of perishable seed, but of imperishable, through the living and enduring word of God. For [and here Peter quotes from Isaiah 40:6–8],
>
> "All men are like grass,
>   and all their glory is like the flowers of the field;
> the grass withers and the flowers fall,
>   but the word of the Lord stands forever."
> And this is the word that was preached to you (1 Peter 1:22–25).

Prayer to God encompasses three vital steps. The first principle and first step in beginning to listen to God is to take the sacred texts into our very spirits and souls by meditating on them prayerfully. His word then "abides in us," burning as an inner light, and we just naturally cry out to God. This spontaneous word spoken back to God is the second step in prayer. Our forebears in the faith termed it *oratio,* which is responsive speech born of God's word aflame within us. As God speaks through His word we respond— through our own needs and through the Spirit's prodding. These responses include questions where fuller understanding is needed as well as thanksgiving, praise, and petitions for wisdom, understanding, guidance, and so on.

We then move into the third step of prayer—listening to God. Because this is so neglected today it is the main subject of the second part of this book. This listening exercises our spiritual ears, preparing us to receive from God any word He might send even in the more hectic parts of our days and lives.

We must fully appreciate the importance and centrality of the Scriptures before delving into this subject. The Bible—the revealed Word of God—is a vital part of prayer. Those with a low view of the Bible should not attempt listening prayer, for it can lead into dangerous gnostic listening. (Chapter 14 is devoted to this subject.) Some with a high view of the Scriptures, in contrast, are prone to cordon the Bible off as though it was not a vital part of prayer. These people first study the Scriptures and *then* pray. But because God's basic way of revealing Himself to us is through His Son and the Holy Scriptures that bear witness to Him, we can delight in listening to God even as we read them.[1]

Therefore, I open my prayer journal to the Word section as I reach for the Scriptures each morning. By this, I am ready for the second step in prayer, *oratio*, my response to the word God is speaking to my heart. I record my strong responses that are born both of my own need and of the Spirit's prodding. These responses concern guidance, exhortation, and the further understanding that is needed. I will return to them in the vital third step of prayer, listening to God.

Always in prayer we seek to gain the Lord's mind on the matter at hand, and for an increase of wisdom and understanding from the Spirit. Sometimes this prayer is answered right away; other times we need to wait patiently on the Lord. Turning St. Paul's prayer from Ephesians 1:17–18 into ours we can pray:

> Glorious Father, grant to me [us] the Spirit of wisdom and revelation in increasing measure, larger and larger, that I [we] may know You better. Thank You for greater knowledge of who You are and what Your will is.
>
> Open the eyes of my heart and fill them with Your light, that I might know the hope to which You have called me—my glorious inheritance; that I may know Your incomparably great power—that which You exerted in Christ when He was raised from the dead.

We do not always know why a portion of Scripture grips us so. On first coming to Christ as an adult and seeking Him with all my might, God spoke strongly to me through two verses of Isaiah 45.

In the Scriptures these words were spoken of and to the man anointed to conquer and then rebuild Jerusalem, although he did not yet serve the living God. Even so, I could not escape them; they were spoken to me as well.

> I will go before you
>   and will level the mountains,
> I will break down gates of bronze
>   and cut through bars of iron.
> I will give you the treasures of darkness,
>   riches stored in secret places,
> so that you may know that I am the LORD,
>   the God of Israel, who summons you by name (Isaiah 45:2–3).

Thirty years ago this verse was transferred to the Petition section of my journal where it remains. I still ponder deeply what "the treasures of darkness, riches stored in secret places" means for me personally. I think it relates to my understanding of the healing of the soul. By the end of my life I will probably know it has more to do with the ongoing discovery of who God is!

At the same time in my life Ezekiel's writings spoke deeply to me. This too is not usually one of the writers a young Christian opens to and remains in, but I could hardly leave his pages. Ezekiel's call in chapters two and three gripped me. I returned to them and sensed God speaking to me:

> . . . Go now to the house of Israel and speak my words to them. You are not being sent to a people of obscure speech and difficult language, but to the house of Israel—not to many peoples of obscure speech and difficult language, whose words you cannot understand. Surely if I had sent you to them, they would have listened to you. But the house of Israel is not willing to listen to you because they are not willing to listen to me, for the whole house of Israel is hardened and obstinate. But I will make you as unyielding and hardened as they are. *I will make your forehead like the hardest stone, harder than flint.* Do not be afraid of them or terrified by them, though they are a rebellious house (Ezekiel 3:4–9, italics mine).

Now I know that this struck me so strongly because my vocation was to be a prophetic one. I would be calling the people of God to repentance in such a way that they could find healing. None of this I knew then, but I did know that God's promises to Ezekiel were also promises to me. It was years before I understood my calling, but I knew early on that my forehead was like Ezekiel's, and that God had made it very hard against many of the lies to which God's people were listening.

Into this Word section I also jot down particularly meaningful meditations by others. I have journaled most every chapter of Thomas à Kempis's *The Imitation of Christ*, and only heaven will reveal the influence the works of Adam Clarke, F. B. Meyer, and R. A. Torrey have had on me.

Truth, wherever it is found, is God's truth. As I happen on it, I put it into this part of my journal where it can be "prayed." The following lines from Alexander Pope's poetry, for example, gripped and held me. I turned them into prayer as I talked to God about them:

> A little learning is a dangerous thing;
> Drink deep, or taste not the Pierian spring:
> There shallow drafts intoxicate the brain,
> And drinking largely sobers us again.

At the time I was deciding about whether or not to pursue higher education. I knew I was to "drink deeply" or not at all. I had to count the cost before the Lord before entering academe (see Luke 14:28 and following). Those lines were transferred to my Petition section where they were "prayed" for a number of years.

Another meditation that in all likelihood changed my life was John Gaynor Banks's on Thomas Traherne's words, "Desire like a God that you may be satisfied like a God":

> Desire is a mighty force, one of your most divine attributes! Whatsoever things ye desire when ye pray, believe that ye have received them and ye shall have them! See the Godlike quality of desire. For it is part of the Atomic energy of the soul. The Kingdom of Heaven within you is operated through desire. Do not quench it or crush

it or suppress it. Rather offer it to Me. Offer Me your most elementary desires, your craving for happiness, for love, for self-expression, for well-being, for success, for joy, on any level of your being—offer these freely and without shame to Me and I will transmute them so that you shall achieve release and fulfillment and complete freedom from frustration.[2]

Banks's meditation on desire somehow made particular Scriptures that have to do with desire more understandable. Such promises as Psalm 37:4, "Delight yourself in the Lord and he will give you the desires of your heart," were already prominent in my journal. Through Banks's words I proceeded to a greater understanding of the true or real self, in contrast to the old, and the need to accept it so as to desire without shame, in freedom.

In this same vein, about the same time, another "listening" of Banks's was transferred to my Petition section to be held before the Lord:

Cast aside the last vestige of unbelief and embrace that destiny which you feared to accept on account of your limitation. These handicaps are now transcended by the might of My indwelling Spirit.[3]

These were important words in my process of self-acceptance. In praying them, they played a part in chasing away my fear of the true self and the vocation to which God had called me.

The above are examples of how this main section of the prayer journal has worked for me from the beginning of my walk in the Spirit. The meditations would have long ago been lost within the pages of my journals had I not transferred them into the Intercession, Petition, and Forgiveness sections to be prayed over often. Moses asked the Jews to bind the words that come from God on their foreheads, hands, and door lintels. I never quite figured out how to do that, but in our day when pen and paper—or even computers!—are plentiful, journaling seems a much more effective way. It provides a wondrous wealth to be able to look back through the years and note not only how God so wondrously answers prayer, but how our very mode of praying has the power to change our lives.

Thomas Traherne's meditation on the cross from *Centuries of Meditations* is presently in my Word section but seems destined for one of my prayer lists because I am always having to thumb back through the dated journal entries to find it. It will find a berth close to one of my prime petitions for the ministry, one in which I ask the Lord for strength and power to lift Him and His cross high. Here it is, replete in its seventeenth-century dress (spelling):

> The Cross is the Abyss of Wonders, the Centre of Desires, the Schole of Virtues, the Hous of Wisdom, the Throne of Lov, the Theatre of Joys and the Place of Sorrows; It is the Root of Happiness, and the Gate of Heaven.

I know of no modern poet who could have penned these words. Maybe there is such a person today whose lifelong meditation on Christ's act of redeeming the world approaches the depth of understanding this seventeenth-century Anglican poet-clergyman had. But this person, like C. S. Lewis, would be something of an old dinosaur, an antiquated anomaly, in this century. Only one who has listened long and well—and with the full Judeo/Christian symbolic system intact—could have written such a thing.

The Lord's Prayer

Somewhere in these first and second steps of prayer I launch into the "Our Father" and all its aspects of prayer as the other dividers are meant to help us with. I then return to this Word section where all is brought together in the third step of prayer, that of listening for the word God is sending in response to the prayer of the day. As I receive His word, I write it in this main section of the prayer journal.

3

Praise and Thanksgiving

Shout for joy to the LORD, all the earth.
  Worship the LORD with gladness;
  come before him with joyful songs.
Know that the LORD is God.
  It is he who made us, and we are his;
  we are his people, the sheep of his pasture.
Enter his gates with thanksgiving
  and his courts with praise;
  give thanks to him and praise his name.
For the LORD is good and his love endures for-
      ever;
  his faithfulness continues through all genera-
      tions (Psalm 100).

From the noncanonical but sacred writings of the Apocrypha:

Worship is the outward expression of wisdom,
and the Lord himself inspires it (Ecclesiasticus
15:10, NEB).

Our Father, Who Art in Heaven, Hallowed Be Thy Name

In this section we write down our aids for giving praise and thanksgiving to God. "Praise is our highest exercise," F. B. Meyer reminds us.

We thank God for what He has done for us; we praise Him for what He is in Himself. In praise we come nearest to the worship of Heaven where the Angels and the Redeemed find the loftiest exercises of their faculties in ascribing praise and honour, and glory to God.[1]

To praise God and give Him thanks is to pray: "Our Father, who art in heaven, hallowed be thy Name." Therefore these first words of the prayer Christ taught us always top this section in my prayer journal.

The Mere Mechanics

Into this section of my journal go the scriptural passages, hymns, and insights from the saints of all ages that give me a boost into praise and thanksgiving when needed. When earthbound and muddled by the particulars of daily existence, these are the wings up and into the spacious—even universal and eternal—perspective that God intends His children to have.

With some exceptions, these passages differ from year to year. On New Year's Eve, I put in new pages not only to receive fresh inspirational "manna" but because the old pages are scribbled over with notes and insights. I file the old sheets away and often (sometimes years later!) reinsert them in this section. In one way or another, that which has been "much prayed" continues to be a blessing.

Besides these aids to praise, I keep a list of current answers to prayer and other unexpected bounties for which I give thanks to God. Another list reflects a custom of New Year's Eve, a time when I go through the past year's prayer journal and write down the blessings of the year. I then have quite a list of people, blessings, and answered prayer to lift in thanksgiving to God.

This Praise and Thanksgiving section helps us "continually offer to God a sacrifice of praise—the fruit of lips that confess his Name" (Hebrews 13:15). There are some special things to note about worship that I hope will add new dimensions to the way your soul comprehends the great Christian disciplines of praise and thanksgiving.

Thanksgiving

Sacrifice thank offerings to God,
    fulfill your vows to the Most High,
and call upon me in the day of trouble;
    I will deliver you, and you will honor me (Psalm 50:14–15).

In Old Testament times, thank offerings were made on special occasions. They always included praise of the LORD for His answer to prayer. Our liturgies—formal or informal—provide sufficient opportunity for us to make this necessary response only when the "making of Eucharist" is rightly taught, understood, and practiced. Besides our daily thanksgiving, we can take great bounties and answers to prayer as special "sacrifices" to Holy Communion, where we can make special gifts to God at the same time.

When our hearts are full of thanks and praise to God we need to be able to express it. At times in our healing missions the people's hearts are so full of thanksgiving to God that they must express it in some tangible way in order to receive even more from Him! On one occasion, when the people had experienced many miracles of God's presence, I was suddenly aware that we could not continue the teaching until the people were able to express a "sacrifice of praise and thanksgiving." The way that came to mind was simply to invite those who were "popping" with thanksgiving to come before the altar of the church and wave their thanks to God. Over three hundred people surged forward, each having received healing from the Lord. All were waving upraised hands before the Lord, some crying, some laughing, some leaping, all praising. And He descended even more powerfully into our midst, for He always honors true thanksgiving and praise.

A Scripture on thanksgiving that I can never omit from this Praise and Thanksgiving section is:

The Lord is near. Do not be anxious about anything, but in everything, by prayer and petition, *with thanksgiving*, present your requests to God (Philippians 4:5–6, italics mine).

Anxiety and worry can creep into our souls on little cat's paws. We need to recognize them at the outset. For that reason, I keep this passage before my eyes, because it acts as a barometer. The moment I glimpse it, I realize any anxious or worried feelings in my heart. Sometimes concern and worry is learned behavior; we may even think we *ought* to be doing it! But in this passage St. Paul actually forbids the activity. He then tells us what to do with it—a most remarkable healing solution. We can lift every care, *with thanksgiving*, up to God. There is a place for anxiety and worry to go: "Cast all your anxiety on him because he cares for you" (1 Peter 5:7).

The simple truth is that God does unending miracles to those with a thankful heart. If in reading this, you realize your heart is hardened through unthankfulness, simply confess your condition as sin. Ask him to give you a thankful heart as you continue through these remarkable scriptural mandates. You may even want to prepare a journal page of thanksgivings of your life from your first memories on through, say, seven-year segments. Ask God to show you all that you are to give thanks for even as He releases you from the early anxieties and worries your heart held as a child.

Hallowing God's Name

If we first hallow God's Name . . . we are delivered from all evil, and all things are ours.[2]

P. T. Forsyth's words are never removed from this section; they are fathomless. To truly hallow God's name is to love and praise Him aright. It is to exult in who He is and His essential nature. This exulting is an awesome activity; our minds and hearts are rightly boggled by the Object of our worship.

In praising God, the soul grows in its capacity both to love and to understand. As we command our souls, following King David's example, "Praise the Lord, O my soul!" we begin not only to hear but to clutch close to ourselves this first and greatest commandment, "Love the Lord your God with all your heart and with all your soul and with all your mind and with all your strength"

(Mark 12:30). This Scripture holds a prominent place in this Praise section as a way to ensure against any slippage of my main focus—in which case the giving of praise and thanksgiving will have suffered.

A hymn that adds immeasurably to this section of my prayer journal and hallows God's name and greatness in such a way that we appropriate it *upon and into ourselves* is the mighty hymn of St. Patrick's, "I Bind Unto Myself" (St. Patrick's Breastplate).

1. I bind unto myself today the strong Name of the Trinity, by invocation of the same, the Three in One, and One in Three.
2. I bind this day to me forever, by power of faith, Christ's Incarnation; his baptism in the Jordan river; his death on cross for my salvation; his bursting from the spiced tomb; his riding up the heavenly way; his coming at the day of doom: I bind unto myself today.
3. I bind unto myself the power of the great love of cherubim, the sweet "Well done" in judgment hour; the service of the seraphim; the confessor's faith, apostles' word, the patriarchs' prayers, the prophets' scrolls; all good deeds done unto the Lord, and purity or virgin souls.
4. I bind unto myself today the virtues of the starlit heaven, the glorious sun's life-giving ray, the whiteness of the moon at even, the flashing of the lightning free, the whirling wind's tempestuous shocks, the stable earth, the deep salt sea, around the old eternal rocks.
5. I bind unto myself today the power of God to hold and lead, his eye to watch, his might to stay, his ear to hearken to my need: the wisdom of my God to teach, his hand to guide, his shield to ward; the world of God to give me speech, his heavenly host to be my guard.
6. Christ be with me, Christ within me, Christ behind me, Christ before me, Christ beside me, Christ to win me, Christ to comfort and restore me, Christ beneath me, Christ above me, Christ in quiet, Christ in danger, Christ in hearts of all that love me, Christ in mouth of friend and stranger.
7. I bind unto myself the Name, the strong Name of the Trinity, by invocation of the same, the Three in One, and One in

Three. Of whom all nature hath creation, eternal Father, Spirit, Word: praise to the Lord of my salvation, salvation is of Christ the Lord.

Through praise, then, we the finite and created are increasingly enabled to love and trust the Infinite and Uncreated. We who are fallen and darkened are lifted up into the One who is All-Good and All-Light. We begin to cry out with the Psalmist, "In your light we see light" (Psalm 36:9). Though limited and incomplete in ourselves we grow in relationship to the All-powerful and Complete because of *incarnational reality*, God's real presence with us.

Incarnational Reality

But thou art holy, O thou that inhabitest the praises of Israel (Psalm 22:3, KJV).

We enthrone God in our praises and He condescends to inhabit them. His presence in our praise reflects the pattern of the incarnation—the way God comes to us, drawing us ever more into Himself. Quoting C. S. Lewis,

The central miracle asserted by Christians is the Incarnation. They say that God became Man. Every other miracle prepares for this, or exhibits this, or results from this. Just as every natural event is the manifestation at a particular place and moment of Nature's total character, so every particular Christian miracle manifests at a particular place and moment the character and significance of the Incarnation.[3]

God's love for us is so great that as we wait in His presence, praising Him who is perfect love, He descends anew to and into us, drawing us into Himself. We become incarnate of His love, wisdom, and righteousness. We thereby always have love to give back to Him. In "looking, longing, loving, we become like the One we vision."[4] This is a built-in incarnational principle. C. S. Lewis puts it this way:

In the Christian story God descends to reascend. He comes down; down from the heights of absolute being into time and space, down . . . to the very roots and sea-bed of the Nature he has created. But He goes down to come up again and bring the whole ruined world up with Him.[5]

In praise, as in all true prayer and worship, we clothe ourselves anew with the Lord. There is a fresh mantle of His presence. We take on God's character and take in Christ's mind. That is, we "put on the New Man" and as a happy corollary we die anew and increasingly to the "Old Man," which is the old self-in-sinful isolation. In such a union, praise is as natural as breathing.[6]

Praise with the Great Dance in Mind and Heart

The heaven and the heaven of heavens cannot contain thee (1 Kings 8:27, KJV).

We often feel inadequate in our praises. This is only to be expected because God is so very great and we are so very small and limited. All who enter freely into worship soon know what the songwriter felt when, lifted into high praise and with the full inspiration to sing a new song of praise to God, he cried out for the angels, sun, and moon to help him:

Angels help us to adore Him
Ye behold Him face to face
Sun and Moon bow down before Him
Dwellers all in time and space.[7]

In this praise we recognize the heavens as the early Jewish people understood them. God created them, they are utterly real, they are with us, and they are full of the glory of God. In Dallas Willard's words, these are "first, the heavens of the birds and the clouds (the ones closest to us), second, the heaven of the stars, and third, the heaven of the angels."[8]

As he states, this is standard material, which we do not hear much about anymore. "The church in other ages knew more of it" and had Latin phrases for these heavens.

> The Third Heaven is out of space, it is so far. . . . God is so big that this huge universe cannot contain Him. . . . We have to get over the idea of a little God flitting around in a big universe sort of waving His hands impotently and trying to get things to behave. No, it's a little universe and a God who is so big.[9]

When Jesus says, "Repent, for the kingdom of heaven is near" (Matthew 3:2), He is speaking of the reality of the highest heaven. May the Lord restore to us the hope of heaven and eternal life, a hope so vibrant that our intellects and imaginations no longer shut out the unseen realities of the heavens and earth—much less the infinitely greater God who created, sustains, and fills them with His glory. We will then love and fear God aright, and praise will issue forth from us. We will learn to celebrate our smallness. When we most keenly feel ourselves too small of a channel for the praise welling up within us, we can deliberately envision and take our place in the whole universe with all the saints and angels, and indeed with all creation throughout all time and space, as it praises its Creator and Sustainer, the all-powerful, holy, and good.

This is yet another principle in praise: when a special charism of praise is given us,[10] whether we are alone or with the worshipping congregation, we automatically cry out for the whole of creation to join us in praise of Him! When we are in a worshipping body of Christians, praising God with every instrument at hand and with full voices, we are most often lifted into high praise. These times are breathtaking with joy, light, and healing. They could not be otherwise for they are filled with God's presence. Together as we praise Him, He has so much more to inhabit. We have all the more praises on which to enthrone Him.

To summarize, we are to praise God as individuals in prayer, but as we do this, we find that we were created to praise God together with His people, and indeed, with all He has made.

Praise in the Great Congregation

> ... Four thousand are to praise the LORD with the musical instruments I have provided for that purpose (1 Chronicles 23:5).

Some people have difficulty entering into praise because they have not seen it adequately modeled in their churches. Therefore they do not have the corporate experience of such true worship. Friends of mine, ministering in a country recently released from the bondage of atheistic communism, attended a church service in one of its historic cathedrals. Within the context of the Eucharistic feast, that nation's leading musicians and their symphony orchestras led the great throng of people in giving thanks to God for their newfound liberty. My friends could hardly describe their awe at what occurred as these heartfelt praises to God ascended. They understood as never before what accrues to the people of God when He is rightly glorified by His congregation. An inner candle aflame with praise and thanksgiving to God was lit within individual hearts—and undoubtedly many today praise God whose hearts never before had the capacity to do so.

I am especially blessed with the musicians on my ministry team. Though few in number, their worship and praise of God is so *vertical* that those who never knew corporate praise before are quickly caught up into it. These newcomers to true praise soon find that the schism between head and heart begins to close and an integration of personality starts to take place.

When led by the Spirit to do so, these musicians invite other song leaders to minister with them. It is wonderful to see how their special charism in leading worship is then passed on to others. Christian leaders everywhere comment to me on the incredible blessing they bring to our conferences. Connie Boerner and Patsy Casey, who most often lead the singing, were born and reared in the Catholic church. This may account for a certain phenomenon that others besides myself have noted. Although weighed down by the big guitars they play, at times their feet barely touch the floor when leading us in praise. Until being blessed by Connie and Patsy in the leading of worship, I never understood St. Theresa and the old pictures that showed her feet off the ground in praise of God. I now have no difficulty under-standing "levitation" in its Christian form![11]

The key for successful leading in worship lies in the focus of the song leader. Not the slightest hint of the performer or "the artist" is to come through. To the degree the personal focus has shifted—from worship of God to getting the best "performance" out of the singing congregation or choir, perfection in musi-cianship, excess personal regard for reputation as a musician, and so on—the person will be unsuitable as a worship leader, no matter how greatly trained and gifted he or she may be. If the leaders themselves are not worshipping, they cannot lead oth-ers into it. Both they and the music they produce will be self-conscious, not God-conscious. There will be a deadening kind of *lateralness* that fails to help us lift our praises to God; there will not be the *verticalness*, the straight-up-ness, that makes a pathway for the Spirit's descent on our heads and hearts. Great worship leaders are first of all men and women of prayer. Like St. Theresa, they have waited and worshipped in the *presence* to the point that their hearts (if not their feet!) are no longer earth-bound.

Those who deeply desire more freedom in praise may need to seek out those who have attained it in corporate worship. I can-not imagine being without it, either in my church or in the min-istry God has entrusted to me.

The Divine Poverty

> For you know the grace of our Lord Jesus Christ, that though he was rich, yet for your sakes he became poor, so that you through his poverty might become rich (2 Corinthians 8:9).

A friend of mine, interceding for a newborn baby in the hands of a pathologically selfish mother, could not sleep for her extreme concern for the child. She had tried to procure help for the baby, but all her efforts (and seemingly even her prayers) had failed. "I had the feeling I was taken in a battle and could nearly hear the clash of the arms." She was immersed in a vicious circle of neg-ative thoughts. In her despair and crying out to God she picked up the New Testament, determining to read it until she came to the answer. She was quickly led to the account of Christ's birth and suddenly, in a profound night vision, she was taken by the Spirit to the crèche of the Infant Christ—whose very life on earth was endangered from the beginning. Looking in, she experienced for a brief moment something of the unthinkable humbling and vulnerability of the Babe who was human but also God. She understood what this impoverishment had cost Him. In grieving over the powerlessness of the newborn she was so concerned about, she was thus reminded of the Christ child's utter powerlessness, a poverty He chose to take upon Himself so that He might bear ours.

My friend was supernaturally comforted and enabled to pray in faith for the baby born into the care of an unfit mother. At this Christmastide when she and I were in the midst of other difficulties—even some strong spiritual warfare—and the going was the roughest, she would say to me in hushed tones, "Oh, just go look into the crèche; Oh, just go and look at the Baby." An intuition far beyond the ordinary of what Christ's incarnation—the central miracle of all time—*really means*, together with a tiny hint of what it had cost Him and the Father, was afforded her. She would never again be quite the same.

The incarnation of Christ is staggering. That the Creator of all worlds yearns to be our Father and gave Himself to us in such a special way in His Son—the Son whom He sent into our dark world through the womb of Mary to grow in the form and flesh of man—is something to be grasped only as the Father Himself gives the power. And we, like Mary, believe in order to receive that "Holy Thing." Then we find ourselves as extensions of the incarnation by the pouring out of God's Spirit on us. This too we can only grasp as our Father gives it to us, pouring out on us our personal Pentecost. Even then it is staggering to the imagination. That the God of all that *is* not only redeems but reveals His mysteries and presence to mite-sized people is almost more than the human mind can at first receive.

Meditating on this, I was particularly struck with these last words of Christ before His ascension:

All power is given unto me in heaven and in earth. Go ye therefore, and teach all nations, baptizing them in the name of the
Father, and of the Son, and of the Holy Ghost: Teaching them to
observe all things whatsoever I have commanded you: and, lo, I
am with you alway, even unto the end of the world (Matthew
28:18–20, KJV, emphasis mine).

The "all power" is in such contrast to the poverty and humility He knew as the divine Son who "laid aside His glory" and
"emptied Himself." His state of vulnerability never once veered
but rather culminated in the cross and His full sacrifice for our
sin. And Paul says that we should *imitate* Christ's humility, even
that our attitude should be as His:

> Who, being in very nature God, did not consider equality with God
> something to be grasped, but made himself nothing, taking the very
> nature of a servant, being made in human likeness. And being found
> in appearance as a man, he humbled himself and became obedi-
> ent to death—even death on a cross! Therefore God exalted him to
> the highest place and gave him the name that is above every name,
> that at the name of Jesus every knee should bow, in heaven and on
> earth and under the earth, and every tongue confess that Jesus
> Christ is Lord, to the glory of God the Father (Philippians 2:6–11).

The immensity of who we worship, and who we become—*real
persons*—sons and daughters of God by adoption into Christ, prepares us to look at the divine humbling and the incredible scriptural mandate to imitate it.

In Praise of the Incarnation
and the Reality That Accrues to Us

> I in them and you in me (John 17:23).

From the beginning of my adult walk with God, I have been
struck by the mystery of the birth of Christ into human form and
history, and what it means to those of us who accept Him as the
divine son of man, the Messiah and suffering servant. These seven
words of Jesus' to the Father, "I in them and you in me," express

the central thought and point of everything Christian. He came, He died, He rose again, He lives forever. All this so that we might know this two-fold incarnation of the Father in the Son and the Son centered in us, the people of God.

This Christmas season, as I continue to gaze into the crèche at the God-Baby who humbled Himself to put on our flesh, I am again reminded of the poverty of spirit, soul, and body I knew when I was separated from Christ, and from holy converse with Him. My blind and deaf state into which He descended and confronted was one of terrible vulnerability.

While in the midst of these thoughts, my heart overflowing anew with wonder and thanksgiving to Him whose acts utterly changed my life, a cousin whom I had not heard from in many years contacted me. "Leanne," she said, "I'm so amazed at what you've done," and here she faltered, saying *and from such a poor beginning.* Afraid her candor would be taken amiss, she had no idea how her words blessed me, affirming what my heart was remembering. For a moment she seemed to stand with me in awe at the God who takes broken lives and not only mends them but gives them meaning. And of course I cried out, "It was the Lord!" This was no trite reply—it welled up from a sure knowledge of what would have happened to me apart from the gift of incarnation, the gift of Christ's life in me. After talking with her, I cried out in praise to God:

O Lord, it was You
It *is* You, O Lord
I heard you in the midst of my extreme need;
I heard you say, "You have not because you ask not."

And I asked largely of You,
And You *gave.* . . .

O Lord, long ago I trusted in You, and You saved me utterly.
You took me up from the ash heap,
    a place of powerlessness and death
And made me fruitful.

You made me as a tree whose branches reach out in every direction,
Bearing Your rich fruits of all kinds and dripping healing waters,
    resins, and oils.

You caused my roots to grow down deep
To tap into hidden reserves of goodness, beauty, and life.

I put You on anew, O Lord
I cry out to You anew. . . .

Writing my prayer as fast as I could before the Lord, I continued to praise Him. A number of very special blessings and honors came my way, ones I had never expected to receive, and I cried out, "Lord, it is *all* gift. Why me, Lord, why me?" And here again I realized this joy of fruitfulness is for all who are willing to "put on Christ" and imitate Him in His poverty. It is merely what the good news of the gospel promises. It is merely answered prayer. It is for all who hear Him say, "Put Me on, receive Me into your deepest selves, walk with Me in obedience."

Putting on Christ

Clothe yourselves with the Lord Jesus Christ . . . (Romans 13:14).

There is a sense in which we "put on" the good—we wear it, as it were, allowing its benevolent influences to seep to the very core of our being. For example, if we have not yet learned to enter into praise, we can "put on" the mantle of praise.[12] Furthermore, St. Paul tells the Colossian Christians to put on all the virtues:

Therefore as God's chosen people, holy and dearly loved, clothe yourselves with compassion, kindness, humility, gentleness and patience. Bear with each other and forgive whatever grievances you may have against one another. Forgive as the Lord forgave you. And over all these virtues put on love, which binds them all together in perfect unity (Colossians 3:12–14).

We have mainly considered the gracious acts of God in our lives; His descents into our praises and into our hearts. Now we need to look briefly at what we do—the way our actions compliment grace. This has to do with the "human side" of the incarnation, with the human will and the way our choices are key in the matter of casting off the old and the diseased as well as in putting on the new and the good.[13] In fact we are commanded to "put on Christ," to "put off the old self," in effect to imitate God in whose image we are created. In faith we do these things:

> You were taught, with regard to your former way of life, to put off your old self, which is being corrupted by its deceitful desires; to be made new in the attitude of your minds; and to put on the new self, created to be like God in true righteousness and holiness (Ephesians 4:22–24).

Among Elizabeth Goudge's many extraordinary novels, a trilogy—beginning with *The Bird and the Tree*—provides a wonderful fictional example of the way this works in our lives. Two women who did not love their husbands honored their marriage vows and "put on" love for them. This occurred only after both had nearly left home and children for men with whom they thought themselves to be "in love." In doing the right thing, they not only came to love their husbands and children, but lived to see the day when they wondered why they had ever thought themselves "in love" with the men they had so compulsively and selfishly desired.

Here Miss Goudge is concerned with right action and the way it serves truth. Her women characters, being of this century, were concerned with the "truth" of their feelings. This was even to the point of rationalizing that truth would be better served if they were "honest" about their (subjective) feelings rather than about faithfulness to some (objective) moral good. Two generations of this family were strongly tempted to destroy themselves in this way. In both cases, the moral good prevailed once the women chose it; the family was saved. From the mouth of the beloved grandmother, Lucilla, who as a very young and beautiful wife came close to destroying her marriage and family, are words of wisdom meant to preserve her family when it is again threatened in such a way:

> I thought it out and I said to myself that true action is the creation of perfection while lying action is the creation of something that falls

short of the Ideal. . . . I had to struggle on by myself to the idea that if truth is the creation of perfection, then it is action and has nothing to do with feeling. And the nearest we can get to creating perfection in this world is to create good for the greatest number, for the community or the family, not just for ourselves; to create for ourselves means misery and confusion for everybody. That made me see that acting a part is not always synonymous with lying, it is far more often the best way of serving the truth. It is more truthful to act what we should feel if the community is to be well served rather than behave as we actually do feel in our selfish private feelings.[14]

C. S. Lewis points to the same lesson in its basic form when he says:

Do not waste time bothering whether you "love" your neighbor; act as if you did. As soon as we do this we find one of the great secrets. When you are behaving as if you loved someone, you will presently come to love him. If you injure someone you dislike, you will find yourself disliking him more. If you do him a good turn you will find yourself disliking him less.[15]

The deceitfulness of sin and of what eventually happens to our inner being when we "put on" and wear a vice is a horrifying thing to contemplate. These lines of Scripture picture the ugly reality perfectly: "He wore cursing as his garment; it entered into his body like water, into his bones like oil" (Psalm 109:18). Just substitute cursing with any of the vices, especially any you are aware of in your own life. "He wore anger as a garment" . . . or envy, lust, lying, hypocrisy, ambition, pride, hatred, bitterness, and so on. Whatever dark cloak we put on, its influence enters into us with dreadful octopus-like tentacles. Eventually we find our outer covering "reflecting" a deep and dreadful inner reality. We are no longer merely afflicted with anger, lust, or whatever—we have *become* essentially that. We have become in our own bodies veritable temples of that particular vice. The outer image we once put on now reflects an inner condition we perhaps never, at first, could have imagined.

When God instructs us through the Scriptures to put off the sin that defiles us, He knows well of the deliverance we need not only from sin but from that sin's diseased tendrils (offshoots) that have found their way into our deepest selves. Only through Christ can these be uprooted and pulled out of us. The virtues and the vices are real things—real capacities for good or evil common to all of us. Out of the virtues issue good actions, good character traits, and in conjunction with the Holy Spirit, even the fruits of the Spirit. Out of the vices issue specific sins and the vicious habits that form bad character. We are instructed to put the one on and to pull the other off. The fact that our actions are commanded does not mean that we attempt to do either apart from God's grace.

Many of the older writers made statements about the saints having "shined outwardly with great virtues and grace." We seldom see these kind of statements anymore, and it is a loss. The virtues as such are disdained today, as though we have nothing to do with practicing them or putting them on. The vices and the individual acts of sin that spring from them go unnamed today. The irony is that legalism replaces the teaching on the one hand, or outright antinomianism[16] on the other. What these earlier writers noted is that to "put on" the Christian virtues is to practice the presence of Christ. It is to put on Christ as a wholly good cloak. The end result is observable in the physical world.

Hypocrisy: When Merely the Outer Image Is Prized

To a phenomenal degree, appearance has replaced reality.[17]

We can "put on" an outer image that has nothing to do with the practice of the presence of God, or even of the virtues as the virtuous pagan understood. In such a case, the outer image is maintained as a means to please or even deceive others.

The vice of merely valuing one's outer image is blatantly exploited by the media today in the interest of emptying pocketbooks. The world of mammon puts a premium on shallowness and hypocrisy. No doubt this is a chief way in which worldliness gains a foothold in the church. At any rate, many today, as the Pharisees of old, chiefly prize their public image. Such a person may have a well-polished "Christian" persona but has inside, rooted deep into the soul, some of the vilest mental and spiritual conditions. Only recently I have seen some of the worst instances imaginable, cases where the one who wears the mask of pious Christian is filled with resentment, hatred, and anger toward God and either some or all Christians. These are not cases where hatred of one's parents or church is displaced onto God, though the individuals may have started out that way. Rather, these are fearful examples of absolute refusal to forsake resentments, forgive others, and lay before God the terrible pride that refuses to allow Him access to their hearts.

Of all the vices in such hearts, it seems that *unbelief* is the main one. If I have put on a Christian persona in order to keep up appearances, then I am in the grip of unbelief. My love and fear of God will be missing. My heart will be hardened by the deceitfulness of sin—those sins that spring from unbelief and usurp the place of a genuine love and fear of God. Instead there will be fear of others and what they think of me.

When in this way outward decorum and respectability are prized as ends in themselves, then the mere *appearance* of good (such as certain of the Pharisees prized) will substitute for the *reality* itself. My heart, bereft of the *real*—the virtuous habits, the fruits of the Holy Spirit, and God Himself—hardens. I become that "whited sepulchre"—that walking dead person that Christ named in certain religious leaders of His day.

In contrast to the pride of hypocrites is the humility of the saints. To put on Christ is to increase in the understanding of the fallen heart's condition apart from Him. All the vices are native to the heart of fallen humanity. The greater the knowledge of God's goodness in the saints' hearts, the more they know that their very best apart from God is not good enough. They know that such a good degenerates and does not stand the test of time. In choosing to fear God rather than others, they opt for inner integrity, a change from the inside out that ends in fullness of being. They hate and eschew the empty shell—the mere persona or showcase outer image.

To summarize: The saints valued the transcendent good and knew that to be *in Christ* was to be enveloped in an awesome and objective good. They knew they could yield their members to that highest good rather than to sinful compulsions (carnal desires and feelings), and thereby form virtuous habits while being loosed from vicious ones. They knew that to yield to the virtues rather than to the vices was to form good behavior and character rather than their sinful counterparts. They knew this to be a vital—not an optional—part of the discipline that enabled them to obey God and remain in His presence.

> The LORD is with you when you are with him. If you seek him, he will be found by you, but if you forsake him, he will forsake you (2 Chronicles 15:2).

This understanding of "putting on" the mind and virtues of God, this veritable practice of the presence of God and the transcendent good, is key to personal wholeness. As the traditional saying goes, "Sow a thought, reap an action; sow an action, reap a habit; sow a habit, reap a character; sow a character, reap a destiny."[18] The discipline of putting on God is critically important in the healing of sick souls. Indeed, it is crucial to the healing of everyone.

A Drama Unfolds As We Put On Christian Habits

That good which we "put on" sinks to the core of our being and connects with the *imago dei* within us. We begin to collaborate with the Spirit to do the will of the Father. We "imitate Christ" as St. Paul admonishes:

> Be imitators of God, therefore, as dearly loved children and live a life of love, just as Christ loved us and gave himself up for us as a fragrant offering and sacrifice to God (Ephesians 5:1).

It is interesting that St. Paul immediately follows up these words with admonitions not to yield to lust. Why are these exhortations, particularly in this context, so necessary?

It is because the moment we put on Christ and the transcendent good, our real, new self starts clamoring at the bars of any foul thing that imprisons it. It then breaks those bars and bursts through to truth and substantive reality; it rises to connect with a holy presence. It races forward in the Presence and then turns and challenges the old self with all its illusionary, disintegrative activity (that which would choose lust over love, evil over the good) to a mortal combat. It spears it through, utterly mortifies it, and then casts it off as the filthy cloak that it is.

Putting On the Virtues of Praise and Thanksgiving

Let us then, in this first part of prayer, put on the virtues of praise and thanksgiving. This mantle creates the conditions whereby our very beings become temples of worship. I invite you to pray the following prayer:

Lord, descend anew and always to renew and remake us. Cause my face to be alight with your presence, may all the virtues of your presence find a home in me.

4

Intercession

> I urge, then, first of all, that requests, prayers, intercession and thanksgiving be made for everyone—for kings and all those in authority, that we may live peaceful and quiet lives in all godliness and holiness. This is good and pleases God our Savior, who wants all men to be saved and to come to a knowledge of the truth. For there is one God and one mediator between God and men, the man Christ Jesus, who gave himself as a ransom for all men—the testimony given in its proper time (1 Timothy 2:1–6).

Thy Kingdom Come, Thy Will Be Done, on Earth As It Is in Heaven

When we intercede, we pray in effect "Thy kingdom come, Thy will be done, on earth as it is in heaven." "Biblical spirituality," as Donald Bloesch points out,

> entails not withdrawal from the turmoils of the world but identification with the world in its shame and affliction. Personal petition would become egocentric if it were not held in balance with

intercession, adoration, and thanksgiving.... We pray not simply for personal happiness or for protection (as in primitive prayer) but for the advancement and extension of the kingdom of God.[1]

Because God is interested in the whole world, therefore we are too. His creative will and purpose is to love the world through us. Soon we realize that the work of intercessory prayer is no small thing.

The Mere Mechanics

This section of our journal contains our intercessory prayer lists and whatever aids us in praying for others. We may want one list for family members, another for certain Christian leaders and congregations, another for special needs in our neighborhoods, another for our country, and another for international concerns. When we have lived in a number of places it is helpful to keep "geographical" lists so we remember to pray for friends of the past. Some people on my lists have been there for over thirty years. I do not pray these lists every day or even every week, but I pray them often enough that the Lord can lay these persons on my heart when prayer is needed.

Our more personal intercessions go in the next section under the Petition heading. Following that is the Forgiveness section, in which I have special lists on prayer for our enemies.

The Lord waits to give us His mind on how to pray in all these intercessions. It is most exciting. As we intercede for others, the Holy Spirit often ministers to us, revealing another way to pray or words of wisdom and knowledge. Therefore, these prayer lists are soon scribbled over with new insights, faith, and Scripture promises.

> ... The Spirit himself intercedes for us with groans that words cannot express. And he who searches our hearts knows the mind of the Spirit, because the Spirit intercedes for the saints in accordance with God's will (Romans 8:26–27).

The Scriptural Mandate

The Scriptures admonish us to pray for all people in authority, the church and her ministers, those above and below us—masters and servants—children, friends, fellow citizens, the sick, those who persecute us, our enemies, those who envy us, those who forsake us, and even those who murmur against God. In short we are to pray for all people everywhere.

This is easily overwhelming, especially in our age when the troubles of the world come to us daily, in technicolor, at the switch of a television dial. Although our intercessions should encompass the globe, we cannot deal with the fears and dark happenings of even one of our smaller cities, much less the world. If we try, we are soon overcome by the vast needs in the world, and end up praying effectively for no one. That is one reason why this section in our prayer journal is so important. In it we list those persons, leaders, communities, churches, and Christian endeavors that we are to keep before God in intercessory prayer.

One's focus in prayer must be kept clear. All prayer is made *unto* God, and therefore our prayers are made in identification with Christ, the light of the world. When we keep this focus strong and clear, we will not overidentify with the darkness in the world. Our prayers will be aglow with faith.

Christ is our model. He focuses on God the Father. His command to intercede is an easy one when we focus on "the Lord of the harvest" and not on the immensity of the need in the world.

The harvest is plentiful but the workers are few. Ask the Lord of the harvest, therefore, to send out workers into his harvest field (Matthew 9:37–38).

The Global Perspective

Many years ago I heard of Dr. Bob Pierce, the founder of World Vision, sobbing with his arms stretched around a large globe of the world. He was praying for the orphaned children of the world. God entrusted him with a special mission in regard to them, and his vision was in line with God's—it was global. He had acquired the Lord's mind on how to pray and how to follow up those prayers.

This habit of Dr. Pierce's made such a deep impression on me that I now always keep a globe at hand. On first hearing of his custom, I could hardly imagine that God could use me globally. But throwing my arms around a globe, I cried out for God to somehow, in some way, love this needy planet through me. "Lord, love Your world through me" is a prayer that has been with me ever since. In group intercessions, we on the Pastoral Care Ministries team at times reach for the globe in order to focus our intercessions on particular countries or areas.

We try to pray as specifically as possible for the work of the gospel He has entrusted to us. We pray that it will find its way throughout the world, into wounded, seeking, hungry hearts everywhere. As we intercede together for upcoming Pastoral Care Ministries (PCM) missions, both in this country and abroad, we are continually awed over how the Holy Spirit leads, often quite specifically, on *how* and *what* to pray. At times we are exhorted, warned, and even given instructions ahead of time that prepare us for the unknown difficulties we will face.

I have noted how God graciously blesses "mixed" or interdenominational groups. We are not called to make converts to any specific denomination. Instead we are commanded to teach the gospel in such a way as souls everywhere are converted to Christ. The PCM team is made up of Episcopalians, Baptists, Lutherans, Catholics, and various others, and a very special blessing accrues because of this. For one thing, we know that God does not call intercessors to "shore up" crumbling denominational walls. If we are the church (the fellowship of the Holy Spirit) and we faithfully hold up Christ, converts to Him will reform organizational church structures as a matter of course. Here again, we must keep first things first, and then secondary matters will take care of themselves.

In our individual and home-group intercessions we can focus too much on local concerns and lose the greater perspective. Or in contrast, we can easily pray only for needs "at a distance" and neglect those within our communities or even our homes. But true global prayers—ones that are not so general as to seem routine or so problem-weighted as to overwhelm us—are not only immensely effective *as prayer,* but keep us healthy as prayer groups. Christ died for all who will come to Him; His redemptive plan is global. We are to go into all the world—in our prayers. Then we are all the more effective in prayer for the needs closer at hand.[2]

Ways Not to Intercede

In every church tradition some make intercessory prayer an excessively grueling work. Sometimes even those who are especially gifted in intercessory prayer do this. Their emotional pathology and need for a sounder theology are usually all too apparent. A. W. Tozer has a balancing word in an article entitled, "Born After Midnight":

> Among revival-minded Christians I have heard the saying, "Revivals are born after midnight." This is one of those proverbs which, while not quite literally true, yet points to something very true. If we understand the saying to mean that prayer offered when we are tired and worn out has greater power than prayer made when we are rested and fresh, again it is not true. God would need to be very austere indeed to require us to turn our prayer into penance, or to enjoy seeing us punish ourselves by intercession. Traces of such ascetical notions are still found among some gospel Christians and while these brethren are to be commended for their zeal, they are not to be excused for unconsciously attributing to God a streak of sadism unworthy of fallen man.[3]

Only yesterday I opened a letter from an anxious soul who felt that all her previous intercessions were "fleshly" or carnal because they were not borne out of this grueling, wailing, travailing, kind of prayer. She was in agony because she believed that she had never "loved enough" and so on. She represents the damage that can be done to people when false asceticism comes in. Such an orientation in prayer tends finally to center us in on ourselves—how much we suffer, love, "put the body under," and so on. Thus we are soon overly oriented toward the "work" of prayer, specifically *our* work, and lose sight of the *object* of our prayers.

If this continues long enough, we begin to suffer a serious case of the "disease of introspection," that unhappy and fragmenting condition that takes us over when we kneel to pray, and instead of praying to God we analyze ourselves, our prayers, and our motives for prayer. In this introspective age, we easily substitute our subjective feelings about ourselves (all that we think needs correction and healing) for the objective gift of God's listening, loving ear, and the forgiveness and healing word He speaks to us. If we are on our knees hating ourselves, we are not likely to look up and out of the depressed self to receive from God—much less pray in faith for others. Instead, we have sunk into an inculcated, emotional state of feeling toward the self, an emotional view we have had so long we hardly notice it. This is not prayer. It is a common and serious barrier to all communication with God, not just intercessory prayer.[4]

When we receive the gift of tears and strong crying out to God in intercession, we are not given special merit. Rather it is a gracious "work" of God's Spirit. We should be grateful and thank God for it. Trying to duplicate this grace is folly and gets in the way of intercession. Much of our best work of prayer will be done without sensible knowledge of this grace. When it comes, we simply give thanks for it.

Having said this, there are bona fide ascetic practices that, when absent from our lives, pretty well guarantee that we will not do much interceding. We are powerless when fasting, solitude, silence, and the classic ways of training our bodies to be temples of the Holy Spirit—as we see in our Lord, those He taught, and the early church—are missing in our lives. Dallas Willard's book, *The Spirit of the Disciplines*,[5] should be read by all who are serious about true ascetics as applied to prayer and the Christian walk.[6]

Besides the matter of false ascetics with its misbegotten ideas about God or ourselves, two other practices that hinder us in prayer are widespread today. One involves the practice of *substitution*. This occurs when we pray to take someone else's pain, illness, fear, or sorrow into or upon ourselves. In such a case, we do not intercede to God for them but try to substitute for them. Rather than looking to Christ as the One who died to take their pain, sin, or darkness *into Himself,* we ask to take it upon and into ourselves. Rather than looking to the Savior, we attempt to be one. Instead of helping someone carry their burden of guilt, pain, sickness, or whatever to God in prayer, we ourselves fail to trust God. We attempt to carry the person's need in our own strength.

Substitution occurs, then, when we blur the distinction between being a savior-redeemer—something only Jesus could ever be and do—and being His disciple, a sacramental channel through whom His life is to flow. To substitute is to attempt to do the work Christ has already finished, while simultaneously missing our own proper work. To take upon or into ourselves as mediators the darkness of others is at best based in ignorance, at worst based in pride. Either way, we fall into a messiah or savior complex and will have to confess pride to get out of it.

One of the great dangers in substitution lies in the fact that spiritual forces we do not understand or fail to discern can be directly involved in sicknesses of spirit, soul, and body. In the case of demonic presences, these are quite amenable to "transferring" themselves from the sick person to the one who asks to "substitute." Such a person unwittingly opens his or her soul and body to darkness, saying to the enemy "Come in" while simultaneously sending messages to his or her own mind and body, "Disintegrate, I give you full permission."

This action, of course, is not rooted in looking to and trusting God—that is, in true prayer. The well-publicized movie *The Exorcist* did not feature an exorcism at all, but a substitution. A priest, failing to pray to God and exercise the authority of his office, instead took into himself the demonic force afflicting a child. The movie ends with the priest leaping from a window to his death. This illustrates most graphically the price to pay in substitutions. This price is not one connected with legitimate Christian suffering.[7]

An interesting sidelight here: in PCM conferences, we bring the gospel to bear on the healing of souls. Since we are psychosomatic unities—body and soul—our bodies begin to heal as a natural course and sometimes even instantly. Near the end of each conference, we are often led to pray for physical healings,

especially those connected to the emotional and spiritual healings received by the people. Invariably, however, when people
have the opportunity to renounce their substitutions, we see dramatic and instantaneous physical healings—as well as mental
and emotional. There have been miraculous healings of cancer,
emphysema, and others from these renunciations. Healings, such
as those connected to the practice of substitution, do not seem
to occur apart from specific teaching and opportunities to pray
for them. Our grief is that there is never enough time in these
meetings to get all the teaching and healing prayer exercises in.

If after reading the above, you know or even think that "maybe"
there has been a substitution of this kind, now is the moment to
name it, repent of it, and renounce it. You can look straight up to
God and pray as follows:

> "Lord, I asked to take on [so and so's] pain, disease, or darkness of
> [name the spiritual darkness, physical disease such as blindness,
> crippling condition, or mental and emotional depression or dark-
> ness of whatever kind]. I name my foolishness and pride before
> You right now. You alone are Savior-Redeemer. My faith in you was
> lacking, and I asked to do what You have already done—You car-
> ried our sicknesses, our sins, our sorrows. Forgive me, Lord, even
> as I renounce this substitution."

The substitution is then renounced, specifically:

> "Lord, I have confessed as sin the pride and unbelief that was in
> this substitution. I now renounce it before You. [Renounce as
> specifically as possible the substitution you made, for instance,
> 'Lord, I asked to take on so and so's blindness, I renounce that sub-
> stitution, confessing as sin the pride and unbelief that was in it.']
> I look directly to You for [so and so's] health and wholeness, and
> thank you for removing from me, as far as the East is from the West,
> this malady I've suffered due to this wrongful practice."

This prayer ends in praise and thanksgiving to God for His forgiveness, for His release from the substitution, and for all the healing that accrues from it.[8]

Another mistaken practice is unbelievably widespread today, and is being taught as a means to "do spiritual warfare." Instead of focusing solely on God in prayer, people focus on demons and "principalities and powers" in order to "bind" them. The following sections are adapted from chapter 14 of *Restoring the Christian Soul Through Healing Prayer,* entitled "Wrong Ways to Do Battle."

Wrongly Personifying Sin

> Then the LORD said to Cain, "Why are you angry? Why is your face downcast? If you do what is right, will you not be accepted? But if you do not do what is right, sin is crouching at your door; it desires to have you, but you must master it" (Genesis 4:6–7).

Sin is personified in this remarkable passage. A biblical commentator explains the origins of this metaphoric speech: "The Hebrew word for crouching is the same as an ancient Babylonian word referring to an evil demon crouching at the door of a building to threaten the people inside. Sin may thus be pictured here as just such a demon, waiting to pounce on Cain—it desires to have him."[9]

Sin within the human heart is a destroyer. There could hardly be a better metaphor for evil than we have here. This personification of sin enables us to better comprehend its power to devour. The scriptural symbols, metaphors, similes, parables, and figures of speech are invaluable in helping us express these grave matters so that the heart can fully grasp them.

It is one thing, however, to understand sin as figuratively demonic. It is quite another to see sin in the human breast as though it were a demonic entity rather than a transgression for which the soul is held responsible before God.

In this day of ignorance about the soul, many Christians turn to the terminology of deliverance from evil spirits and name these motions of the soul (or lack of them) as demons. They identify not only the absence of the holy graces and good emotions within a soul, but the corresponding profusion of sinful vices, fantasies, feelings, and attitudes as demonic infestations. This is not only to fail to discern the problem aright—the sin as well as the psychological deficiencies and problems. Even more seriously it is to fail to see the person needing help as human at all. We become thoroughgoing gnostics who spiritualize away the human element—a grievous kind of ignorance that is nowhere modeled for us in the Scriptures. Jesus dealt with *persons,* men and women with full souls. He helped these souls name and renounce their sins. He never failed to see them as persons.

We are souls, with a spirit at our center that is either linked with Christ or not. In failing to recognize the full soul that is another person, we effectually cross out all that is uniquely human about that person's creation. We delete the human. If we fail to see and revere the unique person in the one for whom we pray, we will fail to help that person deal effectively with the real sin and emotional difficulties. We may even, in our ignorance and zeal to help the person, name these things as demons and fancy ourselves as "binding" and casting them out. But it is the *sin* that is to be bound and the *person* to be loosed from it. In contrast, the wounds are to be healed. If these have provided a place for demons to hide, we can easily enough expel them once they are discerned.

In ministry that fails to recognize the above, people are robbed of the great privilege of coming present to their own hearts. There—in the presence of God—they will finally understand who they are. Rather than helping people recognize and repent of their sin, changing their diseased attitudes and allowing God to create in them new hearts, we cast out nonexistent demons of this or that. We will actually be attempting to "cast out" character traits and deficiencies. Too—just as tragically—all that is positive and unique within that soul will be overlooked. Through ignoring the good, it will go unaffirmed. In effect it will be denied existence. It will not be called into life. A vital step in prayer for this person's healing will be missed.

Thus today well-meaning Christians pray for others through speaking to demons—mostly nonexistent ones.[10] These people need more instruction in the theology of the cross and repentance, and the authentic gift of discerning of spirits needs to be clarified. All too often, the authentic gifts of wisdom and discernment are obscured and then replaced by a faulty theology, often developed from a mistaken exegesis of the Scriptures. A faulty "methodology" quickly follows.

In any one of the three great barriers to wholeness (the lack of self-acceptance, failure to forgive others, and failure to receive forgiveness) a demon may be found hiding away in a nest that a sin or wound has made for it. In ministry to the person, these demons manifest themselves, and even as Christ would command, "Come out!" or "Be muzzled!" and always simply, "Depart!"—so do we. This is the easiest part of healing prayer once people confess their sin or are released from the effects of another's sins against them. But grievous hurt is done, and prayers for others are needlessly ineffective when, rather than being able to listen to God and to that unique and precious human soul that is looking up to God, we start clamoring about demons and commanding imaginary ones to depart.

I will next address this unscriptural *practice of the presence of the powers of darkness* and the very grave dangers involved in such a practice. Also, I want to issue a strong warning about those (again principally those within certain parts of the renewal movement) who fail to understand which planes of spiritual battle are properly ours and which properly belong to God and His angelic hosts. To fail to understand this ends in the error of the practice of the presence of our archenemy and his minions—not the practice of the presence of God. And when we practice the evil one's presence long and seriously enough, he shows up. In focusing on him, we eventually manage to make a pathway for him to come.

Focus on God—Not on Satan, Demons, or Principalities and Powers

> There are two equal and opposite errors into which our race can fall about devils. One is to disbelieve in their existence. The other is to believe, and to feel an excessive and unhealthy interest in them. They themselves are equally pleased by both errors, and hail a materialist or a magician with the same delight.[11]

Many today who lecture on spiritual warfare start out with the vital statement that we are not to focus on Satan. Then, however, the overall effect of their teaching leads both themselves and their disciples to do just that. Often, in warning those they teach, they will even quote C. S. Lewis in his familiar statement quoted above and thoroughly agree with it. But then they live something else out.

Two practices, both that focus on the demonic, have come together to do the most mischief. One involves "doing spiritual warfare" *against* principalities and powers, done by those who fail to understand what planes of battle are properly ours and those that properly belong to God and His angelic hosts. The second concerns the misuse of the terms "binding and loosing"— the misapplying of those terms to demons and then the resulting mistaken practice of *praying against Satan* rather than to God. We pray to God for those souls under Satan's foul aegis, helping them to confess their sins and thereby come out from under the control of principalities and powers. This does not mean that we will not sometimes discern strongholds over people, nations, cities, or communities. But it does mean we must be very careful of our focus. We will always be found ministering to God— singing and speaking to Him in worship, thanksgiving, and praise. We will always be found practicing the presence of God. In so doing, when we discern demons, principalities, or powers directly in our path, we speak directly to them and command them to leave.

Planes of Warfare

Christians are easily confused about what it means to "do spiritual warfare" because of ignorance about the true nature of our souls, of misteaching, and of a failure to abide by the scriptural model of the gift of battle. Any confusion causes us to think the battle is ours rather than the Lord's, and we then battle according to our own understanding and strength. To do this even in part is dangerous, and there is really no excuse for it. The Scriptures are very clear here regarding not only the way Christ and the apostles modeled the warfare for us but also the plane of battle that is properly ours.

Christians who fail to understand this practice can be dangerous to anyone who comes under their influence. The enemy, through gaining these Christians' focus, will have found a "landing platform" through which to "touch down" and bring in all manner of mischief and deception.

One of the most difficult experiences along this line that the PCM team has encountered reveals even further how dangerous such practices can be. This situation involved intercession and a seriously misguided group's attempt to "bind principalities and powers over a city."

A number of years back, several Christian leaders approached me within a short time span with a word they had received from the Lord regarding PCM's need for intercessors. One was awakened in the middle of the night to intercede for us and was given visions of the battle we are in, especially in regard to ministering to persons with sexual neuroses. Another had a specific prophetic word that he spoke over the PCM team, a word about the increasingly vital and even critical part those who are called to intercede for this ministry will play. Part of that word admonished us: "Pray that an army of intercessors be raised up, and they will go before you, springing the snares and traps of the enemy."

We did just this, asking for intercessors through our newsletter. God mercifully raised up many to pray for us, and only heaven will reveal the incredible blessing this has been. We are amazed to see how faithful God is to spring the snares and the traps of the enemy.

In publishing our need, however, we unearthed the dangerous, unscriptural ways of interceding that some people have gotten into. Unfortunately, we drew them toward us as well. These misguided ones had one thing in common—the idea that to "do spiritual warfare" was to focus on demons and on principalities and powers over cities and to "bind" them. To "bind" them was to take control over them through verbal assertions—spoken out into the airwaves but aimed toward "them."

These people, influenced by an extreme teaching (referred to by some as "Faith Formula Theology"[12]), attempt to "control" our Almighty and all-knowing holy God in the same way, believing that if they state their objectives in certain ways and affirm them in "faith," they thereby "force" God to do their bidding. This is not scriptural faith, I must add, but an inducing of a certain psychological mindset. These intercessors see themselves as binding demonic powers by talking to them—in effect praying to demons and by repeating over and over such things as, "I bind you, (whatever name the demon or principality or power appeared to have), and I take authority over you." This is what they called being an intercessor or "doing spiritual warfare."

The first time the team and I were exposed to the darkness that comes out of these dangerous prayer practices we were to minister in a church where many had gathered both to learn to pray for others and for help for themselves. Several teachers of these wrong ways of focusing on the demonic had come—not to learn—but to try to impress us. It did not take long for us to be *impressed* in a most negative fashion, for never have we known the unleashing of such darkness in the context of conducting a prayer and healing service. We knew immediately that these people had inadvertently invited and stirred up the darkness. Their practices were exceedingly confusing and dangerous to any naive soul who might get caught up in them.

Before the first service, their leader said to me: "We pray and fast against principalities and powers [meaning demonic forces], in advance, before we ever go to a place, and we have done this for you. You are now safe because we have accomplished this, we have *bound* the principalities and powers in the high places over this city. . . ."

Right away I knew they were in serious trouble. I could not help them, however, for they spoke only a bleak "spiritualized" language that was overcharged and left no room for reasoned interaction, communication, or fellowship. For them, there was no room for the truly beautiful, either from the realm of nature and the fully human or from the heavenly. There were only demons, and these were to be sought out and dealt with. There was no practice of the presence for these people—only an imagination filled with the demonic.

Unknowingly, they were caught up in a spiritual pride beyond the ordinary. They had said to me in effect, "We are the only ones really who know how to 'bind' the devil, how to deliver the seriously demonized person, because we really know how to do spiritual warfare. We seek and engage the 'biggies' themselves, the principalities and powers. We've come to do this for you and show you how it is done."

Thinking themselves to be intercessors extraordinaire and the only ones "doing" spiritual warfare, they were actually practicing the presence of demons. They had drawn the attention of dark powers toward the body of Christ in that place by *praying to them* and through pridefully seeing themselves as "binding" them. As it turned out, they became a channel through which a "principality and power"—a ruling spirit over that city—descended into our midst. It was one meant to be withstood in spiritual battle only by the holy angels as we battled properly for the salvation of souls.

As we began the ministry there, our hearts were opened to discern the huge entity. It named itself and threatened each one of us on the team. There were bizarre happenings and unbelievable confusion as we called on the power of God to quell the dark power.

Needless to say, we were brought into a spiritual conflict of unusual proportions, one that need never occurred. These folk, thinking they were intercessors, had merely succeeded in informing the powers of darkness in, over, and around that city that we were coming! In listening to them proudly relate all their hair-raising tussles with dark powers, I realized they take this "gift" every place they go. The way they pray assures that the people they are involved with will have dramatic and terrible confrontations with evil powers, and that some of them will come under serious demonic deception. This is dangerous error.

I only tell of this extreme practice because it is no longer a rare circumstance. These practices are spreading (usually in milder forms) to well-meaning people who intercede daily. Too, as one who helps people to wholeness in Christ, I am aware of the many who attempt to cope with life by the usually unconscious striving to control events or others around themselves—named today the codependent personality. Often these people, in fear of the demonic, attempt to "control" it in these ways of prayer—and thereby hope to stave off the evil. Thus "talking to the devil" and practicing his foul presence becomes a dangerous adjunct to the codependence from which these people already suffer. Fearing conflict of any kind, they attempt to safeguard themselves through "controlling" character traits in others, traits they may come to perceive as demons.

Some, when shown what they are doing, will ask, "But how can I pray?" In other words, precious Christian souls out there now no longer know how to pray without talking to the devil. "How," they ask, when embroiled in spiritual battle with their enemies, "do I pray about this lie," or "this slander," or this darkness of any kind? "Shall I get up an hour early and do spiritual warfare?" by which they mean, "Shall I arise an hour early and focus on demons and bind them?" No, this is not what to do. It is wonderful to rise an hour early and focus on God, affirm the fact that He has won the victory, and ask Him how we should trust Him in the face of the darkness and slander coming against us.

But we have no need to control that darkness and slander. He is doing it, and we trust our present and future entirely to Him! It is not by focusing on "demons" of lying, slander, and so on, by finding names for them, or by "binding" them continually in prayer. That way only brings one into striving and fear at best, and demonic oppression and even deception at worst.[13] Instead we look straight up to God and talk to Him. Christ has bound the enemy, and ours is merely the mop-up action. In showing us how to pray, the Scriptures record no one focusing on demons. Rather, as Christ taught us, we pray, "But deliver us from the evil one." In other words, "You do it, Lord."

We do not get involved in "works" prayers to be free of principalities and powers. We trust God and He sends out His holy angels to do the warfare. If a demonic power happens across our path, once we have discerned it then we command it to leave. Only then do we speak to it—a foul presence that the Holy Spirit has shown us is there. And we expel it with a word: "In Christ's name, be gone!"

We won a great victory in the place where this dark incident happened. God is faithful, and people were reborn—spiritually and psychologically. Many came out of the deep darkness that characterizes our culture today. This included people with backgrounds in the occult, witchcraft, sexual perversion, and so on. We are well accustomed to these circumstances and to dealing with any demonic infestation. But we paid a much higher price than usual, in terms of the intensity of the battle and the sheer physical and spiritual stress such a circumstance exacts. It was absolutely unnecessary.

Two examples here will show how wonderfully true intercession works. We were to minister in another country at a well-known but liberal seminary in a city remarkably corrupt even by today's standards. We knew we were entering into great spiritual warfare for the souls within that university, and especially for those training for theological professorships and the pastorate in many other nations. As we confessed the sins of that city and university—known and unknown—and cried out to God for His anointing to preach, teach, and heal in His name, our spiritual eyes were opened. The Lord showed us the angelic battle going on over the seminary where we would be. We saw, before we ever arrived, the holy angels battling and overcoming the evil angels in answer to our prayers. We had a most incredible ministry there, out of which revival continues to spread. We did not leave there needlessly weakened physically through unnecessary confrontations with evil forces.

Another example is of a conference in England. The Lord was mightily stretching forth His hand to heal and to save. Right in the midst of this, Fr. William Beasley's eyes were opened, and he saw an immense and terrible "principality and power." But it was outside attempting to peer in. It wanted so badly to know what was going on, but it could not find out. The holy angels were always with us, and they had certainly done their part ahead of time. And there had been no misguided group of Christians who—by focusing on this evil entity—had made a pathway for it to insinuate itself into our midst.

Christ Our Model in Intercessory Prayer

For who has known or understood the mind (the counsels and purposes) of the Lord so as to guide and instruct [Him] and give Him knowledge? But we have the mind of Christ, the Messiah, and do hold the thoughts (feelings and purposes) of His heart (1 Corinthians 2:16, The Amplified Bible).

Our intercessions are modeled on Christ's example from the Scriptures. He prayed only to His Father in heaven. He sought and found the mind and will of God in all matters, and so, too, do we.

> . . . Because Jesus lives forever, he has a permanent priesthood. Therefore he is able to save completely those who come to God through him, because he always lives to intercede for them (Hebrews 7:24–25).

It is wonderful to meditate on the fact that Christ's intercessions for us did not end with His death, resurrection, and ascension to heaven and the "right hand of the Father." For He is the ultimate Mediator-Priest, and as such "ever lives to intercede" for us. "Jesus, intercede to the Father for me!" is always my cry when I am most desperate. I often wonder why I waited so long to turn to Him *as Intercessor*. What an immense privilege we have. What an infinite conduit of mercy opens to us when we remember to invoke Him in His office of divine Mediator.

Human Models

> A prayerful life, with a character to match, is a better invitation to prayer than many exhortations.[14]

Just as being in the midst of those who freely praise God immediately gives us a model and a jumpstart in doing the same, so too are we blessed by the saints who model what it means to imitate Christ in intercessory prayer. I was most fortunate in this respect for my mother was such a person. She not only prayed with my sister and me at our table and in our nightly Bible reading and prayer, but closeted herself away on regular occasions for the purpose of intercession. On Saturday mornings she interceded on behalf of the church services the next day and for the Sunday School class she taught. As my mother immersed herself more and more in intercession for others, she would "forget herself," and her voice would slowly rise. Then there would be "strong crying out to God" for the concerns of the church and the nation.

In her praying, there was not the least hint of the prayer being either a legalistic thing or an excessively grueling work. More times than not there was a special sense of God's presence in the home as Mother's intercessions mounted up, and as a child my spirit too would be "infected" with a spirit of prayer. Though not with her in the prayer closet, I would enter into prayer with her. On a few occasions, visiting playmates did the same, a thing that was not altogether understood by their parents.

Mother treasured the writings of Andrew Murray on prayer. I pick up his works on occasion but find them to be an exercise in redundancy, for he and mother were kindred spirits. What he wrote, she lived out before me. As a single, working mother, widowed in her early twenties during the Great Depression, she had little or no leisure time. Intercessory prayer, however, was not deemed peripheral. Her full trust, even for the most basic necessities of life, was in God alone. I could not have had a better model.

She never confused love for others, the church, or the nation, with *feelings* of love for them. She knew that to love others was not to drum up feelings of love. She did not turn from the object of her prayers to examine her feelings. She was singularly lacking in such a vice. Nor was she involved with sentimentalism, a dark and dangerous vice that riddles the organized church today and successfully passes itself off as love.

In her intercessions for others, Mother knew something about what love really is, and the awesomeness of God's true and even terrible love for His people. It does not take interceding long before we find out that in loving others in this way we open the floodgates of heaven on ourselves as well. Besides experiencing the most amazing and miraculous answers to these intercessions, we receive great gifts from time to time as we pray.

Mother, for example, did not belong to a church that emphasized the gifts of the Spirit, but these were quickened in her *as she interceded for others*. During prayer for others she received the gift of a prayer language. She did not tell me about this until I was an adult; I think she hardly knew how to explain it. It was a gracious gift of God and a great aid in intercessory prayer.

It was also during prayer for others that she experienced the love of God in such a way as to be forever changed and strengthened. She named this a "baptism" of God's love. She described it as "liquid love" that came upon her, wave after wave. Each wave came in vivid colors beyond her power to describe. Love, in its very essence, seemed to wash over and into her as the Shekinah Glory, she said—almost more than she could bear and still live. To the end of her life she wisely shared this with very few people. Such *joy* as this, especially when not understood, can dissipate when shared indiscriminately. But it can multiply in its healing effects—even to others—when rightly garnered and stewarded.

Later, as a young adult, I too found that in prayer for others— though we do not intercede for personal gain—God surprises us by unexpected and good gifts. I recall going to my pastor and insisting that prayer must surely be a sacrament for so much grace flows through it. I came to realize what an incredible "means" of grace intercessory prayer is. In fact, at the time I was almost bowled over by it. I had learned the lesson that the woman who, fearful that all her prayers had been in vain because she had not striven and therefore "loved enough," is in need of learning. F. B. Meyer puts it this way:

> Probably the only way to know the love of Christ is to begin to show it. The emotionalist, who is easily affected by appeals to the senses, does not know it; the theorist or rhapsodist does not know it, but the soul that endeavors to *show* the love of Christ, knows it. As Christ's love through you broadens, lengthens, deepens, heightens, you will know the love of Christ, not intellectually, but experimentally.[15]

5

Petition

Give us each day our daily bread. Forgive us our
sins, for we also forgive everyone who sins
against us. And lead us not into temptation
(Luke 11:3–4).

In the Bible petition and intercession are primary, though adoration, thanksgiving, and confession also have a role. Yet the petitionary element is present in all these forms of prayer.
Biblical prayer is crying to God out of the
depths; (1 Sam. 1:15; Pss. 88:1–2; 130:1–2; Lam.
2:19; Matt. 7:7–8; Phil. 4:6; Heb. 5:7). It often
takes the form of importunity, passionate
pleading to God, even wrestling with God. (F. B.
Meyer)[1]

Give Us This Day Our Daily Bread

In contrast to our intercessions for others and for the Lord's
work throughout the earth, the Petition section in our prayer journal is set aside for our more personal petitions. Here we pray, as
Christ taught us, "Give us this day our daily bread." These peti-

tions often lead directly into intercession for others, even as in intercessory prayer we are often brought face to face with our more personal needs. This is as it should be. Our prayer to God will always burst the boundaries of our little categories, transcending them by far.

There are those, however, who think personal petition to be somehow inferior or even selfish. But the truth is that we need to pay attention to the heart's personal needs and desires, and take care to spread them out before the Lord:

> Prayer in the Christian sense does not . . . accept the idea of a higher stage of prayer where petition is left behind. The progress that it sees in the spiritual life is from the prayer of rote to the prayer of the heart.[2]

The Mere Mechanics

The Lord moves mightily on behalf of those who *wait* for and before Him. Mary understood this well as she sat at Jesus' feet, risking Martha's wrath as she "did nothing" but talk with Jesus. As we wait for the Lord we fill this section with our personal petitions, great and small, that require ongoing prayer and even perseverance. I jot most of my personal petitions in the Word section, simply and as they occur naturally in daily prayer. The ones listed in this section, however, require further *listening*. They are those about which I need sit at the Master's feet and talk to Him.

As we continue to lift up our longings before the Lord we gain understanding of our own hearts. We also grow in the knowledge of how best to pray for ourselves, others, and the situations surrounding us. At times, therefore, we modify or even strike through a petition and replace it with something better. In this activity we grow in wisdom, understanding, and knowledge as we gain the will of God. We even gain the mind of Christ in regard to our petitions.

Prayer is powerful. We can release our faith amiss, or in the wrong timing. Christ has said:

> Ask and it will be given to you; seek and you will find; knock and the door will be opened to you. For everyone who asks receives;

he who seeks finds; and to him who knocks, the door will be opened (Matthew 7:7–8).

It is important, therefore, to ask always for God's mind and even His most perfect will on our petitions. To persevere with God in this way is a needful thing. We ask, we seek, we continue to knock, and like the persistent widow of Luke 18:5, we receive.

Persevering with God

Prayer in biblical or evangelical spirituality is rooted in both the experience of Godforsakenness and in the sense of the presence of God. It is inspired by both the felt need of God and gratitude for his work of reconciliation and redemption in Jesus Christ.[3]

Until we learn to yield to God all the needs, cries, and desires of our hearts in petition, we will know neither Him nor our hearts as we should. To come present to Him and to our hearts is to cry out our personal petitions. Then we must have ears to hear His heart for us: His desires, promises, exhortations, and commands. In this way, we no longer pray merely by rote but achieve the "prayer of the heart."

I will never forget the joy of first coming into this prayer of the heart. I had much need and therefore much to lay out before Him. As I was finding and holding close to my heart His promises, my petitions began to multiply. After all, does it not say in James: "You do not have because you do not ask"? (4:2) From early on, this section in my journal has been a large one.

I learned to head my petitionary lists with Scriptures that urged me on to greater faith, such as, "Until now you have not asked for anything in my name. Ask and you will receive, and your joy will be complete" (John 16:24) and "If you believe, you will receive whatever you ask for in prayer" (Matthew 21:22). It is wonderful to go back through my journals and recount God's answers to prayer. Sometimes when something remarkable has happened, I find in reviewing some old prayer journal where I specifically petitioned the Lord for this thing. "No wonder this marvelous thing has happened!" I find myself exclaiming aloud. There is nothing surer on this earth than the truth that God hears and answers prayer. It has been said that it is a rule of the Father's house that we *ask* for what we get. The Scriptures certainly admonish us to ask. Then we need only learn to *receive* of the abundance He sends.

In those first days of learning to lay my heart before God—which is what the prayer of petition enabled me to do—I received more healing and understanding than one could well imagine. The Psalms, with their wonderful promises, provided a bounteous and boundless seedbed of petitions in my early journaling. "Delight yourself in the LORD and he will give you the desires of your heart" (37:4) especially exercised me. Just how does one delight oneself in the Lord, I asked over and over. What were the desires of my heart? I did not know. They were too repressed; I had little hope for them. I searched the Scriptures for clues, and those that proclaim God's presence with us stood out. King David had the answer: "In thy presence is fulness of joy" (Psalm 16:11, KJV). From the Amplified Bible, Psalm 27, verses 4 and 8, I wrote in my journal:

> One thing have I asked of the Lord: That I may dwell in His Presence. You have said: Seek My face, My Presence. My heart says: Your face, Your Presence will I seek.

"Yes, Lord, I will seek your face! I will look straight up to You. With all my might Lord, I will seek your presence." I journaled all the Scriptures about God's presence *with* and *within* us, turning them into petitionary prayers. I meditated on them, asked questions of the Lord about them, listened to hear what He would speak to me about them—and was led straight into the practice of the presence!

Perhaps no other discipline has been more used of God to change my life than the practice of the presence. This is the simple acknowledgment that He is with me and never leaves me. I prayed the following daily until the discipline was set into my life:

> I affirm: I will persevere to practice Your presence today.
> I affirm: Christ who is my life is made manifest today.

Undoubtedly journaling these petitions played a vital part in making this a reality in my soul. Had I not kept this matter before the Lord and journaled the related Scriptures, I probably would have gone on to pray about the next most pressing thing—as we distracted moderns are prone to do. Yet how simple are the things and ways God uses to help us walk in the Spirit.

A humble missionary whose name I do not know gave me another petition. As guest minister in church he shared his personal petition, which gripped my heart. I immediately made it part of my daily petitioning.

My life is short
And I (apart from You) am nothing
Help me to communicate one perfect Jesus Christ to the world.

Believing not only that God *is* but that no yawning chasm exists between us opens our hearts to great inroads of joy. There is no delighting ourselves *in Him* if we seek and strain after Him as though He were absent from our lives! This affirmation of His nearness, then, together with actively listening to Him in prayer, puts us in touch with the desires of our hearts.

Desires of the Heart: The Soul's Atomic Energy

It is no small thing to get in touch with one's truest desires. I had known what it was to follow my own will apart from God— my evil or selfish desires. I knew the kind of trouble that caused. Therefore I earnestly petitioned: "Lord, I desire that my will be one with Yours." This prayer then led me to take every scriptural command of Christ as if He gave it to me personally, and to write it out. This comprised an individual section in my first journal. I cannot overstate its profound effect on me.

God waits and even yearns to speak to us about His commands and promises and how they apply to our needs and desires. Early in life I knew *regeneration*—being born from above. God had certainly done His part. Now, through petitioning and listening to God's response, I was being thoroughly *converted.* My will was undergoing conversion, a continued process that is other than the soul's initial regeneration.

The more our souls grow, the more there is to be converted. As we come present to God and our own hearts, that which is below the conscious level rises to consciousness. It too is acknowledged and yielded up to God. This full and ongoing conversion of our will enables us to desire greatly without fear. We are free of fear of disappointment, fear that we will misuse what God gives, or even fear that we are unworthy of God's favor. We know that our heart's desire has become one with His even as we make our wills one with His. We trust Him to show us when our desires are amiss, or simply not His chosen best for us.

Once our will is converted, and we spread out before the Lord the desires of our heart—"the atomic energy of the soul"[4]—we get in touch with our fears, limitations, and even the outright negative feelings about ourselves. We find that we are afraid of the *true* self. In fact we run from it because we are afraid of its creative energies, such as its capacity to envision and thereby desire a higher good and greater goal for itself and others. I discovered a deep sense of inferiority in regard to my ability to give to others. I felt my handicaps. "Lord, I am *after all* a divorcée," I would pray and then remind Him of many other ways I had failed. "You see, Lord, these feelings of powerlessness and vulnerability . . ."—only to hear Him say:

> Confess your pride and unbelief. Of course you are a sinner but a forgiven one; of course you are powerless and vulnerable. "Apart from Me, you can do nothing," nothing of lasting significance. But I AM with you. Practice My presence. Know that with Me you transcend your limitations, even all your handicaps. Only love Me, and allow Me to love others through you. Embrace My will for you, the destiny you fear as long as there is pride and unbelief.

In my unbelief (and I was not calling it that at first), I was unable to *receive* from God. In my pride, I feared exposure: fears of being criticized for past failures, fears of being shown to be inadequate. I journaled each one of these fears. In the process I learned the meaning of "Whoever cares for his own safety is lost; but if a man

will let himself be lost for my sake, he will find his true self"
(Matthew 16:25, NEB). To care for my life would be to lose it. I had
to be willing to lose all to gain Christ. What did it matter if I lost
everything so long as I pleased God! Everything had to be placed
freely on the altar, with no strings attached.

What I ended up losing were my attempts to be justified in the
eyes of others, to please and be affirmed by humankind. What a
relief to let all that go; I merely wanted to please God. What an
incredible role petitionary prayer plays in this release. I learned
to celebrate my inadequacy, which became a most important
part of the practice of the presence of God. I took God's righteousness and all-sufficiency for my own and was released from
useless striving.

> It is indeed a memorable moment in the history of the human
> spirit, when we suddenly wake up to see that the Almighty is the
> All-Loving Father, that the righteousness of God is no longer a
> ground of anxiety and fear, but of assured hope.[5]

One petition I prayed regularly was for the ability to see myself
and others through God's eyes. Over time this wrought changes
in how I perceived both, and in how I prayed. Great personal benefit comes to anyone who prays in this way because feelings of
both inferiority and superiority are overcome. Both, of course,
belong to pride, and must be confessed as such.

As I listened to God the Father I was gaining the great virtue of
self-acceptance. I was also being healed of many things—chiefly,
the effects of being fatherless from age three. God the Father was
fathering me, meeting my needs for guidance and affirmation as
a person and a woman. Without a doubt, profound healing comes
to the soul that recognizes and petitions its needs before God. As
F. B. Meyer has said:

> You may take your journey into a far country and waste the pre-
> cious formative years in selfish indulgence. But if you will let the
> Great Father work out His full purpose in your training, [in] your
> unfolding and becoming, [and in your] *prayer life* specially, you

will find with Isaiah, that eye hath not seen, nor ear heard such an One as our God, who worketh for him that waiteth for Him.[6]

These early petitions helped my spiritual formation and are still deeply meaningful to me. Today my Petition section bulges with the needs of the ministry, and with my needs and desires from this stage of my pilgrimage with God.

Lest I give the impression that only prayers for spiritual growth and well-being find their way into this section, let me hasten to add that any personal thing that proves knotty to resolve ends up in these lists. For example, prayer for help to find the right physician or the trustworthy plumber is often a crucial matter that is not always easy to solve. And until these details are taken care of, especially if they pile up, our prayers can be interrupted with niggling worries about them.

I have learned to jot down my more mundane petitions. This allows me not only to consider them later if need be, but ensures that they will no longer erupt into my thoughts while praying or reading the Scriptures. If, however, I become desperate over such mundane things as, for example, where to find clothes that fit and a suitable wardrobe for speaking and travel, into this section such a petition goes. Knowing that I will not search this huge metropolis to mix and match, I will add something such as the following: "And please, Lord, let these clothes be found in one place so as not to take up too much time and energy!" I always thank God in advance for answering these prayers. It is perfectly amazing how He answers once we get needy enough to ask.

Several years ago, after the desire had become so strong I could no longer deny it, I prayed for a home. Not just any house. I went through the usual heart searching where I asked for deliverance from self-indulgence and the like if this desire was not of Him. Then I wrote out before the Lord what I desired, even to the location. I asked that this house be filled with light, be accessible to woods, have trails for walking and bicycling, be utterly suitable for animals, and be the best for freedom from allergies. I asked for beautiful trees and flowers. To ask for such in this area of the country was to ask for a miracle. Heading that petition for the "impossible" was: "Ask what ye will and it shall be done."

Now that I am in my home—an incredible gift straight from the heart of God—I realize more and more my extreme need for it. Not only beautiful trees, grass, and flowers surround me, but a prairie marsh is close at hand with white and blue herons, turtles, beavers, and many other birds and creatures. The healing beauty and quiet of nature helps offset the pressures of the growing ministry.

In answer to such specific petitions as "Lord, enable me to fulfill Your purpose for me," the Lord Himself inspired and strengthened this desire in me. This miracle of quiet, unpretentious beauty, and simplicity is necessary if I am to complete the work God asks of me. This home helps me to continue in the strength God gives even as I grow older.

Petitioning for Strength

> If anyone speaks, he should do it as one speaking the very words of God. If anyone serves, he should do it with the strength God provides (1 Peter 4:11).

Prayer for strength is evermore prominent in these pages of my journal. Never have King David's words, "I love you, O Lord, my strength" (Psalm 18:1), meant more to me than now. Never have the scriptural passages and promises concerning strength brought such blessing.

This is not so much because I have known exhaustion (which I have), nor even because these Scriptures are illuminated as I grow older. It is chiefly because I have known God's faithfulness. I feel saturated, through and through, with His loving kindness. This surely is one of the rewards of journaling answers to prayer faithfully. Truly, in regard to the work He has called us to do, He gives us His very strength.

Physical strength has long eluded me, and an immunopathy that causes chronic allergic fatigue has steadily worsened. Many days I have only a few hours of "good energy"; some days I have none. Every day I have to be careful. Like Paul, I have asked the Lord repeatedly to remove this "thorn in the flesh" only to hear Him remind me that His strength is sufficient for me and that in my weakness, He is strong. And through it all, He gives me the most amazing promises.

> The righteous will flourish like a palm tree,
>   they will grow like a cedar of Lebanon;
> planted in the house of the LORD,
>   they will flourish in the courts of our God.
> They will still bear fruit in old age,
>   they will stay fresh and green,
> proclaiming, "The LORD is upright;
>   he is my Rock, and there is no wickedness in him"
>   (Psalm 92:12–15).

These past months the "listening prayer" part of my journal is alive with words from God regarding a continual "greening" and blossoming of the work He has given me to do. The fruitbearing is not to stop; it will even multiply. I am to stay fresh and green! And the Lord has affirmed these words through others in several wonderful ways. This "thorn in the flesh" may yet be taken from me. In the meantime, however, the Lord has turned even it to good use in my life. I know beyond all shadow of doubt that I walk in the Lord's strength.

Besides needing great strength of concentration to write, it seems I need at least two lifetimes in order to write what is in my heart. I put each subject before the Lord in petitionary form. One by one—ever so slowly it seems—they are birthed. It is an understatement to say that I never know how they got done; I just know that by some miracle they do. One petition I pray regularly in regard to all this is the following:

> Strengthen my mind—Lord, should I live to old, old age may it be sharper then than now . . . and that because I will have grown in You, Your wisdom, righteousness, understanding, power.

People with immune difficulties such as I have do not travel, much less minister publicly. Yet I continue to do both. I am amazed at the special strength and grace I am given. From early on, one of my petitions has been, "Lord, I ask for glowing good health, even unto old, old age, so as always to be able to lift high Your cross and propagate Your Gospel." And strange as it may seem, I know the Lord has heard and answered this prayer. There are even ways in which I seem to have extraordinary strength, health, and the power to accomplish.

I do not tempt the Lord here by failing to seek His face (together with my team who are also my prayer partners) about where I should go or what I should do. But as He leads, I go in the strength He gives. At the time of this writing, the condition has been severe—only a few hours each day with physical and mental energy. This has been going on for months. Yet next week I go to Germany! I thought surely the Lord would say it was right to cancel this time. My team went to prayer, however, and heard the Lord say something quite different. And they heard aright!

Someday I look forward to asking Paul what his "thorn" was, a condition that no doubt seemed as nothing compared to his "people" problems. Already we know who's strength he went in when he rose after he was beaten and left for dead, was shipwrecked in stormy seas and yet undrowned, was snakebitten and yet alive and ministering to others. Nothing stopped Paul! Surely he left an example no one else has since equaled. To look at his life is to see the impossible accomplished at every turn. To really see the Apostle Paul is to marvel at myself as weakling.

Even so, my prayers for physical strength are only one of the "impossibles" through which I see God regularly help me. In regard to many things, it often seems I petition for the impossible, humanly speaking. But the desire for "the impossible" has been strong in my heart and tested before Him. Therefore, I know to lay it before God in all its fullness. In other words, I ask *largely* of God and continue to pray about it. Then, when it is done, I always see that it was really such a small thing for God!

Petitioning for Wisdom

The fear of the LORD is the beginning of wisdom (Psalm 111:10).

Wisdom is supreme; therefore get wisdom.
    Though it cost you all you have, get understanding.

Esteem her, and she will exalt you;
   embrace her, and she will honor you.
She will set a garland of grace on your head
   and present you with a crown of splendor (Proverbs 4:7–9).

Some of the strongest petitioning in my early journals was for wisdom. My besetting defect and sin seemed to be impulsiveness. My mother, with not an impulsive bone in her body, often had to say to me from infancy onward: "Child, you must learn to look before you leap." But in my impatience to live I often reversed those two things and had to learn the hard way.

On returning to Christ as an adult, greatly chastened, I thought about this character flaw, despaired over it, and wondered if God could or would remove my "blind spot." He could and did, of course, but only as I confessed my foolishness as both sin and defect[7] to Him, asking Him to replace it with His wisdom. "Foolishness is bound up in the heart of a child" so the Scriptures tell us. I was still struggling to come up and out of the immature, "under-the-law," unaffirmed state. I was straining toward the walk in the Spirit and maturity in Christ. In order to make the transition into spiritual maturity, only God's wisdom would suffice. This required learning to wait on God; it required *persevering* in His presence. As I did, of course, the Lord unstopped my spiritual ears and enabled me to hear and be led of Him.

Wisdom is an attribute of God that we are to seek and find. Interestingly, the book of Proverbs and wisdom literature personalizes wisdom as feminine. As an attribute of God, she was active in creation of the world (see Proverbs 8:22–31). Here we see wisdom advance in the joy of "making":

Then I was the craftsman at his side.
   I was filled with delight day after day,
rejoicing always in his presence,
   rejoicing in his whole world and delighting in mankind
   (Proverbs 8:30–31).

To find wisdom is to find an outlet for our capacity *to make* as craftsmen at the Creator's side; it is to turn our impulsivity into creativity. With it we find release from our own striving and activism, our unaided reason. As importantly, we find the capacity *simply to be* in His presence, a condition whereby we are affirmed in the very center of our beings as children of God. We gain solidity. We gain *place* and are at home within. Our actions then come from this center, a quiet place where we take our cues from God.

In training his son, Solomon posits wisdom, the transcendent feminine as it were, over and against the seductive and worldly wisdom of the harlot—the false feminine that brings death, not life. The essence of the true feminine is response to God, others, and all that *is*. As a quality in God, we all—men and women alike—are to participate in her and receive her capacity to say, with Mary, "Be it unto me according to Thy will." We then conceive within the womb of our spirits more of God and more of all that is true, beautiful, and good.

In the story of Mary and Martha, Mary chose to sit receptively before the Lord. Hers was the true feminine response, which affirms and strengthens the true feminine within. We receive wisdom from God. Men are only healed in their true masculine— the power to initiate and to do the full will of God—as they are strengthened in their bridal identity. This is the power to respond and be penetrated, through and through, with the fear of the Lord—the fear of a masculine that is so powerful that we are all feminine in relation to it.

If anyone has not yet seriously petitioned the Lord for wisdom, now is certainly the time to do so. God promises it to all who ask in faith (James 1:5–8). Radical changes take place when we ask because wisdom is "a tree of life"; to "embrace her" is to find a source, an eternal and free-flowing fountain, of life (Proverbs 3:18). To journal the Scriptures and petition God for wisdom is to grow in the fear and the knowledge of the Lord. Indeed it is to grow in all that truly *is*. To gain wisdom is therefore to grow in love. The more we come to know and understand, the more there is to *love*. Our hearts and minds then have to expand out of necessity. To petition God for wisdom, therefore, ranks with the first things in importance.

Now as always most of my petitions are pleas for wisdom: wisdom to use time wisely and overcome sloth or any other vice as it lifts its ugly head; wisdom to write and teach in such a way as never to lead another soul astray; wisdom above all in regard to my relationship with God; wisdom to prepare aright for judgment and death.

Petitioning for Guidance

> God's impressions within and His Word without are always corroborated by His Providence around, and we should quietly wait until those three focus into one point.[8]

Petitioning for wisdom and guidance are together in my mind. In seeking guidance for the future we pray for God's wisdom in regard to moving forward in His will; we do not attempt to *divine* the future. This is an important distinction. In petitionary prayer, then, we often seek God's guidance for our future. The right attitude of heart reflects trust in a God who holds and knows our future, while the wrong one attempts to see the future in order to be at peace. The wrong attitude of mind in this respect will pervert the power to listen to God.

In seeking guidance, whether on how to pray or how to find God's will for our lives, the principles for receiving that guidance reside in trusting God with all our hearts, minds, and bodies. F. B. Meyer's wonderful wisdom, quoted above, *together with learning to receive wisdom from the Lord in listening prayer,* is the prescription for knowing and receiving God's will for our prayers and for our lives. There is a time to wait on God. That waiting requires our ears to be open to hear what the Spirit speaks when He speaks.

Dallas Willard's book *In Search of Guidance: Developing a Conversational Relationship with God* is the finest on this subject, combining as it does the insights of F. B. Meyer with insights on listening prayer.

Blocks to Gaining the Lord's Mind on How to Pray

We do not gain the Lord's mind on how to pray if we need or desire to control or manipulate Him or others. We must deal with our bentness in these ways (commonly referred to as codependency today) or it will interfere with our prayer lives. In these cases, our motives are impure; our eye is not "single" (Matthew 6:22). Rather than trusting God, we trust in our own power to "fix" things.

We do not acquire the mind of the Lord and receive from Him if we are out to please others or look good in their sight. To please God is often to displease others—in fact we often confound them. And the silly language of popular psychology can easily confuse us at this point. For example, by way of excusing one bishop who was pleasing others rather than God by ordaining sexually perverted priests, one Christian said: "But he's such a gentle and good man; he just *can't stand conflict.*"

That is not an excuse God would give any Christian, much less a bishop. Christ calls such a one as this a people-pleaser—an idolater and false prophet. And He laments the fate of sheep put under such a "gentle and good" shepherd. Christ knew well that these would be the people who crucified Him. He reminded men like this bishop that they always killed the true prophets before Him. People-pleasers are idolaters—those who look to others and not to God to get their (in the language of today) ego needs met. Someone or something has replaced the living God, trust in Him, and the word of truth He always speaks.

We do not get the mind of God on how to pray if there is the least inclination in us toward using prayer as a crystal ball. In petitionary prayer, we are often seeking God's will and *guidance for the future*, which is absolutely right, good, and necessary to the walk in the Spirit. This is in contrast to any attempt to *divine* the future.

Trust in God for a future only He can see is an underlying principle in gaining the Lord's direction for our lives. This is not to say that God never gives us a prophetic insight into the future toward which He is leading us. He does. The right attitude of heart does not seek to know the future, and does not need to know it in order to be at peace.

Prophets Who Speak to Itching Ears

We do not receive the mind of God on how to pray if we idolatrously attempt to use others as crystal balls either. Sadly, there is a need to issue warning to Christians who seek out "prophets" who may "have a word" for them—in other words, those who will "divine" their futures for them. The kind of prophets who oblige these seekers are proliferating. Many of them are active in the various sectors of the church.

On the one hand, these false prophets include those whose gifts were given by God but have since become mixed with powers of divination. Demonic spirits of divination now accompany them, giving them personal details about another soul that are fruitless for that soul's growth in Christ. Instead this knowledge builds up the "prophets" themselves as some kind of powerful spiritual magicians. Although parts of these prophecies are simply scriptural promises given generally, other parts are simultaneously slanted to appeal to the subjective ego needs of those who seek them out. Actually, they constellate a carnal "drive toward power" in them.

As I write I see numerous instances of pastors who are in trouble because they have received false prophecies concerning how they were to succeed personally and how their churches would expand in power and number. These men damaged or even destroyed their ministries by believing the words of false prophets that constellated within them a false masculine activism and appealed strongly to their emotional and spiritual needs for affirmation as men.

These prophets are often considered safe by the immature or the undiscerning because they inveigh against New Age paganism. But the irony is that these prophets themselves have fallen into what amounts to the same practices. Things become all the more confusing for those who follow such a prophet and hold onto the "prophecies" laid upon them, often through laying-on-of-hands. In many cases they have received their only scriptural teachings from this person—there has been good teaching mixed in with the bad prophecies. Thus it is extremely difficult for the needy or immature Christian to untangle the good from the confusing and the bad. This makes it difficult for them to come out of the confusion into which these "mixed" and therefore false prophecies lead. When the prophecies are received, spiritual deception is the end result.

On the other end of the spectrum, some people will not receive the words and images of these false or misguided "prophets" into their spirits but they fall into what amounts to the same thing. They become deceived by "Christianized" secular psychologies that assign innocence to sin and evil. Sin and evil in a person or situation are renamed, with evil being called good and good being called evil. God and evil are thereby "synthesized"—made one and reconciled. These systems of understanding the soul are pagan and gnostic, as I have described in chapter 14. As the early Christians knew well, it takes only a tiny pinch of gnosticism to bring one under spiritual deception. Just a little bit of that leaven goes a long way in perverting a soul—or a congregation of souls.

New Age neognosticism is being spread throughout the church today, covered with a veneer of psychological (mostly Jungian) terminology. Therefore, as people attempt to divine their own soul and "story" or journey, they completely leave out a transforming moment with God that brings the soul into union with a transcendent Holy Other. Rather, their "transforming moment" is union with themselves. Their wisdom and guidance comes from discovering and interpreting the images of their own heart. They accept a neognostic (Jungian) interpretation of those images, including dreams. The individual's feelings, radiating out of ego needs, send up a variety of messages and images that lead astray when misinterpreted. Objectivity is lost. A subjectivity that is ego-related is elevated to the point that these people literally live from their subjective feeling being—a narcissism that makes the feeling being one's center. The self then becomes god. "Story" replaces objective reality, including divine revelation, Holy Writ. Those so deceived are no longer open to objective wisdom. Undoubtedly they are faced with a false prophet—their own hearts. The old paganism completely replaces trust in God.

Fleeing the Carnal and Demonic Mixtures

False prophets always batten off the church. Always, too, they mix the language of the gospel with the pagan practices they advance. Out and out evil is easy enough to see. But we need to flee the mixture of good and evil. This can be less obvious to the undiscerning. These dreadful mixtures follow a diabolical principle best seen in witchcraft and the satanic. They require that the good and true be present—that which has been set into the church and hallowed. The satanic aim is to insinuate the obscene and the perverted into the good and the holy, the lying falsehood into the midst of the true.

What we see today in the "divining" prophets has occurred partly because of a lack of knowledge. Ignorance, mixed with a taste for the superficial and the more dramatic "supernatural," has been coupled with a machismo-like need to lord it over others. Our day seems ripe for almost anything of this nature to take place. This has, unfortunately, made people wary of the true gift (*gift*, in contrast to office of prophet) of prophecy. But even so its proper function in the church's ministry should not be deterred. The least attention the gift commands, the better; what is important is that the true gift is maintained and matures.

At times God gives a personal promise for the future, along with comfort and guidance. We, like Mary, are to hide it away in our hearts, saying "Be it unto me according to thy word." We remember it before God in prayer. This foretelling is a valid and vital need of the soul, which this gift fulfills most wonderfully. The Scriptures tell us not to despise it.

I write this so that we might quickly detect any subtle shift from trusting in God to trusting in some means of controlling the present or divining the future. We must not allow this into our prayer or ministry life. We also need to be aware of this in the lives of those to whom we minister. Some people will always seek a word from or through a minister in order to avoid the more strenuous duty of learning to trust in God and hear Him for themselves. The next step in their healing is surely for the minister to show them what they are doing and point them strongly toward God and His revealed word to them:

Your statutes are wonderful; therefore I obey them.
The unfolding [literally *opening*] of your words gives light;
it gives understanding to the simple (Psalm 119:129–130).

Preparing for Death and Judgment

"She's gone, dear," said the district nurse. The elderly woman on the other side of the bed sighed and said, "Well, poor soul, it's a happy release."

Both were silent a moment out of respect for the dead and then Mrs. Croft, the nurse, said briskly, "Well, dear, we'd better get cracking, for I'm pressed for time."

The old-fashioned room was filled with the quietness of the deep country and the light of a marvelous sunset. Mrs. Baker, who had loved the dead woman, was touched to awe by the tide of gold. It was like water, she thought, flooding into the room, and she was unusually silent as she and Mrs. Croft performed the last offices with the gentle yet swift dexterity of long practice.

"Nothing on your mind, dear?" asked Mrs. Croft, for Mrs. Baker was by nature chatty. "The way you looked after the poor old dear, year after year, you've nothing to reproach yourself with. A few hours a week were all you were paid for, as well I know, and you were here morning, noon and night."

Mrs. Baker, a wiry, doughty little country woman, said simply, "I was fond of her. No, I've nothing on my mind. I was remembering her last words."

"What did she say, dear?" asked Mrs. Croft soothingly. Mrs. Baker, she perceived, was in her own fashion taking this death hard, and it was always best to let them talk.

"She said something about sailing out on living water."

"Wandering," said Mrs. Croft.

"She had been, but not then. She was quite clear in her mind, like they so often are. Living water, she said. This gold put me in mind of it."

Mrs. Croft returned to practical matters. "Do you think she would have wished to be laid out in her wig?"

"Of course," said Mrs. Baker tartly. "She was always one to make the best of herself."

A little later, the auburn wig in place and their work done, they stood back to admire their handiwork, in which each took the pleasure of an artist.

"Looks peaceful," said Mrs. Croft. "Funny how quickly they change." A few hours ago a very grotesque old woman had been dying in the curtained bed but now the sculptured face already wore the stamp of beauty. "Must have been a lovely woman once."

Though life and death were equally all in the day's work for both women the mystery held them for a moment. Then Mrs. Croft turned briskly to the door. "Well, dear, I must be getting on. I've a baby due any time up at the farm."

Mrs. Baker was not listening. "It was herself that she meant," she said.[9]

With this scene and these words, Elizabeth Goudge begins one of her finest novels, my favorite. This and another scene from *The Scent of Water*, one of a healing of self-hatred, are two of the profoundest in this century's literature. "Sailing out on living water"—this is the kind of death for which we petition God.

In my childhood, my mother and grandmother told me of death scenes of Christians in the family. The dying spoke of seeing into heaven as they left this earthly life. Some even spoke of seeing other members of the family coming to greet them. In the most meaningful story to me, my father came to welcome his sister as she began her last journey. The other stories were before my time, but this one occurred when I was a child. I recall how awed my mother and I were by this. Once in a great while I asked her to tell me again of what happened as my Aunt Mary lay dying.

With the death of my father very early in life, I learned that a loved one could be quickly taken from among the living, that "our days on earth are as a shadow." I also knew, however, that we sail out on living water. I knew that those who are in Christ are alive in a way that far surpasses and fulfills our lives here. In part due to this consciousness, perhaps, I have always devoted part of my Petition section to death and judgment. It is filled with Scriptures that admonish and prepare us for both.

There is nothing depressing about this—though people with a decidedly morbid cast of mind could make it so. The historic church even has teachings that contribute to the morbid and to the hatred of our time on earth and our incarnation into a physical body. But this is not Christian. Yet there is tension in the sense that death is our last enemy, as even the Bible teaches. We need to come to grips with this fact and pray the relevant Scriptures. We need to prepare for our own deaths. I make these self-evident statements because of the modern Christian's denial regarding death.

As one in the healing ministry, it is difficult to teach on physical healing because of this modern denial. For example, some think that if their bodies are not healed, their souls will not be either. Though irrational and certainly contrary to Christian teaching, these notions are widespread. They are part of the modern's denial of death—the failure to accept the fact that even one's own body is destined to die once and then to face judgment. But this has not always been so. In the past the church has better prepared her people for these ultimate matters.

Petitions for myself and others close to my heart include prayer that we be spared a calamitous and untimely death. I ask that we be given (even should we die as Stephen the protomartyr did) a peaceful Christian death—one with a window right into glory. It is right to pray in this way because we learn better how to listen to the Spirit's warning when we are in danger. We also keep heaven in view.

For the Christian to prepare for death and judgment through journaling the teachings of the Scriptures on these matters is to regain the full hope of heaven—the prize that awaits us. To sail out on living water is to come finally into a harbor where an "exceeding and eternal weight of glory" is ours, an inheritance eternal and incorruptible.

Receiving from God

"If you remain in me and my words remain in you, ask whatever you wish, and it will be given you. This is to my Father's glory, that you bear much fruit, showing yourselves to be my disciples" (Jesus, John 15:7–8).

Let us then approach the throne of grace with confidence, so that we may receive mercy and find grace to help us in our time of need (Hebrews 4:16).

In him and through faith in him we may approach God with freedom and confidence (Ephesians 3:12).

"If you believe, you will receive whatever you ask for in prayer" (Jesus, Matthew 21:22).

You need to persevere so that when you have done the will of God, you will receive what he has promised (Hebrews 10:36).

An important part of petitionary prayer is that of appropriation, the moment in which we *receive* God's answer by faith. We are not passive but active in this *receiving;* we open our hearts to receive that which we have asked for in prayer. This involves a release of our faith.

To believe in Christ is to know Him; to know Him is to be *in Him*. This *union*—our personal relationship with Him—*is* faith in the primary sense. This faith is already there. As it were, we dwell in it and it dwells in us. From this status, then, of being in faith—being in Christ—our trust (faith in a secondary sense) goes out to God. We lay hold of and appropriate that for which we have petitioned.

This is the confidence we have in approaching God: that if we ask anything according to his will, he hears us. And if we know that he hears us—whatever we ask—we know that we have what we asked of him (1 John 5:14–15).

The failure to receive forgiveness from God is a grave and widespread problem among Christians today. Even after we confess our sins to Him and He stretches out His hand filled to overflowing with forgiveness, we fail to receive it.[10] But forgiveness is not the only thing we have difficulty receiving from God. In a day when we are out of touch with the soul and its ways of communicating and interacting with God, we have to learn anew how to receive from Him. It is really very simple. Through an act of the will we release our faith in confidence and receive what we have asked for, thanking God in advance for the answer. But we must not overlook this action in prayer.

Releasing Prayer in Faith

Many people fail to receive from God, oftentimes because of the misguided practice of excessive striving. I mentioned this earlier in writing about what to avoid in intercessory prayer. Where we lack understanding or power of appropriation we will necessarily employ these onerous practices of striving and struggling.

We do well to pray without ceasing. This is largely what *practicing the presence* is all about. It results in an extraordinarily peaceful trust, which is anything but static. We move continually toward God, the object of our faith. In excessive striving, however, we do far too much supplicating as we fail to appropriate the answer we seek. To be stuck in this way leaves one spent rather than strengthened in faith and hope. The Scriptures indicate that God wearies of it as well.

In order to release the prayer offered in faith (James 5:15), first we must obtain the mind of God on how to pray. We ask, "How, Lord, would you have me pray about this matter?" As we lay the matter before Him we gain His wisdom on it sooner or later (James 1:5). Second, we make our request specifically and simply. Third, we release our prayer offered in faith. Fourth, after releasing our prayer in faith, we *receive* (appropriate) the answer to our prayer. We thank God most sincerely in advance for hearing and answering our prayer. None of this is difficult if our will is one with God's. Actually it is the natural way of believing prayer. The Scriptures teach and model it.[11]

Some people automatically and even unconsciously appropriate and receive answers in prayer. However it is done, it involves the mind and heart's picture—however dim—of the good end and God's acceptance of it. But if we have missed this step routinely we can learn it easily. We merely take a moment to "see" with our hearts God's will being done. We start out by simply picturing with the mind's eye what we have requested from God. We hold it before Him in such a way that He can continue to speak to us about it. It is amazing how often, by this exercise, God modifies or changes our picture to be more in line with His will. Thus we receive additional wisdom from above, and even a word from God. Just as He modifies the way we think and feel in line with His will, so He corrects and often expands the way our hearts picture-think.

To see God's will being done with the eyes of our heart involves the same principle that Isaiah speaks of when he says: "Without a vision the people perish." As in all things, in prayer we must have a vision of the good and the goal, or we do not release the faith needed to attain it. It is the creative principle at work.[12] As such it differs drastically from its carnal and demonic imitations—the attempts to create, control, or divine the future.[13]

6

Forgiveness

If I had cherished sin in my heart,
  the LORD would not have listened;
but God has surely listened
  and heard my voice in prayer (Psalm
    66:18–19).

And Forgive Us Our Trespasses, As We Forgive Those Who Trespass against Us. And Lead Us Not into Temptation, But Deliver Us from Evil

This section of the Lord's Prayer has three vital petitions we are to incorporate into our prayer life. Because of their unique importance they should be placed as a separate section in our prayer journals. Repenting of our sins, forgiving others their sins against us, and gaining deliverance in temptation and from the evil one are central to everything Christian. Without forgiveness or freedom from evil we are subject to sickness of spirit, soul, and—eventually—body as well.

There are three great barriers to personal healing and wholeness—failing to receive forgiveness, forgive others, and gain the great virtue of self-acceptance. We overcome these barriers when we repent with all our hearts, receive forgiveness, and renounce the evil one and all his works. I have written at length about these matters in *Restoring the Christian Soul through Healing Prayer: The Three Great Barriers to Personal and Spiritual Completion in Christ*. Those who have not done their vital work of repentance and forgiveness—especially those who are in need of spiritual and emotional healing—should work through that book carefully in conjunction with this part of their prayer journal.

Notice that *sins* is plural in the phrase "forgive us our sins." Because we have been born from above, we are *in Christ* and are forgiven the sin (singular) of separation from God. That big one, so to speak, has been forgiven; it is settled. But we are to confess our *sins* (plural) of omission and commission immediately as our consciences and the Holy Spirit reveal them. Then, as importantly, we are to receive forgiveness for these sins; in other words, forgiveness is to be appropriated through a deliberate step of faith. Our repentance and confession of sin, then, together with bestowing forgiveness on others and loving even our enemies, is the larger part of what this section of our prayer journal is about.

Most often our petitions for forgiveness and protection are simply breathed up in prayer; if noted, we record them in the daily prayer section. But when any of these concerns proves stubborn, needing ongoing prayer, we are to journal them in this section.

When we journal our concerns regarding either deliverance from temptation or from the demonic, we listen to God in a way that enables us to avoid the grievous sins and pitfalls that can so easily ensnare us. And we also prepare ourselves to stand in the day of spiritual battle and win the war waged against us by the evil one. In Christ's righteousness we overcome all the wiles and fiery darts of the enemies of our souls.

As we pray these petitions as Christ has taught us, we trust Him to shine His light on any unconfessed sin in our lives so that we can repent of it instantly (Psalm 139:23–24). We also ask Him to show us if we need to forgive others their sins against us. This does not mean that we descend into an overly introspective or examining stance in our daily prayers. That would take our focus from God, turning our attention inward in an unhealthy way. But it does mean that we ask Christ, in as much of His radiance as we can bear, to shine into any space in our hearts and lives—inner or outer, conscious or unconscious—where we may be "cherishing iniquity" or failing to forgive another from our heart. As David cried out in the Psalms, "Surely You desire truth in the inner parts; You teach me wisdom in the inmost place" (51:6).

> Blessed is he
>> whose transgressions are forgiven,
>> whose sins are covered.
> Blessed is the man
>> whose sin the LORD does not count against him
>> and in whose spirit is no deceit (Psalm 32:1–2).

The Mere Mechanics

The best way to start in this Forgiveness section is to take four sheets of paper and place the following headings on them: (1) "Forgive us our sins as we forgive everyone who sins against us"; (2) "And lead us not into temptation"; (3) "But deliver us from evil"; (4) Prayer for enemies.

As we need to petition the Lord under any of these headings we then journal the pertinent Scriptures through which God speaks to our hearts. It is also helpful to journal the writings of others whose insight gives clarity and greater understanding to us. We write out our confessions before the Lord as specifically as possible, as well as the forgiveness we extend to others.

This section of my journal is chock-full of Scriptures that have been quickened in me as the different spiritual temptations and battles have come. These Scriptures now act as blueprints for action, for overcoming in the face of trial. They are solid reminders of past victories.

Forgive Us Our Sins As We Forgive Everyone Who Sins against Us

New converts to Christ will benefit greatly by allowing the Lord to shine His light over their entire lives. We can do this by taking our life in manageable segments—such as seven-year periods or early childhood, grade-school years, junior-high years, and so on—and spread before the Lord any memory of our sin or our grievous reactions to the sin of another. In this way we root out unforgiveness, fully confess our sins, and carefully *receive* (and perhaps even record!) God's forgiveness.

In forgiveness of injuries done to us, Christ is our supreme example and teacher. When crucified, He prayed, "Father, forgive them, for they know not what they do" (Luke 23:34). And over and over again, He taught us

> ... When you stand praying, if you hold anything against anyone, forgive him, so that your Father in heaven may forgive you your sins (Mark 11:25).

Jesus has taught us to love and forgive even our worst enemies. We will explore how to do so later in this chapter. Once again, I urge all who remain in an immature state because of issues of forgiveness and confession of sin to see my book *Restoring the Christian Soul through Healing Prayer*.

And Lead Us Not into Temptation

> When tempted, no one should say, "God is tempting me." For God cannot be tempted by evil, nor does he tempt anyone; but each one is tempted when, by his own evil desire, he is dragged away and enticed. Then, after desire has conceived, it gives birth to sin; and sin, when it is full-grown, gives birth to death (James 1:13–15).

Satan is the author of temptation. As the master deceiver he uses his powers of deception. If we studied the temptations we have "entered into," we would see the three stages St. James points to: first carnal desire, then sin, then death. But most of us do not do such analysis because it is painful and humbling, especially after a fall. Instead we are relieved merely to confess our sin heartily, forgetting how we fell into deception in the first place. We can see these three stages easily enough in Bible characters;

Eve is the first and primal example. C. G. Kromminga points out that

> Satan avoids making a frontal attack. . . . Instead he sows the seeds of doubt, unbelief, and rebellion. The temptation of Eve is typical. *She is made to feel that God has unwisely and unfairly withheld a legitimate objective good from man.* In Job's trials the strategy is different, but the end sought is the same—the rejection of God's will and way as just and good.[1]

To charge God "unwisely and unfairly" is a demonic temptation. When we yield to it we enter spiritual deception. I shudder at Christian counselors who affirm and enable counselees in their temptations to charge God amiss. These counselors usually do so by sympathizing with their patients' "need to express their feelings." In such cases, neither counselor nor counselee seems to realize that in charging God with some kind of evil, they have willingly entered into temptation.

Many people, angry with father or mother or the church they grew up in, transfer this anger onto God. Thus not only do the problems of denial and unforgiveness need to be dealt with, but displaced anger as well. And there will also be *unbelief*, either in needing to know God more truly or in failing to know the true God at all. In these cases the misbegotten feelings must be acknowledged *as such* to sort them out before God and counselors learned in His wisdom. Wise counsel helps such people uncover the true objects of fear and anger in their lives.

The Retired Sphere of the Leasts

> Be self-controlled and alert. Your enemy the devil prowls around like a roaring lion looking for someone to devour. Resist him, standing firm in the faith, because you know that your brothers throughout the world are undergoing the same kind of sufferings (1 Peter 5:8–9).

> *Watch and pray, that ye enter not into temptation* (Matthew 26:41, KJV, emphasis mine).

Oswald Chambers warns us that some of our most subtle temptations come in the form of "the retired sphere of the leasts." He warns us that "the Bible characters fell on their strong points, never on their weak ones." Quoting the tragic words about a once loyal military leader turned traitor from 1 Kings 2:28, "Joab had turned after Adonijah, though he turned not after Absalom," Chambers writes:

> Joab stood the big test, he remained absolutely loyal and true to David and did not turn after the fascinating and ambitious Absalom, but yet towards the end of his life he turned after the craven Adonijah.[2]

Chambers's words and the related scriptural admonitions, such as "take heed lest you fall," are writ large in my heart today. I do not want to have run the race this far to lose it through the failure to be watchful.

Throughout my life the lure of material comfort has certainly been on my "retired sphere of the leasts." If it ever was a temptation, it was "retired" years ago. In order to minister as I have, I never had a home until I was past fifty years of age. It was not as if I eschewed it. But to be faithful to my vocation, I had to pour my energy into that rather than in earning enough to buy and support a home. So I mostly lived in rooms—usually in someone's basement or attic.

Now, however, that God has provided a home and income is more certain, I have noted a sense of concern lest something happen—to either the place or the steadier income. I have started taking care of *things:* gifts from people from all over the world, such as paintings by artist friends, a beautifully carved crucifix, and so on. That which never trapped me before—never seemed quite so important—is now something to be worried about, insured, and so on. I could a little more easily elect not to go out in ministry but (with all my good excuses of age and health) elect to stay in my home. It could become my treasure.

Noting this and the fact that the lure of physical and material comfort is no longer necessarily on my "retired sphere of the leasts," I have prayed, "Lead me not into temptation." I have journaled this before the Lord. I have acknowledged and confessed the danger and temptation of a little less trust in Him for the future, a little more trust in the gifts He has so graciously given.

We are to give hearty thanks for His gifts, delighting in them as such. But we must be watchful for the shift from thankfulness to an idolatrous dependence on these gifts. The *moment* we see something like this at work in our lives we must journal it. Therefore we keep a straight account with our God, resting in the knowledge that:

> No temptation has seized you except what is common to man. And God is faithful; he will not let you be tempted beyond what you can bear. But when you are tempted, he will also provide a way out so that you can stand up under it (1 Corinthians 10:13–14).

But Deliver Us from Evil

> The Lord will rescue me from every evil attack and will bring me safely to his heavenly kingdom (2 Timothy 4:18).

The Lord protects us from the evil that strikes at us both through others (human evil) and through demonic spirits. As in all things divine, we need to learn how to receive (appropriate) this protection and *move in it.* That is, we need to know how to collaborate with God—listening to Him—in the midst of spiritual battle and win in the power of His love, righteousness, and wisdom. In this way, we are most assuredly "kept by the power of God" for we are *in* Him. This does not mean we will not suffer, but rather that good will come from the suffering; it will be redemptive in contrast to being merely remedial.[3] We "who through faith are shielded by God's power" (1 Peter 1:5) listen to God, appropriate His promises, and are led by Him. This protection is ours as we remain *in* Him.

A recent example here illustrates this further. I have been concerned that each member of the PCM ministry team learn to appropriate protection from God. We are often attacked because this ministry speaks truth and light into places where particularly vile strongholds of lies and darkness rule. And though we have enjoyed the faithful, powerful protection of our God, we need to keep in mind the part we are to play faithfully. There are

> two sides to the perseverance of the Christian. He is shielded (1) by God's power and (2) by his own faith. Thus he is never kept contrary to his will nor apart from God's activity.[4]

The practice of the presence, together with listening prayer, takes all wrongful striving out of the act of releasing our faith. Our faith is not in our faith, but in Christ who is in and with us. We simply acknowledge that fact, trusting the one whom the Father has sent.

Releasing our faith and appropriating this protection is actually a simple step. Only yesterday we prayed for one in special need of protection. Jabez's prayer for both protection and blessing was quickened in me (1 Chronicles 4:10), along with several other Scriptures. We "prayed" them, thanking God in advance for His answer to this prayer. I then prayed for a "wall of God's holy fire" around this team member through which no evil could penetrate. As he *received* in prayer he opened the eyes of his heart to see this holy fire encircling him. In doing this his faith was released and God amplified the picture. He saw that the fire was rising from a ring of blood surrounding him. Like the protection the blood on the lentil post symbolized and afforded the ancient Israelite, he appropriated the saving protection of the blood of Christ.

Protection from Evil People

> An enormously good gift to give someone evil is to foil their effort to win. Evil is used to winning. It uses conscienceless seduction and shameless mockery to win ground and frighten others away from taking it back. . . . One of the greatest gifts one can give a person inclined to evil is the strength to frustrate their attempts to dominate.[5]

We do not forgive evil. The soul so deeply wounded by an evil person often does not understand this fact. We hate evil (Proverbs

8:13; Romans 12:9). But we find the grace to *forgive* those in the grip of evil.[6] We begin by confessing their specific sins against us.[7]

The severely wounded soul fears forgiving the evildoer, thinking that doing so will put him or her back under the power of the evil one. But hating evil while releasing the evildoer from unforgiveness on our part does not mean that we remain under his or her power to destroy us. Instead we gain Christ's strength to defeat and utterly overcome the effects of that evil on ourselves.

> Such strength must be full of cunning and precision. Evil can never be overthrown through rational, reasonable argumentation. It may dialogue and debate, but its direction is already determined. Evil will never stop long enough to consider its destructiveness unless it is held accountable, under strong, clear, and unwavering consequences of righteousness.[8]

One of the key ways to love an evil person is to place the proper boundaries around ourselves. These protect us from his or her will to use and destroy us. We must extricate ourselves from the evilly constructed web of lies—the dark personal myth or story—that protect the evildoer from reality. This person shuns the insight into and acknowledgment of his or her sin; he or she also rationalizes his or her scapegoating maneuvers.

To construct such boundaries we must learn to speak the truth objectively and judiciously, not to rescue or try to change such a one through our own power, but to hold up the only standard of truth whereby both perpetrator and victim can find salvation and freedom. For full healing we all must choose reality over illusion, truth over lie, heaven over hell. The loving action we must finally take toward the one whose evil is hardened and unremitting is that of *excommunicating* him or her from our lives.

To confess the specific sins of others against us does not mean that those who commit evil deeds find forgiveness of sin apart from their own personal repentance. It means that we as Christians have the privilege, in Christ, of breaking the power those sins continue to have over us. Confessing the sins committed against us by those who are yet unrepentant, and extending forgiveness to them, opens the doorway to freedom from the effects of that sin on us.

I have often seen a weakening of the stronghold of sin over the evildoer as well after this prayer, together with a special moment of grace. There will be an unusual "window" of light and opportunity to choose God, to choose heaven over and against hell, truth over and against the lies that make up the personal "myths," *life* now and eternally as over and against death. But those who consistently refuse to acknowledge their sin—their evil behavior as evil—often, sadly, refuse this bright window of opportunity.

Those whose childhood years were dominated by evildoers and the environments they create need much wise counsel and prayer to come to terms with the circumstances of their early lives. Obviously, they had no power either to name or excommunicate the evil behavior of the adults over them.

Along with their need for healing and deliverance from evil, these people need to understand their lives in the light of what is straight and normal. Their struggle to come up and out of *denial* (a strong defense mechanism) about what all actually occurred will be steep and fraught with pain. This is especially so when denial is so strong that traumatic memories and circumstances are repressed and blotted out from conscious memory. When healing begins in these people, the painful memories often come up fully loaded with all the original pain. And to confuse matters even more, these repressed memories come up in disguised forms.

One precious young woman, deeply wounded by parents who were known as religious leaders in their small community, stayed in my home for a while. Healing had commenced in her, but her stress was almost unbearable as repressed memories threatened to come up. Indeed they were coming up, but in disguised and fearful forms. She was so terrified of these memories coming to consciousness that she could hardly sleep at all—and then only with a full light on in her bedroom.

She picked up a copy of M. Scott Peck's *The People of the Lie* from my bookshelf and began to read. He has written about evil in the one who covers it over with a moral or religious veneer. In reading this she was freed to name the evil she had suffered.[9] She could finally name the evil aright. This understanding brought her out of the last stronghold her defense mechanisms of denial had on her. She said:

> I knew my parents had stepped over the line somewhere, had become evil, but I did not understand what made them evil, and why they were. They created the illusion that they were perfect, and though they never said it in so many words, they demanded that I think they were. . . . They convinced me that I was evil.

I asked her to share the passages from Dr. Peck's book that helped her. This was easy for her to do since she had written them out in her prayer journal.

She headed these passages with the exclamation, "Key!" Here she finally had the words to name and understand her particular situation. Some of them are reprinted below:

> When a child is grossly confronted by significant evil in its parents, it will most likely misinterpret the situation and believe that the evil resides in itself.[10]

> It is not their sins per se that characterize evil people, rather it is the subtlety and persistence and consistency of their sins. This is because the central defect of the evil is not the sin but the REFUSAL TO ACKNOWLEDGE IT.[11]

> Those who have "crossed over the line" are characterized by their absolute refusal to tolerate the sense of their own sinfulness.[12]

> Evil is not committed by people who feel uncertain about their righteousness, who question their motives, who worry about betraying themselves. The evil in this world is committed by the . . . Pharisees of our own day, the self-righteous. . . . It is out of their failure to put themselves on trial that their evil arises.[13]

> Whenever there is a major deficit in parental love, the child will, in all likelihood, respond to that deficit by assuming itself to be

the cause of the deficit, thereby developing an unrealistically negative self-image.[14]

Forever fleeing the light of self-exposure and the voice of their own conscience, they [evil persons] are the most frightened of human beings. They live their lives in sheer terror. They need not be consigned to any hell; they are already in it.
   Because in their hearts they consider themselves above reproach, they must lash out at anyone who does reproach them. They sacrifice others to preserve their self-image of perfection.[15]

Scapegoating works through a mechanism psychiatrists call projection.[16]

They project their own evil onto the world. They never see themselves as evil; they consequently see much evil in others. Evil people are often destructive because they are attempting to destroy evil. The problem is that they misplace the locus of the evil. Instead of destroying others they should be destroying the sickness in themselves.[17]

One of the characteristics of evil is its desire to confuse.[18]

I hope the above is helpful to those who need to identify evil behavior and draw the proper boundaries between themselves and the ongoing abuse they have suffered through it. The very nature of evil causes confusion in its victims. They are often the last to be able to name it rightly, realizing that they themselves are not the cause of it. We must understand this in the context of what it means to love our enemies (not some sentimentalized "love" that enables the evildoer) while simultaneously hating, naming, and *excommunicating or exorcising* the evil that they bring or have brought into our own lives. This is vital for growth in Christian maturity and joy.
   When Mario Bergner lectures in our PCM conferences, people who have suffered in this way as children receive great understanding and healing. His book *Setting Love in Order* will help all such as these.[19]

Prayer for Our Enemies: The Gift of Battle

As we learn to love and forgive our worst enemies we gain "the gift of battle." Because of their supreme importance today, this and the following sections have been adapted from chapter 12 of *Restoring the Christian Soul.*

Jesus said, "But I tell you, Do not resist an evil person. If someone strikes you on the right cheek, turn to him the other also" (Matthew 5:39). Jesus makes a number of statements like this one in the Sermon on the Mount. In doing so, He contradicts and overturns the best Jewish wisdom of the day. As Oswald Chambers says, a study of these words reveals

> the humiliation of being a Christian. Naturally, if a man does not hit back, it is because he is a coward; but spiritually if a man does not hit back, it is a manifestation of the Son of God in him. When you are insulted, you must not only not resent it, but make it an occasion to exhibit the Son of God. You cannot imitate the disposition of Jesus; it is either there or it is not. To the saint personal insult becomes the occasion of revealing the incredible sweetness of the Lord Jesus.[20]

We can never understand or live out our Lord's words by ourselves. This can only be done because another—the one crucified for sin—lives in us. We are to listen for a higher wisdom and collaborate with it. If we are to be victorious in spiritual conflict we must move forward not only in the knowledge of Christ's presence with us but in the gifts of the Holy Spirit as they operate through listening prayer.

As we truly experience spiritual battle we will understand what real enemies are. Nothing sends us back to Christ's words about loving our enemies more quickly than a skirmish with those who hate the word of truth—Christ and His gospel—and therefore hate and malign us. We will soon find out if we are battling partly in our own strength. If so, we must cry out for mercy to battle only in His.

In *Crumbling Foundations*, Donald Bloesch writes of our need to pray for the "gift of battle." He reminds us that "Christians can only live out their vocation by discovering and exercising the gifts of the Holy Spirit." He believes the gift of battle is an additional gift that both Testaments allude to and is crucially significant for our day:

> Christians who are under the cross of persecution need to pray for the gift of battle, the ability to endure under trial, the boldness to challenge immorality and heresy in high places. The gift of battle is properly included in the gift of might or power (Isaiah 11:2). It is the power to enter into conflict and the stamina not to grow weary. It must be accompanied by and fulfilled in the gift of love, since we cannot wage war against sin successfully unless we love the sinner. We must speak the truth, but we must speak the truth in love.[21]

Speaking the truth in a love born of God is the greater part of the gift of battle. There is nothing weak about this love, for fully orbed and aptly spoken truth is incredibly powerful.

Thus a first principle in spiritual warfare is knowing that we cannot function in the gift of battle without *agape,* the gift of divine love that comes from God's life within us. We know that we must trust Him completely and look to no other power than to Him. As we look straight to God and receive His battle plan we come to understand that we are to hate sin but not our enemy.

The following prayer from a Greek Orthodox liturgy has a permanent and prominent place in my journal. It helps me pray aright for my enemy when the battle is raging and I am least able to muster my own words for such a prayer. It echoes the true spirit of Christ's Sermon on the Mount.

> Save, O Lord, and have mercy upon those that envy and affront me and do me mischief, and let them not perish through me, a sinner.

Such prayer as this is what loving our enemy is all about.

A second principle is that we cannot function in the gift of battle apart from mature prayer partners. These foot soldiers trudge alongside us, persevering in the same battle:

Christians who enter the battle against the powers of darkness cannot persevere without a life-support system, without a supportive fellowship that continually holds up its members in intercession to the living God.[22]

Those of us who have these "life-support" systems are deeply grateful for them, as I have mentioned elsewhere in this book. Those who do not have prayer partners must pray earnestly for them. The intercessions of the saints who gather together in Christ's name to pray are absolutely vital in the Christian walk, and most assuredly so in spiritual warfare. God's gift of precious souls that not only intercede but hear and pass on the word that God is speaking when we are sore besieged and fainting is true wealth.

We must engage in the gift of battle because the archaccuser of our souls, the enemy who would deceive and bring us under dark deception, plans the full destruction of us as persons. We overcome under the Lord's banner—His holy cross and its way of love (Hebrews 2:10)—not according to the way the world fights:

> For though we live in the world, we do not wage war as the world does. The weapons we fight with are not the weapons of the world. On the contrary, they have divine power to demolish strongholds. We demolish arguments and every pretension that sets itself up against the knowledge of God, and we take captive every thought to make it obedient to Christ (2 Corinthians 10:3–5).

The Scriptures are filled with references to this battle, some of which I have included for easy reference in Appendix A. This battle engages the whole of our being as a good warfare (1 Timothy 1:18–19) and "the good fight of faith" (1 Timothy 6:12). It is against "the world" (John 16:33; 1 John 5:4–5), the flesh (Romans 7:23; 1 Corinthians 9:25–27; 2 Corinthians 12:7; 1 Peter 2:11), our enemies (Psalm 38:19; 56:2–4; 59:3), and Satan himself (Genesis 3:15; 2 Corinthians 2:11; James 4:7–10; Ephesians 6:12; 1 Peter 5:89; Revelation 12:17).

The Scriptures exhort us to diligence in the warfare (1 Timothy 6:12; Jude 3). We are to undertake it with faith and good conscience (1 Timothy 1:18–19), steadfastness (1 Corinthians 16:13; 1 Peter 5:8–9; Hebrews 10:23), watchfulness (1 Corinthians 16:13–14), sobriety (1 Thessalonians 5:6–8), endurance (2 Timothy 2:3, 10), self-denial (1 Corinthians 9:25–27), confidence in God (Psalm 27:1–3), and prayer (Psalm 35:1–3).

I never cease to be amazed at the myriad and unexpected ways God protects (Psalm 140:7), delivers (2 Timothy 4:18), helps (Psalm 118:13; Isaiah 41:13–14), comforts (2 Corinthians 7:5–7), encourages (Isaiah 41:11–12; 51:12; 1 John 4:4), and strengthens (Psalm 20:2; 27:14; Isaiah 41:10; 2 Corinthians 12:9; 2 Timothy 4:17) in the midst of spiritual battle—even the worst warfare. Although now we see through a glass darkly, someday our Lord will enlighten us about spiritual battle. In the meantime it suffices to say that we, as the body of Christ, have hardly started to draw on the divine resources our God longs to send. There is joy and victory in the midst of real battle and suffering.

When the Enemy Is the Beloved Enemy

> For a son dishonors his father, a daughter rises up against her mother, a daughter-in-law against her mother-in-law—a man's enemies are the members of his own household (Micah 7:6).

Often the enemy takes advantage of opposition that arises within our most intimate circles—our close relatives or friends in the body of Christ—to stir up the most heartrending kind of spiritual warfare. This especially occurs when a groundbreaking ministry is at stake. There will always be slander and lies in such demonized warfare. I have yet to see a case like this where a root sin of envy was not exposed and reckoned with as well. Oddly enough, that dread vice is rarely recognized for what it is today.

I have experienced this kind of opposition especially when I first began teaching on the healing of relationships through the forgiveness of sin. The most bizarre and irrational opposition, lies, and slander came from certain quarters. The situation was rife with demonic spirits, which also surprised me. I went flat on my face before God. Spiritual battle brings all manner of confusion, so I had a lot of "thinking through" to do with God. I had to forgive and keep forgiving the same people, interceding again and again for them.

To do all this and keep track of the understanding God was giving me through the Scriptures and the ways He was leading me to pray, I set aside the section in my prayer journal (the fourth sheet I mentioned in the Mere Mechanics section) entitled "Beloved Enemies." This section is filled both with Scriptures that deeply ministered to me and with prayers God gave me to pray for these dear ones. I can call them that with all sincerity, for they truly are loved. Had I not learned to pray for them effectively, I do not believe I could make that statement. Perhaps I would not have been able to stand in the ministry at all, for the enemy's plan was to bring it down through discouraging me personally. The nature of the warfare would most surely have disheartened me had I not learned to pray for my beloved enemies—those closest to me who opposed the work God has called me to do.

"Painting the Dragon Red"

The Lord delights in showing us how to pray. The sooner we ask Him for help in each situation, the better off we will be. When I seemed to be getting nowhere in my battle, I finally cried out in desperation, "Lord, what and how am I to pray for my enemies? How can I pray for those beloved ones who slander me and the work You've given me to do?"

And God promised to give me a blueprint. We on the team call this our "paint-the-dragon-red" prayer. Many other Christians embroiled in spiritual battle have been helped through it, for it contains sound principles that we all seem to need once the battle is joined:

First, pray that the eyes of all who surround these people will be opened to see the situation as it really is.

Second, pray that their associates will be given ways to speak truth and light into the situation.

In these first two steps, we pray for godly illumination and wisdom for those who can minister truth and peace into the situation while simultaneously praying for their safety. We ask that these stable people be spared from being caught up in the dark net of spiritual confusion and deception—a very present danger in spiritual warfare—and that they can help others who are ensnared.

As I meditated on these first two ways of prayer, the Lord greatly ministered the story of David and Goliath to me, and this truth from 1 Samuel 17:47 in particular: ". . . it is not by sword or spear that the LORD saves; for the battle is the LORD's. . . ." I asked, "Jesus, what is the smooth stone, slung at your command, that will stop the Goliaths of envy, slander, murderous hate, and all that is the enemy of Your cross, Your message?"

And immediately I heard in my spirit, "Truth, truth will out—it will hit the mark." Then the following instruction is why we call this way of interceding the "paint-the-dragon-red" prayer:

Third, pray that any demonic power within these people or situations manifest itself—that it may be clearly discerned and seen by all.

C. S. Lewis has rightly said that "Love is something more stern and splendid than mere kindness."[23] The "beloved enemy" will only be healed through this discernment. In answer to this prayer, God causes the real enemy of our souls to be revealed for all to see.

Some, of course, will be unwilling to see and repent. They are blind by the rationalizing of their sin. Here the root sin of envy is often revealed—the sin that opens the door for the demonic dragon to enter, providing a nest from which it can strike and harbor others of its demonic kind. When this happens, we invoke and practice the presence of God and find that, "Wherever Jesus is, the storms of life become a calm."[24] We find also that He is doing a work within ourselves that could never have been done apart from the disciplines we learn through sustained spiritual warfare.

After this third point, the Lord quickened 1 Samuel 14:15 to me. That verse gave me further insight into the model for taking the offensive in intercessory prayer. I saw that Jonathan and his armor-bearer—merely two men—put the entire Philistine army to flight as they fought for God's people. They stepped out in faith, speaking the word of truth. The Lord worked with them: "Then panic struck the whole army . . . and the ground shook. It was a panic sent by God."

Here we see so clearly what it means to be used by God in *His* (not our) battlings. When we step out at His command, He sends the panic or whatever else is needed. Evil has an illusory nature. It attempts to win through bluff—through puffing itself up to horrendous size. But one word of truth, spoken in the power of the Holy Spirit, solid as a rock and splendid as eternity, flies swift as the surest arrow to puncture evil's swelled balloon of lies, posturing, and bravado. Then panic sets in. There are times when we pray, "Send Your panic, Lord," and He does. We do not fight with words—we speak and live the truth. God does the fighting.

The fourth step the Lord gave in this "paint-the-dragon-red" prayer is ever so important. It underlines the fact that our battle is against sin and not against the sinner.

Finally, ask that what can be salvaged (in this situation and in the lives of your enemies) be saved, humbled, and blessed by the Spirit of God.

With this, I wrote out these instructions from the Lord:

> Pray for the health, the wholeness, of your enemies. Pray for the salvaging of all that is good, beautiful, and true within them. I do a great work, one that will amaze you. Be at rest now from all that besets, offends, attacks—love, write, pray, live in peace in My presence. Enter the timelessness of My joy and peace.

That our God is faithful to hear and answer all prayer, including these prayers, is something I want to shout from the housetop. With the prophet Micah, I was given the grace to say: "But as for me, I watch in hope for the LORD, I wait for God my Savior; my God will hear me" (Micah 7:7).

And He does. If we are obedient and stand in Him, our God turns our battle wounds into healing power for others even while He pours His healing grace and light into the worst of our gashes.

7

Listening for God's Response

We have now completed the "Our Father" and are ready for a full committal of ourselves and our day to God: "For thine is the kingdom, and the power, and the glory, for ever and ever. Amen." This is best done as we turn back in our journals to the Word section, ready to make this committal and listen for any word the Lord may be speaking in response to our prayer.

It is not possible to describe the "mere mechanics" of listening prayer. Matters concerning *being* itself (our union with God where we stand with the wax out of our ears and the blinders off of our eyes) come quickly to the fore and overcome any how-to's I may have to give. Nevertheless, certain "methods"—such as the keeping of this prayer journal—can help us make time and space for our "Mary work." They prepare the ground of our hearts to retain the word of God once we receive it.

After we have moved through the first two steps of prayer— taking the holy Scriptures into our souls and meditating on them, and then responding to God—we enter the vital third step. Now is the time to listen for God's response to the day's petitions and cries for intercession, forgiveness, guidance, and healing. We listen for any further word the Lord would quicken to our hearts.

For this third step in prayer we turn back to the Word section of our prayer journals, pen in hand. We are ready to write out any requests or questions we may have and receive God's response.

By this point, we have meditated on His revealed Word and usually have several lines of Scripture jotted down—those the Holy Spirit has quickened to us in one way or another. We have praised and thanked Him, we have lifted up our intercessions and petitions to Him, we have forgiven and received forgiveness where needed. Now we come to that hallowed space and time of listening to what God may be saying in response. By an act of the will—with no striving—we simply open our hearts to receive His word, insight, exhortation, or guidance.

In my experience, before this point as I have praised, petitioned, and so forth, God has answered many of my questions. Just as importantly, the desires of my heart have been revealed and laid before God; He has given me insight and understanding even as I have meditated on the Scriptures and prayed. I have been listening to God all along. But prayer to this point may simply have prepared me for the larger picture—the fuller will of God that is to be woven into the tapestry.

As I enter this third step in prayer my questionings, desires, and need for insight and/or forgiveness may be lifted to yet another level. Or this may be the moment when I once again hear the Lord's invitation, "Come, let us reason together." In effect He says, "let us think deeply together about these matters and I will shine a light and truth on them that transcends the understanding and insight you now have." This too is listening prayer; it is one of the most frequent ways that God chooses to speak to us. To reason together with the Lord is to plow up the soil of our heart, preparing it to receive the seed of His word, His mind, His wisdom.

Mental sloth is a terrible thing, an evil vice. The best way I know to overcome it is by "thinking through" all things with God. In this way our hearts are revealed and we know more of what is in them. We know more of how to repent, how to pray, what to rejoice about. This thinking through with God is wonderful. Usually we find that the time allotted for prayer is all too short—some will have to wait for later.

I write out my petitions before the Lord and then write down the words He sends. At times this word comes as a strong impression on my thoughts; it comes as a picture or pictures another; many times a word does not come but I know the answer will come in His good time and way.

PART 2

Listening to God

8

Listening to God

This is what the LORD says:
  "Stand at the crossroads and look;
      ask for the ancient paths,
  ask where the good way is, and walk in it,
      and you will find rest for your souls" (Jere-
          miah 6:16).

"Consider carefully what you hear . . ." (Jesus,
Matthew 4:24).

"He who has ears, let him hear" (Jesus, Matthew
11:15).

K nowing that Jesus is truly Emmanuel, God with us, and
learning to hear His voice is vital to becoming spiritually mature. Listening to God—which is a key part of
practicing His presence—is not a method, but a walk with a person. There is always an ongoing dialogue in this walk, as the Scriptures and our experience plainly show.

The Fruit of Listening Prayer Is Wisdom from Above

To listen to God in prayer is to look up to Him with the intuitive-thinking organ the Bible calls the heart. Through the eyes and the ears of the heart we see and hear God; through it we apprehend the transcendent—that which is beyond the merely physical or material. The Scriptures graciously invite us to look up and see the invisible.

The Bible is full of these examples. We look to God and are radiant as the Psalmist and Isaiah tell us (Psalm 34:5, Isaiah 60:5). Ezekiel (as well as Isaiah) looked and saw the glory of the LORD fill His temple (Ezekiel 44:4). Ezra tells us that "The gracious hand of our God is on everyone who looks to him" (8:22). Sometimes the impartations are such that everyone around is affected, such as when

> . . . Stephen, full of the Holy Spirit, looked up to heaven and saw the glory of God, and Jesus standing at the right hand of God. "Look," he said, "I see heaven open and the Son of Man standing at the right hand of God" (Acts 7:55–56).

More to the point of listening prayer, if less dramatic, is the wonderful word of Habakkuk: "I will look to see what he will say to me" (2:1). In order to hear we look up and out of ourselves to the source of all being—the Uncreated, the Objective Real.

To listen in prayer is to receive wisdom from above. God gives transcendent wisdom and knowledge to those who love and wait on Him.

Truly Listening to God Is Obeying Him

> . . . When Christ came into the world, he said:
> "Sacrifice and offering you did not desire,
>   but a body you prepared for me;
> with burnt offerings and sin offerings
>   you were not pleased.
> Then I said, 'Here I am—it is written about me in the scroll—
>   I have come to do your will, O God'" (Hebrews 10:5–7).

When Jesus was eight days old Mary and Joseph took him to the temple (Luke 2:21–40). Simeon, who "was waiting for the consolation of Israel" (v. 25), was there to see, hold, and even proclaim a prophetic word over Him. In Luke's gospel we read that "It had been revealed to him by the Holy Spirit that he would not die before he had seen the Lord's Christ" (Luke 2:26). Simeon was "moved" or nudged by the Holy Spirit to go to the temple at precisely the right moment to see the Messiah for whom he had so long waited and prayed. Again moved by the Spirit of the Lord, he spoke these words over the Infant Christ, which we now know and sing as the Nunc Dimittis:

> Sovereign Lord, as you have promised,
>> you now dismiss your servant in peace.
> For my eyes have seen your salvation,
>> which you have prepared in the sight of all people,
> a light for revelation to the Gentiles
>> and for glory to your people Israel (Luke 2:29–32).

Simeon was not the only one who received words from the Lord that day. The aged widow and prophetess, Anna, who remained in the temple worshipping night and day, instantly recognized the Messiah. She gave thanks to God and proclaimed this Infant "to all who were looking forward to the redemption of Jerusalem" (Luke 2:38). Simeon and Anna received these words from the Lord and acted on them without difficulty because they were seasoned pray-ers. Their hearts had long looked up to God in prayer and were open to receive wisdom from above.

Mary and Joseph marveled at these words. Surely they hid them away in their hearts, even as Mary had done when the Lord told her through the angel Gabriel that she would bear the Son of God. The word of the Lord, coming to Mary and Joseph over the previous eventful months, had prepared them for this day in the temple. On that day the word of the Lord again came and reaffirmed what they had been told. By these words they must have been deeply quieted and strengthened for the lot that had befallen them and for all that lay ahead. Otherwise the holy awe they experienced as they traveled back to Galilee treasuring the Babe entrusted to them would surely have been insupportable. There in Nazareth "... the child grew and became strong; he was filled with wisdom, and the grace of God was upon him" (Luke 2:40).

At the angel's word that she would bear the Son of the Most High, Mary uttered these words: "Behold the handmaid of the Lord; be it unto me according to thy word" (Luke 1:38, KJV). Her divine Son came into the world saying, "Here I am . . . I have come to do your will, O God." And in listening to the Father, He gained the wisdom to do His will. His full vocation of redeeming the world was accomplished.

What is my vocation? For what purpose was I sent into the world? These may be questions you will want to journal, because the obedience that comes out of listening to God puts us securely in our truest vocation. It is a radical place to be—a place of freedom from the words of the world, the flesh, and the devil. No longer slaves to sin, but alive to God's voice, we are brought into that spacious place of genuine creativity. We are *makers,* ourselves made in the image of our Creator God.[1] We learn to collaborate with what we hear the Lord command, and He in turn loves His world through us.

> But first, there must be a dying to any man-centered, need-dominated distortion of the gospel where Christ and his Spirit can be easily reduced to the source of our blessings and the satisfiers and servants of our needs.[2]

In his important book, *The Forgotten Father,* Thomas A. Smail warns us that

> ... The Jesus of the gospels will just not fit into this mould, because it leaves out his chief priority. He was never the servant of the needs that pressed around him; his agenda was not written for him by the insatiable demands of those who thronged him, but rather by his obedience to his heavenly Father. His life was not dominated by the claims of men, but surrendered to the claim of God. To see the place of the Father in the life of Jesus helps us to see that our own greatest need is conversion from an obsession with our needs to an obedience-centred Christianity in which healing is only a

prelude to following, being renewed to giving yourself in sacrifice to the one who has renewed you.[3]

True listening is obedient listening. To listen to God is to obey Him. Wisdom from above is received by those who are prepared to obey it. To listen in prayer for the voice of the Lord is to find the mind of Christ; it is to gain transcendent wisdom, a wisdom that includes understanding, guidance, knowledge, exhortation, and consolation. This is not at all difficult but requires that we be born from above and that we remain centered in that new life. Here our chief priority is one with Christ's. The Christ-life within listens for the voice of the Father. As Oswald Chambers says, "The proof that your old man is crucified with Christ is the amazing ease with which the life of God in you enables you to obey the voice of Jesus Christ."[4]

Christ Listened for Wisdom from Above

. . . I do nothing on my own but speak just what the Father has taught me. The one who sent me is with me; he has not left me alone, for I always do what pleases him (John 8:28–29).

Jesus modeled listening prayer for us throughout his earthly life. He who is Himself the *Word* from before the world began learned listening obedience to the Father as a child. When Joseph and Mary took him as a twelve-year-old to the temple, He astounded the teachers and scholars of His day. They cried out, "How did he get this wisdom?"

Throughout his earthly life, Jesus always practiced the presence of the Father. To see and hear Jesus as He speaks to us through the Scriptures is to see and hear the divine Son in union with the divine Father—always praying to Him and listening for His voice. God the Father, though we cannot see Him, overarches and undergirds the Son, instructing and affirming Him. And Jesus reflects the Father perfectly. This is why Jesus can say to Philip, "Anyone who has seen me has seen the Father" (John 14:9b).

In this way, then, Jesus perfectly models the practice of the presence of the Unseen Real, the Objective Presence outside the self to which we are drawn and made partakers of immortality. We partake of the *Real* that—though unseen—*speaks* to us, calls us by name, and *hears* us when we pray. We in turn become more *real*, taking on more substantiveness and solidity as we listen to Him.

Our Relationship with God

Let us look briefly at the relationship that God is—that Three-in-Oneness into which we, as redeemed ones, step as we listen in obedience. As Smail writes: "It is of the essence of God to be Father and Son, and the nature of this relationship determines everything else."[5]

It is wonderful to study Jesus' way of relating to the Father, for He was in constant listening obedience to God. Of this union, C. S. Lewis writes:

> The union between the Father and the Son is such a live concrete thing that this union itself is also a Person. . . . What grows out of the joint life of the Father and Son is a real Person, is in fact the Third of the three Persons who are God. This third Person is called . . . the Holy Ghost or the "spirit" of God.[6]

To be born from above is to be drawn up into this Union, this listening obedience. This love calls forth the real "I" in each one of us. And from this real "I," or true self, praise is called forth. Love then flows down from the Uncreated into the created, and then into all other created beings.

> A blessed spirit is a mould ever more and more patient of the bright metal poured into it, a body ever more completely uncovered to the meridian blaze of the spiritual sun.[7]

To continue to receive of the "bright metal," each creature must become a channel of this love to others. And by virtue of love flowing through us we begin to bless and name our fellows, calling forth the real "I" in them. We also begin to bless and name the beasts, plants, and even the inanimate creation.

C. S. Lewis wonderfully imagines this incarnational reality as the Great Dance. This magnificent rhythm, harmony, and order has existed from all eternity in the love between the Father and the Son, defining us as "in him we live and move and have our being" (Acts 17:28). Committed absolutely to Him, our will becomes one with His. We enter into union and communion with the source of all love and creativity; we find, within ourselves, that we have become persons.[8]

God's love in us is the divine energy that overcomes not only the Fall in each individual life but the death that intruded into all of nature. Nature too shall be redeemed. Lewis liked to think that God wills to heal nature through human beings, by our obedience to find a pathway through which love can flow to all other creatures. He imagined that as disobedient humanity is taken into the obedient Christ, so dying nature is to be taken into redeemed humanity.

Although the mode of nature's redemption can only be speculated on, the mode of our redemption is a certainty: we are drawn into that three-personal life: "God has come down into the created universe, down to manhood—and come up again, pulling it up with Him."[9] This is the message of love flowing down to us and taking us up into it. This is the message of the cross, where the great reversal of the Fall began. At the cross love and life were injected into a dying creation and from there we begin to tread "Adam's dance backwards."[10]

As we abide in the relationship between the Son and the Father we realize our rightful place as God's children—our sonship. "The *central secret of the Christian life* is that we are adopted into this relationship as children of this Father. . . ."[11] Our sonship differs to that of Christ's. He is the only begotten of the Father; we are adopted *into* Christ.

Jesus alone is *huis* (son), we are always *tekna* (children). . . . The sonship of God's *tekna* consists in the fact that they receive Christ and believe in his name (John 1:12).[12]

For a freeing and proper perspective, we are to bring all our other "relatings"—whether to persons or things—into our union with

God. We experience the necessary and healthy interdependence in our relationships while simultaneously eschewing the idolatrous and emotionally dependent ones in and through Christ and the grace He gives. We no longer bend toward the creature, but stand upright in the presence of our God, who freely bestows His life and love upon us:

> In this relationship creation and all its structures and multiplicity of relationships, redemption and all its way of sacrifice and resurrection, family, state, the whole universe of human interrelatedness find their ultimate significance.[13]

Union with God

I in them and you in me (John 17:23a).

Jesus, praying to the Father for us, said: "I have given them the glory that you gave me, that they may be one as we are one: I in them and you in me" (John 17:22–23a). These remarkable words, comprising one sentence uttered by our Lord, contain the very heart of the gospel and Christian reality. "I in them and you in me" is the ultimate point of *everything* for which Christ came to earth to accomplish. The incarnation and the cross was for this. All He suffered on our behalf was to bring us back *present to the Father.*

Christ, Himself the Word and truth, brings those of us who are *in Him* to the place of ultimate healing—communion with the heavenly Father. Apart from listening prayer there is no dialogue. Today earnest, believing Christians suffer because they lack scriptural teaching and spiritual direction that would remove the intellectual and spiritual blocks to this listening. *In Christ* we are taken to the Father. As we hear Him we come into our full identity; we know who we are and who we were created to be and become. We pass from immaturity to maturity.

When Christ says to the Father that He has given us the glory that was given to Him, He speaks of the Father's presence. The glory of God is the presence of God. Listening to God is an important part of the presence of God we are to practice, that is, acknowledge always. Just as we learn to practice His presence within, without, and all around, so we must learn to open the eyes and ears of our hearts and recognize His voice.

> The LORD thy God in the midst of thee is mighty; he will save, he will rejoice over thee with joy (Zephaniah 3:17, KJV).

Moving Out in Faith

I love the glimpse we have of Moses when God speaks to him and commands the impossible in Exodus 14:10 and following. It is most instructive. Moses faces the lapping waters of the Red Sea on the one side and Pharaoh's army bearing down on him on the other when God tells him to move forward. Moses is told to move not only himself but the entire Israelite nation forward. And the only place to go is into the sea.

Moses apparently murmurs his astonishment because God says to him: "Why are you crying out to me? Tell the Israelites to move on" (v. 15). And this is just the kind of thing God says. Many is the time that, from my limited perspective, I face the impossible and cry out to God. What I hear him say is, "Rise and do my bidding." Those very words are written time and again in my journals. The Lord is saying in effect, "Why are you crying out to me? There is something for *you* to do; arise and obey me, and then I'll tell you what to do next."

That is exactly what happened to Moses. He was responsible to obey and do something to enable the Israelites to go forward: "Raise your staff and stretch out your hand over the sea to divide the water so that the Israelites can go through the sea on dry ground" (v. 16).

In effect God is saying, "Trust me, Moses, and move out in faith." God had fully prepared him for this exercise of faith, this moving forward at the word of God, through a series of smaller steps in faith. Moses saw not only what God will do, but what He is always faithful to do.

When we see how Moses and the great heroes of faith heard God and moved in accordance with His will our hearts are apt to falter. Perhaps we can more easily identify with and even receive such a word as Saul (before God renamed him Paul) received: "Why do you persecute me?" (Acts 9:4) This kind of word suddenly warns the grievous and wayward sinner and confronts our guilty consciences; we must confess our sin.

It seems harder, however, for us to receive such words as came to Paul later and to such stalwarts as Abraham, Moses, Anna, Simeon, Joseph and Mary. We can more easily imitate the immature and the sinner. We have difficulty hearing God in the manner that the mature in Christ do. In the sense of moving forward the kingdom of Christ, hearing God is definitely for the mature in faith. Such feats as Moses accomplished are not ordinarily where we as learners begin in listening prayer.

Teaching listening prayer to the immature and unhealed has been a priority in my life. It is for all believers as part of our inheritance in Christ and our discipling in Him. So where do we begin?

We Begin with Acknowledging the Presence

"And surely I will be with you always, to the very end of the age" (Jesus, Matthew 28:20).

"Remain in me, and I will remain in you" (Jesus, John 15:4).

We begin with the practice of the presence of God. To learn to acknowledge always *the God who is really there* (Psalm 16:8)— immanently with and within us as well as transcendent over and above us—is a way of praying continually as the Scriptures exhort us to do (1 Thessalonians 5:17). When we do this, the eyes and ears of our hearts are opened to receive the word He always speaks. We enter a path of listening obedience we could not find through striving (for example, keeping the law perfectly), a path of freedom where we joyfully realize and acknowledge Jesus as Lord and carry out His will.

But the acknowledgment that God is always with us—even when we are least aware of it in our sensory being—requires discipline. To acknowledge the Unseen Real requires a concerted effort of our will at first. This is why the term *practicing* the presence is so useful.

It is especially easy for us modern people to regard the super-natural world (such as the Holy Spirit, angels, and demons) and activities (such as spiritual warfare) as somehow less real than the world we behold with our senses. As twentieth-century Christians, we live in a materialistic age in which our systems of learning have long based their conclusions on scientific truth alone. The presuppositions of such systems have misled many generations of students, blinding them to the truths of God and the Unseen Real, whether moral or spiritual.

Because of these intellectual blocks, we moderns have more difficulty with invisible realities and perhaps a much greater need for the discipline of *practicing* the presence than did our fore-bears in the faith. In the very beginning of the Christian era, however, St. Paul spoke of the practice by saying: "We fix our eyes not on what is seen, but on what is unseen. For what is seen is temporary, but what is unseen is eternal" (2 Corinthians 4:18). The practice of the presence, then, is simply the discipline of calling to mind the truth that God is with us. When we do this consistently, we are given the miracle of seeing by faith. We begin to see and hear with the eyes and ears of our hearts.

In this listening we come out of our spiritual adolescence—our immaturity—and begin to mature in Christ. To listen to God is to receive wisdom from above. Like Jesus, we grow as we continue to receive it. "And Jesus grew in wisdom and stature, and in favor with God and men" (Luke 2:52).

In every healing seminar I conduct, if broken lives and souls are to be healed, I must begin with teaching the practice of the presence. In this reality alone will the healing of the soul begin, proceed, and end. To abide in the presence of the Lord is to begin to hear Him. To follow through on that hearing is to find healing, self-acceptance, and growth into psychological and spiritual balance and maturity.

The single most striking thing that the religious leaders of Christ's day reacted to was His claim to be one with and present to the Father, the Unseen Real. Those who had invested in earthly religious power and control had to deny this; it was for this that they crucified Him. He claimed to be one with God, to have come from Him, to be listening to Him from before the world began.

Christ was always looking to and listening to our Father in Heaven. He teaches us to do the same.

Listening prayer is a vital facet of God's presence with us. It is a place of freedom from the voices of the world, the flesh, and the devil. Those latter voices, when hearkened to and obeyed, pull us toward nonbeing and death. To fail to listen to God is to be listening to one or another (or all) of those voices. It is to miss the vital walk in the Spirit and our immensely creative collaboration with Him. This collaboration requires the new self—one in union with Christ—that is always maturing in Him.

9

Hindrances
to Listening Prayer

e may agree with all that is stated in the previous chapter and still be unable to enter the freedom of the listening heart. This is a common predicament for us moderns, for we suffer a severe split between head and heart. Listening to God is difficult when we are separated from our own hearts, when in effect we have denied parts of our own souls as valid.

How, for example, can I hear God if I deny the very faculty of my soul created to apprehend Him? By this I mean balancing and rightly integrating the intuitive and imaginative faculty with the more objective, rational faculty. This chapter outlines several hindrances, such as this modern denial, that keep us from listening to God.

The Modern Split between Head and Heart

Most Christians today suffer to one extent or another from the "Post-Enlightenment" mindset—the Cartesian-Kantian split between thought and experience.[1] René Descartes was the seventeenth-century French philosopher who attempted to ground human experience in his own confidence in reason: "I think, therefore I am." Immanuel Kant was the eighteenth-century German philosopher whose rational system epitomizes enlightenment thought. For Kant, the human mind is not equipped to know God either through reason or through metaphysical knowledge. He acknowledged Christ only as a moral teacher and proclaimed that we only know God through our ethical impulses, not through reason. His and Descartes's ideas underlie the confusion in many Christians' thoughts yet today.

This split in most Christians is characterized by an acceptance of their conceptual knowledge *about* God as reality while they simultaneously deny the primary ways of loving, knowing, and walking *with* God. These latter ways are more closely allied to intuitive knowledge, without which we lose the good of reason, the good of conceptual knowledge. These Christians substitute the secondary for reality. This is what Pope John Paul II refers to in his statement that for modern people the sense of God is vanishing from the earth.

As a result of this split between intuitive and rational knowledge we live in an age when few—even among committed Christians—believe in Christ's real presence *with* and *within* us. Søren Kierkegaard, in the last century, cried out a warning to a church sunk in post-Enlightenment thought: "We've forgotten how to *exist*, to be." But we have seemed incapable of hearing it. We can only *think* about being. We can think in terms of Christian dogma, but find it hard to love and obey God because that requires a heart no longer suffering the split. By denying the intuitive ways of knowing we can no longer hear God's voice.

Here is an example of how this split is played out in our midst. A Christian man was grateful beyond words for the healing of this split between head and heart and the way his walk with God changed as a consequence. He shared with another Christian his delight in listening prayer. But the other Christian's response was a withering, "Oh, so you have a direct line to God, do you?" The latter, a committed Christian, merely expressed the type of *unbelief* that the greater part of even the "believing" church shares with Kant.

This is the Kantian split: God cannot be an object of knowledge; the noumena cannot be known in the phenomena. This is an abstract, philosophical way of denying Christ's incarnation and incarnational reality. It denies that the divine Son was born of *matter*—of woman. And it denies that another—even Christ with the Father and the Spirit—lives in Christians:

> For to me, to live is Christ. . . . I no longer live, but Christ lives in me (St. Paul in Philippians 1:21; Galatians 2:20).

In contrast to Kantian ideology, Christians affirm that God Himself speaks to us in the fashion modeled in the Scriptures. He has so designed our souls and given us eyes and ears of supernatural faith—rooted in the fact that He lives in us and we in Him—that we do see, hear, and *know* Him. The noumena, in the sense of a transcendent Good beyond the realm of nature and pure reason, indwells us, the phenomena after Christ's incarnation.

Although faith sees and discerns humbly as "through a glass darkly," yet we see. We hear. The gospel concerns this seeing, this hearing. We were made for fellowship—communication with God. For this reason Christ appeared among us.

When We Seek Experience Over the Presence

Because of the home in which I grew up, I did not suffer the headiness of the Cartesian-Kantian split. My mother saw and lived all of life from a thorough-going Judeo-Christian worldview and passed it on to me. I know very well, however, the confusion accompanying this split due to an *experience orientation* I stumbled into as a child. This dilemma was a fall on the opposite side of the Kantian split—the modernist position.

A firm principle in acknowledging that God is always with us is that we seek God alone and never an *experience* of God, including any word He might send. In other words, practicing the presence is not merely a subjective feeling. God, the Objective Real, is *really there*. As C. S. Lewis said, He is the most concrete reality we can ever know.

As a child, I received what I now know was a most remarkable baptism of the Spirit. This happened in a church where many were drawn to Christ; the Holy Spirit was present in both the preaching and the ministry of prayer around the altar. One Sunday evening when people were called forward to pray I went forward. Kneeling, praying with all my might (only an unction from the Holy Spirit could enable anyone, much less a child, to pray like that), I cried out for God to come. He surely answered that prayer. The Spirit descended upon and into me, and I *knew* God with my entire being. It was as if the living presence entered into me as a holy fire throughout my being and, filling me, ascended both as a holy shout and a holy wine, bubbling up in sheerest, most incredible joy. My very fingers and toes tingled with God's cleansing, healing fire and joy.

I will always be grateful for that experience; I lived long in the glow of it. But a problem developed: I confused the *experience* of God's presence with the objective presence. After the sensory experience faded, I tried to "recapture" it. Failing in this, of course, I entered my early teens fearing that God was no longer with me because I could not sense or feel His presence. Therefore I ended up in the same difficulty as the "heady" Christian; in falsely thinking myself to be estranged from God, I could not hear Him.

A mural-size (larger than life) reproduction of Holman Hunt's painting of Christ as "The Light of the World" stood in the church where I grew up.[2] This painting had a profound impact on me as a young girl. When the sermons did not speak to me or became overlong, I would lose myself in the painting. Was Christ knocking on the door of my heart? Yes. How could I open it to Him? Had I? How I wanted to! This was my plight and my questions even *after* conversion and baptism in the Spirit. Christ was definitely knocking at the door of my heart. He was trying to speak to me but I could not hear. I could not open the door. I needed to hear and receive answers to my questions.

In the painting, briars and weeds have grown around the door, which has not been opened in a long while. There Christ stands in such incredible light. He wants to bring that lamp of glowing light into my heart. "Jesus, help me," I would pray. "Jesus, help me to open the door of my heart to you."

But I could not open the door because I suffered that awful split. I did not know how to affirm God's presence with me, seeing and hearing Him with the eyes and ears of my heart. I did not know how to practice His presence within, thereby coming present to my own soul and heart and its capacity to listen to God. He had entered my heart in my initial regeneration and baptism; as I grew He baptized me in His Spirit. But because I did not *feel* Him, I called to Him as if He were only and always far off. *He was there*, however, all the while as I was calling to Him. The problem was that I was estranged from my own heart; I did not know it and was therefore in effect absent from it and Him.

Being absent from my soul and not understanding it is a very modern kind of problem. I was walking "alongside myself."[3] Like any materialist, I was trying and expecting to apprehend all of reality with my sensory being. At that age, however, I had the problem of being a child who yet lacked the power to integrate subjective experience with objective reality and truth. I had the more or less simplistic black-and-white thinking common to that age. As an aside, parents whose children hear and respond deeply to the gospel as it is preached—thereby opening their hearts fully to experience God's presence—need to explain these matters prayerfully to their children at a level in which they can comprehend.

During adolescence, I gave up striving to experience God and gradually lost my way. This confusion over experience was the problem C. S. Lewis suffered in his attempts to recapture *joy*. He wrote of it so well: taking our eyes off the object from which the joy comes and moving them onto the experience or track it leaves in the sensory being. To keep our eyes on the object is the only way. At any rate, this lesson eluded me for a number of years— years when I left the path God intended for me.

We must note, especially for those who work with young people, that the Kantian split between thought and transcendent experience seems "natural" to puberty and the stage of immaturity. Puberty is a narcissistic and autoerotic period every child passes through before reaching maturity and adulthood. C. S. Lewis wrote about the temporary cessation of his imaginative life (see "Listening Prayer and the True Imagination" in chapter 10) in the period between childhood and "that wonderful reawakening which comes to most of us when puberty is complete."[4]

This boyhood sleep he called the "dark ages," the period "in which the imagination [creative intuition of the unseen real] has slept and the most unideal senses and ambitions have been restlessly, even maniacally, awake."[5] At about fourteen years of age, an imaginative renaissance of joy as *longing* returned to him, bringing with it the gift of an inner awareness of "hungry wastes, starving for Joy."[6]

As so often the case with fallen mortals after awakening from the narcissistic and autoerotic stages of puberty, however, Lewis began to experience life in two modes. The one was his secret imaginative life with its search for joy and its constant aim to "have it again"; the other—with its schoolboy bustle and aims— still clung to attitudes and lusts ("erotic and ambitious fantasies") gained in the "dark ages." We all can be grateful that C. S. Lewis came out of this "double life" with one face before God. He wrote better than anyone else in modern times about the necessity of naming sin and dying to sinful, false modes and selves.

The time came when, humbled and brought to the end of myself, I too knelt in obedience before God. Remembering with a sinking heart my fruitless striving to apprehend God in my early youth, I prayed, "Lord, if I never know Your presence again, if I never make heaven, yet I will serve You. I will obey You the best I can." That, of course, was what the Lord was waiting for.

Living in the Presence

> If you obey my commands, you will remain in my love, just as I have obeyed my Father's commands and remain in his love. I have told you this so that my joy may be in you and that your joy may be complete (John 15:10–11).

My eyes would now be solely on the object—on God Himself. From the Scriptures, I took every command of Christ and personalized it—addressing it to myself by name—and wrote it in a prayer journal. I meditated on these commands and asked God to show me how best to carry them out in the many ways they applied to me—right where I was. Thus I was completely freed from any *experience orientation* and learned to walk by faith. I slowly began to know joy again. I grew in Christ. There came a time too when on occasion I "felt" the manifestation of God's presence and action. But I had come to know fully that He is always with me, whether or not I "sensed" Him in any way. I do not look for sensory experiences; I do not need them. What I seek is God Himself, not experience.

Surely Holman Hunt's painting carries as great a message for the believing church as for the world today. Living in the late nineteenth and early twentieth century, he saw how Christians have distanced their Lord and have lost an incarnational understanding of His indwelling. In this condition Christ's words in the gospels can only enter the Christian's rational mind. So often they cannot penetrate the deep heart where intellect, intuition, will, feeling, imagination, and sensation are finally one—integrated in the knowledge of faith.

If we are born again of the Spirit and are unable to listen to God or receive guidance, consolation, wisdom, and understanding, most of us can take a small practical step to help us over the impasse. This step releases "more of us"—spirit, soul, and body—to participate in prayer.

But first we must start by acknowledging God's presence with and within us. We affirm the *real* that came down to us at our conversion: Through our baptism we took our place in Christ's death, dying with Him to our old sinful nature. In His rising we rise with Him in the *newness* of His Spirit's indwelling. Even as we read, we may want to place our hand over our breasts, thanking God and acknowledging:

There is another who lives in me—Christ, the light of the world, by whose Spirit and Word I am led into all truth, by whose Spirit I can look up to the Father, sovereign over all, transcendent, high and holy, and know Him as my heavenly Father.

Thank You, Lord Jesus Christ, for indwelling me, for linking me to God the Father, for helping me to receive His words of love and affirmation in such a way as I find, accept, and live out my true and full identity as His beloved child, in You and through the redemption You won for me.

And may Your word, together with Your presence within, radiate up throughout my entire being, increasingly granting to me a cleansed and a holy intellect, imagination, and sensory feeling being. I thank you, Lord, even in this moment and in advance, for the answer to this prayer. Amen.

To continue to pray in this way, practicing the presence, will eventually fully deliver a Christian from the Cartesian-Kantian split. A thoroughly Judeo-Christian worldview and symbolic system—a Christian way of seeing God, others, oneself, and all creation—will be gained.

Once such prayer unto God as the above is made, these Christians become rightly oriented in Christian reality. They no longer seek Christ as though they had never been born of the Spirit, being absent from Christ and their own heart. They are not abroad from their hearts where Christ dwells in them, and they in Christ. They are centered in Christ, abiding in Him, and are therefore at home within.

Entering Listening Prayer

Because I have shared my story above, I will use it as an hypothetical example of how a young person with the difficulties I had can be helped to hear the Lord and receive the needed help. I would explain to such a one that to experience God as she has is rare, which is a mercy because such experiences are hard on our mortal bodies. I would tell her that since her new birth into Christ, He has never once left her. Then I would likely take her hand in agreement before God and pray something like this:

Come, Holy Spirit. Come, enter deeply into this child's heart and bring up exactly what we need to talk about. Give me the eyes to see and the ears to hear what we need to pray about, and how we are to pray.

A little practical step is next, a way of praying that can help the Christian who would enter into listening prayer. This prayer helps the person see and hear with the heart. In this case I could pray in a number of ways. But because the Lord so used Holman Hunt's painting in her life, I would likely ask her, with eyes closed, to look up to Jesus with the eyes of her heart and thank Him for that painting. Then, depending on the Holy Spirit's leading, I might ask her to see in memory that painting, with Christ knocking on the door of her heart.[7] I would then speak the truth to her about what was happening: "He is knocking because somehow you've forgotten He is with you. You've forgotten how to talk to Him and hear Him speak to you." Still depending, of course, on the Holy Spirit's leading—and it is perfectly amazing how wonderfully the Holy Spirit leads in these cases—I would ask her to see herself in her own heart and then, once she pictured this, to walk over and open the door and bid Jesus come in and talk with her.

The way God's words and pictures come is truly incredible. They help us both to discern what He is attempting to do in a life and to help others open up and receive. After asking her what she was seeing,[8] I would then ask her to listen to what He would say to her. I would ask, "What is the Lord saying to you, what is He speaking?" And she would hear and tell me.

Only when we pray with a child do we realize the depth and love of God in the way He communicates to a soul. He meets that young child and all of us exactly where we need to be met.

Such a prayer as this would have preserved me from seeing that door as shut. As a young girl I had prayed fervently for the opening of that door. Through a prayer that allowed me to see and hear with my heart—a prayer that allowed the intuitive-imaginative faculty to be exercised—the door would have opened quickly. I would have had ups and downs with feelings as any juvenile does. But I would have known and affirmed, with that one prayer, that God was with me—whether or not I ever experienced Him in my sensory being. And thereafter I would have been able to listen to the Lord and receive in humility and thankfulness the needful word He was speaking to me.

More on Protection from an Experiential Focus

Many who do not understand the experience of God call lis-tening prayer and moving in the gifts of the Holy Spirit exercises in subjectivity, meaning mere emotionalism. The truth is, how-ever, that to learn to pray aright and have real fellowship with God puts us in touch with Objective Reality and truth. To prac-tice the presence of God is to acknowledge always the ultimate, objective reality. In the process, we *are*, and we *walk with* Him in experience and in truth.

When St. Paul says "we have peace with God through our Lord Jesus Christ" (Romans 5:1), this peace, as the New International Version note states, is "not merely a subjective feeling (peace of mind) but primarily an objective status, a new relationship with God: Once we were his enemies, but now we are his friends." Oswald Chambers explains this succinctly:

> . . . Salvation is God's thought, not man's; therefore it is an unfath-omable abyss. Salvation is the great thought of God, not an expe-rience. Experience is only a gateway by which salvation comes into our conscious life. Never preach the experience; "preach the great thought of God behind."[9]

Many who have come to Christ out of secular backgrounds or who are still immature emotionally and intellectually are likely to approach the transcendent and the mystical primarily through experience. They are at risk here, especially if they grew up with-out receiving either sound instruction in the Scriptures or the basics of a good theological education.

In discipling these people and teaching them listening-obedience to God, we should emphasize the fact that the most common way we hear God is through the "still small voice." Of this voice, Jeffrey Satinover remarks in an unpublished article:

> I have often wondered why the voice of God is so quiet and so still. Perhaps He is trying to train us to listen. Just as by his very quiet the gentleman in a room of shouting oafs eventually com-pels attention, perhaps God draws us to His voice not by out-

shouting our inner babble, but by the whispered truths that reveal His character.

This is what we understand as we reason together with God: "Come now, and let us reason together, saith the LORD" (Isaiah 1:18, KJV). We should also emphasize the fact that "high impact" experiences are even mercifully rare in a person's life. Most experiences of God are mediated to us in such a way that our physical frames can endure it. The commoner ways of receiving from God, which I mostly write about, are better suited to our physical frames. And they can be just as profound in their effect.

It is a mistake to pursue experience, to desire "high impact" encounters. There is such a thing as *spiritual lust*. Like the more physical lusts, we must uncover and deal with the motives behind it. We may find, for example, a desire to prove God to oneself or to impress others. We may find the type of unbelief or even ignorance of the immensity of divine reality that leaves us pridefully demanding to walk not by faith but by physical sight.

Incomplete Initiations into Christ

> . . . We preach Christ crucified: a stumbling block to Jews and foolishness to Gentiles, but to those whom God has called, both Jews and Greeks, *Christ the power of God and the wisdom of God* (1 Corinthians 1:23–24, italics mine).

Most people are ill-prepared to receive wisdom from the Spirit because their initiations into Christ—their baptisms—are incomplete. Only a full taking of our place in His dying (by effectively putting to death the old self in experience and truth) and His rising (by effectively receiving the life-giving Spirit in experience and truth) will do. Baptized fully into Jesus Christ, we abide in Him who links us with the Father and who Himself is our wisdom.

> It is because of him [God the Father] that you are in Christ Jesus, who has become for us wisdom from God—that is, our righteousness, holiness and redemption (1 Corinthians 1:30).

The great majority of Christians have missed the spiritual preparations for baptism that enable them to go into the cleansing waters ready both to die to the old self, the self-in-separation, and to be open fully to the "sweet unction of the Holy Spirit." This is the infilling of the Holy Spirit that comes through an effective laying-on-of-hands and anointing (*chrism*) by those who themselves are filled with faith and the Spirit. In such an empowering we come to know ourselves as "God's temple" (1 Corinthians 3:16; 6:19; 2 Timothy 1:14; 1 John 2:27; John 14:26). We are indwelt by Him, the transcendent Word of life, the very wisdom of God.

All those in earnest about opening their hearts to see and hear God must ask for and receive whatever has been lacking in their initiations into Christ. The fullness of baptism, by water and in the Holy Spirit, is not optional.[10]

> ... [T]hey prayed for them that they might receive the Holy Spirit, because the Holy Spirit had not yet come upon any of them; they had simply been baptized into the name of the Lord Jesus. Then Peter and John placed their hands on them and they received the Holy Spirit (Acts 8:15–17).

> If you love me, you will obey what I command. And I will ask the Father, and he will give you another Counselor to be with you forever—the Spirit of truth. The world cannot accept him, because it neither sees him nor knows him. But you know him, for he lives with you and will be in you. I will not leave you as orphans; I will come to you. Before long, the world will not see me anymore, but you will see me. Because I live, you also will live (John 14:15–19).

The teaching and ministry of prayer for the healing of the soul (the work to which my team and I are called) is not merely related to the sacrament or ordinance of baptism; it is a vital part of the work of baptism.[11] As this work is done, people become open to receive from God. "Buried with Him through baptism" they come free from the voices of the world, the flesh, and the devil, along with the laws and regulations that have been clamped down like a grid over their lives. "Raised to life with Him" and quickened in the Spirit, they are enabled to listen and walk uprightly in the Spirit as free men and women.

The Need to Focus on God First

A blurred focus—along with the split between head and heart, the seeking of experience over God, and an incomplete baptism— also keeps us from hearing God's voice. It is especially hazardous for people in full-time ministry where the needs and pressures of the day, centering on the work of the Lord and the helping of others, can cloud our first duty of loving, glorifying, and enjoying God always.

As Oswald Chambers says: "The greatest competitor of devotion to Jesus is service for Him."[12] In the following quotation he states the problem and the solution: "It is never 'Do, do' with the Lord, but 'Be, be' and He will 'do' *through* you."[13] All the terse and wonderful statements Chambers makes about our Christian work presuppose a thorough understanding of Christian reality. The very life of God operates through us and makes our yoke easy because it is Christ's. Faith and belief are easy because it is not merely mental assent but the acknowledgment of a *real presence*—Christ who comes to us bringing the kingdom of heaven with Him.

But this truth is so very difficult for modern people to grasp. Our education, based on materialistic and humanistic presuppositions, has set us up to resist the fact of spiritual reality. Perhaps this is why the following statement by Chambers rings a radical note to the modern ear: "The only way to keep true to God is by a steady persistent refusal to be interested in Christian work and to be interested alone in Jesus Christ."[14]

When the whole world seems spiritually and emotionally sick, and the church by and large is not functioning in its capacity to heal even its own members, then we can easily focus too exclusively on what has been neglected, misunderstood, or misrepresented. For example, when the church and modern Christians are profoundly confused over what a soul within a human body *is*, then we who minister may be tempted to focus merely on the soul and its development. Our supreme interest, however, should be the relationship with God and His glory. Otherwise this fatal shift of focus works against our own spiritual health as well as our capacity to be channels of God's healing to others.

To focus first on God rather than on people's needs is among the first things we are to teach others. Then, as those we disciple are directed toward churches where worship has its full expression, they learn to love the great Unseen Reality and source of all that *is* aright. He becomes personal to them. He becomes God the Father, God the Son, God the Holy Spirit. In praise and thanksgiving, they joyfully enter into their primary duty of loving and relating to God.

To keep this primary reality straight will save us from our worst imbalances, including the inventions of theologies and psychologies that are only partly true and not fully Christian. We start, remain, and end by acknowledging the *real presence* and the practice of that holy presence. Otherwise we lose our focus—and our truest selves and healing ministry. As C. S. Lewis says, "You can't get second things by putting them first—you can get second things only by putting first things first."[15]

Many renewal and healing ministries have failed because of the modern propensity to shift from the primary to the secondary, from the real to merely its shadow image. Even after grievous failure, the leaders rarely recognize the subtle but fatal shift that brings about the grievous loss and failure. P. T. Forsyth speaks powerfully to this tragic condition, one so virulent in the modern mind:

> To make the development of man the supreme interest of God, as popular Christianity sometimes tends to do, instead of making the glory of God the supreme interest of man, is a moral error which invites the only treatment that can cure a civilisation whose religion has become so false—public judgment.[16]

Once God is first in our lives we are ready to learn both what it means to be a human being and what kind of thing a soul *is*. A true understanding of the soul (one's self) in the human person always leads us to highlight His presence with us. Therefore we do not have to worry about overemphasizing the soul. Even to speak of its redemption and healing is to speak of its interaction with God. This is to speak of *incarnational reality*, God *in* us and our becoming in Him, the very thing the gospel is all about. Then we will not have to concern ourselves about neglecting the care of the soul—either our own or another's. What we will be doing and teaching others to do will be in accordance with what we see Christ Himself doing.

Is the Son of God Praying in Me?[17]

The only platform from which the holiest saint on earth is ever heard in heaven is that mentioned in Hebrews 10:19: "We have confidence to enter the Most Holy Place by the blood of Jesus." There is no other way to come into the presence of God. As human beings we approach God and pray acceptably only through the "piece of God" that He has given us.[18]

By and large we Christians do not understand Romans and Galatians, our freedom in Christ. We lack understanding because we have relegated that "piece of God" to the abstract world of doctrine. We do not grasp the greatest, most concrete reality we have as those born of the Spirit—Christ *in us.* Our tendency is to remain in or come back under law and condemnation rather than to walk in the Spirit, listening to and obeying our Lord. Paul cried out to the Romans:

> There is no condemnation for those who are united with Christ Jesus, because in Christ Jesus the life-giving law of the Spirit has set you free from the law of sin and death (Romans 8:1–2, NEB).

The occasion for his outcry was the Romans going back under the law. They were straying from listening to God and the vital walk in the Spirit to which mature Christians are called. Certain teachers were taking them back to the law in order to better "control" and rule over them. This is exactly what happens to Christians today when they fail to come into the freedom of the realized, mature self in Christ.

This is a place where we can always dare to celebrate our smallness and inadequacy apart from Him. We can always acknowledge the fact that He alone is our righteousness, that we cannot keep the law, that He—the Holy Other—must do it for us, and that we alone, apart from Him, cannot hear the Father.

To walk in the Spirit, listening, is to live in the present moment, looking to Christ, practicing His presence, moving in tandem with Him. It is to live from the locus of the true self as the old one is being crucified. This is the center where we are in union with Christ, that completed self that hears and obeys God.

With this we glimpse the eternal child who will be eternally talking to the Father. This self is in starkest contrast to the under-the-law, immature, wounded, complaining child we know as the old self. Oswald Chambers asks, "Is the Eternal Child in you living in the Father's House? . . . Are you so identified with the Lord's life that you are simply a child of God, continually talking to Him and realizing that all things come from His hands?"[19] Yes, indeed, this is how it is. To all who are anxious about us and would keep us in an immature state, we can say with the twelve-year-old Jesus, "Why were you searching for me? Didn't you know I had to be in my Father's house?" (Luke 2:49)

10

Becoming Spiritually Mature through Listening to God

God speaks to us in a number of ways, but like young Samuel in the House of God with Eli, we do not always recognize His voice at first. We need our Eli's, the true prophets and teachers, to help us recognize and respond aright to the voice of God. After Samuel heard God call his name twice and mistook the voice for Eli's, we are told,

> Now Samuel did not yet know the LORD: The word of the LORD had not yet been revealed to him (1 Samuel 3:7).

Samuel had never before experienced a direct word from the Lord. When the Lord called to Samuel yet a third time, Eli realized that the Lord was speaking to the child. He instructed Samuel in how to respond:

> So Eli told Samuel, "Go and lie down, and if he calls you, say, 'Speak, Lord, for your servant is listening' " (1 Samuel 3:9).

This is exactly what Samuel did when again the Lord came and stood in his midst, calling out his name.

Learning to Recognize Wisdom from Above

In our "third step" in prayer, we learn to quiet ourselves and pray as Samuel did: "Speak Lord, for your servant is listening." In all prayer, we forsake our "Martha work" (it will always be there to come back to) and enter into our "Mary work." This is not so much work as an exercising of our God-given capacity simply to *be*, our souls silenced in His presence.

The literal translation of Psalm 62:1 is: "My soul *is silence* in God alone, my salvation comes from Him." In this silence we hear Him speak. This listening is indispensable in the ministry of Christian healing. Henri Nouwen writes that it is "possible to experience the relationship between pastor and counselee as a way of entering together into the loving silence of God and waiting there for the healing Word."[1] This is actually the norm. We are called to listen for the creative, healing word and teach others so to do.

Within this silence our spiritual ears are attuned to receive the word He may need to speak throughout the noisier, more hectic times of the day. In our prayer "cell," as we call the gathering in which Lucy Smith, Connie Boerner, Patsy Casey, and I meet to pray, I was particularly led one Christmas season to pray for our physical safety. My concern was so strong that I asked these women, busier than ever at this time, to add a quiet moment of listening to their schedules as they entered their cars. By way of practicing—calling to mind—the presence of God, I asked them to make the sign of the cross over themselves, look to Jesus, and listen for any word He might be speaking before driving. They agreed and as it turned out, our ears needed this extra tuning.

The most dramatic instance happened to Connie, who then had five teenage daughters, a husband, and a house to care for as well as being a singer and worship leader. On her way to a singing engagement, she dashed into a large grocery store to purchase throat lozenges. She knew exactly how to save steps by ducking under bars and moving directly to the front of the checkout counter where the drops were sold. As she hurriedly headed to the counter she heard the Spirit say, "Stop! Go round the long way." She stopped instantly, muttering to herself: "I don't know why I should do this but I will." Just as she circled around she heard a frightening commotion. A man was aiming with a gun at the cashier, demanding money. Connie came within seconds of thrusting herself between the armed robber and the cashier.

Sometimes when we most need to hear God speak the word comes when we are least inclined to listen. This listening, though it saves lives in every sense of the word, is most needed to remove hazards from the crucial work of the kingdom. This listening helps us do the will of God. When Jesus visited the home of Martha and Mary, this is what Mary did. She silenced her soul and sat in obedience at Jesus' feet to hear His every word. When Martha complained, Jesus told her that Mary had "chosen what is better," and in fact had chosen the "only one thing" needed (Luke 10:38 and following).

We do not know what Jesus imparted to Mary, but young Samuel was entrusted with quite a revelation. God was preparing him to be the great prophet-leader of Israel. The revelation, a difficult one, prepared him for the events that followed. God was giving young Samuel, and through him Eli, the larger picture. This is one of the most outstanding characteristics of listening prayer. In and through it God gives us the larger picture, and wonder of wonders, we can even see—if only a little—our own role.

Our prayer cell meets to listen and gain the Lord's mind and guidance on the ministry He has entrusted to us. Lucy Smith says about this little gathering, "God is always there speaking to us, and we see that He is creating a *whole* picture, a tapestry that is a *masterpiece* of His making. When we look at this big picture we see beautiful strands of all colors woven together, and those strands are made up of the gifts He has given to us."

This is a wonderful description of listening prayer. It describes the creative energy and giftedness God gives as we obey Him. God has given us the *spirituals*,[2] translated from the Greek as *gifts*, which are all related to *listening prayer*. All have to do with listening to God, receiving from Him, and thereby being energized to do His very will throughout the earth. God's multicolored grace flows through those who do His will.

William Barclay puts it well:

Paul uses a great word to describe the grace of God. He calls it *polupoikilos*, which means *many-coloured*. The idea in this word is that the grace of God will match with any situation which life may bring us. There is nothing of light or dark, of sunshine or of shadow, for which it is not triumphantly adequate.[3]

What a tapestry! No matter what our situation, we have God's perspective, and His guidance as we move forward in obedience to His voice.

Ministering in the Presence

The boy Samuel ministered before the Lord under Eli (1 Samuel 3:1).

As Samuel's experience attests, it is hard to minister before the Lord and *not* hear Him. In the context of desiring to do His will with all our hearts, and then in moving out to do it, He speaks most powerfully into our lives, and into and through our ministries. For example, when we on the PCM team come together to do the work of God in a conference, the word of the Lord comes quickly and easily; it is "stepped up" as many find healing of spirit, soul, and body. The degree to which we experience the presence of God and therefore the power to hear the word He is speaking is simply manifested to a greater extent.

Those of us who pray for others during this time never cease to be astounded by this phenomenon. The psychiatrists and depth psychologists among us are amazed at how the word of the Lord comes, bypasses what would be for a person years of therapy, and brings *healing*—not just insight—into the problems. As the gathered church listens and collaborates with God, the word is multiplied. God reveals so much more of the "whole picture"— His desire for an individual, the church, or for the world He loves—and we learn so much more of His intense desire to love and heal His people.

No matter how quietly or powerfully the word comes, the naturalness or "homeliness" of the way it comes is noteworthy. For example, Samuel thought the voice was Eli's. It was not jarring, unearthly, eerie, or spectacularized—as in its carnal or demonic imitations.

Interestingly, when God calls Samuel a third time, He not only speaks an audible word but *comes and stands there* calling Samuel's name. This illustrates the fact that hearing God speak is simply part of experiencing God's presence. Christ is with us, and He, the Word, has never stopped speaking.

A week or so before writing these words, various members of the PCM team came together from different parts of the country to meet and pray. Just before the meeting took place, the women in the cell group were in prayer and the Lord sent a strong word that began with two instructions and a promise for that meeting:

> Take the wax out of your ears, kneel before me, and I will walk among you.

Once again it was the Christmas season. We were excited to be together, were exhausted from traveling, preparations, and so forth, and had not much time for all of us to be together. We had much to talk about and catch up on. By reason of all this, we could have neglected to push through the merriment and exhaustion, removing the wax out of our spiritual ears and getting down on our physical knees to humble ourselves before Him.

When we finally settled down to prayer, I realized very keenly the need for the seemingly strong word from the Lord. It gave me the necessary strength to call us to silence our souls in His presence and enter into listening prayer. Because we treasured the word—the promises He sends—we persevered through the weariness and excitement of the occasion. The Lord indeed walked among us. There were strengthenings and healings amongst us, and we received the word we needed (the "only one thing needful") for starting out in the coming new year of service to Him.

Already, in the short time since, much of great moment has come from that one prayer time. In it and through it God revealed more of the larger picture, the tapestry of our lives lived to the hilt in His kingdom, replete with all the varied colors of His grace that are continually being woven into it. I tell this not because this one prayer time was any more special than another, but because it illustrates the part listening prayer plays in helping us persevere in the face of weariness and even the joy of special occasions. It illustrates what we have come to expect after hundreds of such prayer times. True prayer is the most exciting thing in the world; it is an awesome thing to dialogue with the living God.

Answered Prayer

Except where there is unconfessed and consciously held sin, God hears our prayers and answers them. These answers come in various ways, however, and are often delayed. If we are foolish, we might charge God with not hearing us simply because the answers do not come as we would like or as quickly as we hoped. But as we persevere with God we find out (sometimes a good distance down the road) that He has been at work in the situation we were praying about all along—and in ways we could never have foreseen.

In the past two years I have seen the resolving of a critical situation over which I have been in prayer for almost two decades. This situation could have disabled me altogether from serving the Lord had I not been able to hear Him in the midst of it. But as Christ has promised, it has been lightened for me because He bears it with me. As He tells us, "My yoke is easy, my burden is light" (Matthew 11:30). There is no burden that He does not either lift from us or help us carry. That is what being *in Christ*—being in union with Him and the Father—makes possible. What comes against me, comes against Him.

The importance of listening to Him, gaining His perspective and guidance on my particular situation as year after year rolled by, can never be overestimated. Faith, hope, and love were given me in abundance. And I received the wisdom and knowledge about what to pray and how to pray it—as each and every occasion demanded. This situation was, I believe, designed by the evil one to destroy my capacity to serve God. But as I listened to God, fixing my heart and mind on Him, He used the very darkness of that oppressing situation to sharpen and enhance my work in the kingdom. Layer after layer of fear of what others could do or say to hurt me, or any fear I had of what Satan and his minions could do as they worked in this situation, were dealt with in me. I have been enabled to help many others who lacked courage in such desperate situations.

Sometimes the obstacle blocking the way of an answer to prayer turns out to be our very selves. Most of us know only too well how long it has taken the Lord, gently working with us and wooing us, to bring us to a place where we can stand without falling should He answer certain cries of our hearts according to our timetable and wishes. It takes time for us poor mortals to see and hear aright in regard to certain motives and aspirations in our souls. Some of these are imprinted by the culture in which we live, others by human regulations and laws placed harshly over us by misguided parents or even church fellowships. These "laws," when internalized, can be compelling and even compulsive in nature.

This fact alone should call us to walk in the utmost humility before God. The very nature of some of our most urgent requests, then, require time. God takes time to woo and turn our hearts and the hearts of others to Himself, to bring forth vindication and justice where there has been slander and all manner of evil, and to heal relationships wounded in the fray and fallenness of life.

It must be said, too, that there are certain kinds of prayers God cannot answer. As usual, C. S. Lewis says it best:

> Can a mortal ask questions which God finds unanswerable? Quite easily, I should think. All nonsense questions are unanswerable. How many hours are there in a mile? Is yellow square or round? Probably half the questions we ask—half our great theological and metaphysical problems—are like that.[4]

Nonsense questions come from out of the depths of our foolishness. God seems to suffer us as fools mostly in silence. I have noticed that nonsense questions usually have more than a tinge of unbelief and even atheism in them. "The fool hath said in his heart there is no God," said the Psalmist (14:1, KJV). In our twentieth-century materialism, we have been given over to such foolishness on a universal scale. In fact we have been given over to a corporately depraved mind, which could only and always be asking the wrong questions.

Insofar as many of our nonsense personal prayers are concerned, we Christians have bought into materialism's atheistic psychological reductionism. This is a stellar foolishness so great that we must surely cast a cosmic shadow of fool on the screen of history and time. We are pathetic in our ignorance of God and therefore of the soul created to reflect His image.

For some, the beginning place in prayer is for deliverance out of the quicksand of psychological reductionism—that which blinds us to the transcendent dimension and eternal significance of everything that has real existence, including our own souls. Reduction of ourselves (as in secular and popular psychology) to biologically determined beings without will, spirit, or soul is a bottomless pit. Only in confession and repentance of unbelief, while looking up and out of the self to receive forgiveness and the healing word God is speaking, can we be pulled out of this pit.

God does answer legitimate questions in various ways. These differing ways stretch us and call the whole of us—spirit, soul, and body—out of any sloth or apathy we might be in. Answers to legitimate questions bring us out of the denial that the deceitfulness of sin, whether our own or others, has wrought and hardened in us.

We Walk by Faith, Not by Sight

That we cannot foresee the way God will speak in answer to our prayers is something for which to give thanks. It combats our attempts to live by sight rather than by faith. For example, it hinders any attempt we make to turn listening prayer into some sort of message-on-demand. Such prayer would be akin to crystal-ball gazing. Sadly, there are those who engage in a carnal equivalent of this and call the activity listening prayer. Neither is it the "message-a-minute" view as Dallas Willard calls another common misperception.[5] Listening prayer is in no way related to anything compulsive such as "automatic writing"—a pagan occult imitation that not only employs demons but "uses" a soul as if it were a zombie or a robot. The humble stance of waiting on an awesome God who speaks to His people in His time and in His way—all of which is modeled in the Scriptures—offsets these misperceptions.

Our entire being is involved in true listening:

> We have nothing that we have not received; but part of what we have received is the power of being something more than receptacles.[6]

God does not despise our minds, imaginations, sensory and feeling faculties. He demands that they mature in listening prayer. He calls the whole of us, using our every faculty to respond to Him and His truth. God is interested, as E. Stanley Jones points out, in the development of character. This

> must be the purpose of the Father. That fact should make us use with caution the method of sitting down with a pencil and a blank sheet of paper to write down the instructions of the day. Suppose a parent would dictate to the child minutely everything he is to do during the day. The child would be stunted under that regime. The parent must guide in such a manner, and to the degree, that autonomous character, capable of making right decisions for itself, is produced. God does the same.[7]

We cannot despise our souls and discount their various faculties, so exquisitely fashioned by God to see and hear Him, and then proceed to hear Him aright. He comes to us in and through our thoughts, imaginations, dreams, and visions.

Most who fear listening prayer, or teach against it, have a more or less gnostic view of what it is to hear God. The flesh or human person—all that Christ incarnates—is either underrated or despised in this view. The created mind and heart, in such a view, could not contain or convey the Lord or His presence. In its practical outworking, God would be forced to speak to us as if we were robots—devoid of minds, imaginations, feelings, and senses—because we disregard or despise our own faculties.

> We profanely assume that divine and human action exclude one another like the actions of two fellow-creatures so that "God did

this" and "I did this" cannot both be true of the same act in the sense that each contributed a share.[8]

Such an erroneous view is superficial. It is a "magical" view in the worst sense, for indeed it profanes the Christian incarnational and supernaturalist view. C. S. Lewis, in *The Lion, the Witch, and the Wardrobe*, uses the concept of "magical" in the best sense when he refers to the true Christian view of incarnational reality not as mere magic but as "deep magic from the dawn of time." It is miracle, and we participate in it in our spirits, souls, and bodies.

Earnest Christians who have never entered into this third step of prayer invariably say to me, "Oh, but I am so afraid it would be *just me* speaking!" Although there is validity to that particular caution (see the first part of chapter 14), why is there such fear? When we are one with Christ, why are we afraid to know what "just me" knows—what our own hearts from their depths can speak? This fear parallels our loss of understanding of the soul; for all practical purposes we simply no longer believe in its existence.

Like God Himself, the soul belongs to the unseen real—it too is invisible. Today we are drenched in materialism's denial of what cannot be seen, felt, or touched. We ask how can what we do not recognize as *real* have valid motions, wisdom, knowledge, understanding, and so forth. This difficulty is further compounded by such false teaching as dualistic pagan inroads into the Christian faith. Lacking an incarnational view of reality, they encourage us to fear and despise our thoughts, imaginations, and truly ourselves as created matter—ourselves as souls and bodies.

For this reason, I recommend the following to all who are just beginning to open their hearts to listen to God: "Do not be afraid that what you hear is 'just me.' You need to know what 'just me,' your deep heart, knows. Within a short time you will be able to discern the difference between the knowledge you already have—the wisdom already given you and a part of your heart—and the word God speaks to you afresh. Both are important and needful." I ask these Christians to refrain from overanalyzing a word they receive but rather to look back after several days and then reread it. Then discernment will come easily enough.

They will see that unique difference that we learn as we gain experience in prayer. Dallas Willard describes this difference as "a characteristic type of thought and impulse, which was to me the moving of God on my mind and heart":[9]

> Experience taught me to identify a remarkable difference when it was "just me" talking . . . and when a certain "something more" was taking place.[10]

A point to be made here strongly is that we never try to force a word. As we simply allow time and space for God to speak, we learn both how easily and wonderfully the word comes and the differing ways it comes. But another point, equal in importance, is that it is with our *wills*—the incredible faculty of the soul with which we initiate change, not as robots but as free *persons*—that we deliberately (*consciously*) open the eyes of our hearts and minds to receive the word God sends. We know that He hears and answers prayer; we know the answer will come in His own way and time. Christ is the Word who never stops speaking the very word of truth we need to hear in order to grow and obey Him. Christ truly hears and answers. Having made these qualifications, I am amazed how often He has simply been waiting for the opportunity to speak into my mind and heart.

Listening Prayer and the True Imagination

> I will look to see what he will say to me . . . (Habakkuk 2:1).

To receive a word or picture from God is to know the true imagination in operation. The truly imaginative experience is an intuition of the real. At its highest level, it is the experience of receiving from God, whether by word, vision, or—greatest of all—an incarnation or infilling of the Holy Spirit. The true imagination is engaged when we worshipfully listen in creaturely awe and obedience to God with our heart. Our heart receives pictures from the Lord.

It is important to stress that the picture-making faculty of the heart is not itself the true or higher imagination. Pictures are the language of the heart; like icons they are merely images through which the real shines. If the image is mistaken for the real, it becomes "self-conscious" and thus a "dumb idol." The heart's capacity to image symbolically what it intuits is different from the intuition itself.

When an angel of the Lord appeared to Joseph in a dream and said, "Joseph son of David, do not be afraid to take Mary home with you as your wife, because what is conceived in her is from the Holy Spirit" (Matthew 1:20), Joseph's heart rightly intuited both the presence of the angel and the angel's message. Had he attempted to literalize what he saw by saying, "All angels look like the one who appeared in my dream," he would have mistaken the conscious mind's way of seeing for that of the heart's. He may even have lost the true message in an attempt to make it analytically logical. Similarly, when the angel Gabriel was sent to Mary, he went into Mary's presence in the town of Nazareth and said, "Greetings, you who are highly favored! The Lord is with you" (Luke 1:28). She too intuited Gabriel's presence and message aright.

To most of us the word imagination is a vague one.

> The dictionary defines it as "the action . . . of forming a mental image or concept of what is not present to the senses." Another definition denotes the imaginative faculty itself by which these images or concepts are formed. A third refers to the "power which the mind has of forming concepts beyond those derived from external objects (the 'productive imagination')." This power refers not only to fancy but, more important, to creative or poetic genius, "the power of framing new and striking intellectual conceptions."[11]

This last definition, in its reference to creative or poetic genius, approaches our definition of the true or higher imagination.

Seeing the Unseen with the Eyes of the Heart

Our sole avenue to reality, as C. S. Lewis has said, is through prayer, sacrament, repentance, and adoration[12]—that is, through the deep heart's way of knowing. Seeing with the eyes of the heart is an important part of this *knowing;* it is an important part of listening prayer.

Oswald Chambers understood the heart's need to fix its eyes on God. Commenting on Isaiah 26:3 (RSV), "Thou wilt keep him in perfect peace whose imagination is stayed on Thee," Chambers says:

> Is your imagination stayed on God or is it starved? The starvation of the imagination is one of the most fruitful sources of exhaustion and sapping in a worker's life. If you have never used your imagination to put yourself before God, begin to do it now. It is no use waiting for God to come; you must put your imagination away from the face of idols and look unto Him and be saved. Imagination is the greatest gift God has given us and it ought to be devoted entirely to Him. If you have been bringing every thought into captivity to the obedience of Christ, it will be one of the greatest assets to faith when the time of trial comes, because your faith and the Spirit of God will work together.[13]

Commenting on Isaiah 40:26 (KJV), "Lift up your eyes on high, and behold who hath created these things," Chambers says,

> The people of God in Isaiah's day had starved their imagination by looking on the face of idols, and Isaiah made them look up at the heavens, that is, he made them begin to use their imagination aright. . . .
>   The test of spiritual concentration is bringing the imagination into captivity. Is your imagination looking on the face of an idol? Is the idol yourself? Your work? . . . If your imagination is starved, do not look back to your own experience; it is God Whom you need. Go right out of yourself, away from the face of your idols, away from everything that has been starving your imagination. Rouse yourself, take the gibe that Isaiah gave the people, and deliberately turn your imagination to God.
>   One of the reasons of stultification in prayer is that there is no imagination, no power of putting ourselves deliberately before God. . . . Imagination is the power God gives a saint to posit himself out of himself into relationships he never was in.[14]

Chambers's insight into the heart's way of seeing and knowing is profound and true. In listening prayer we put ourselves deliberately before God and receive the wisdom from above that enables us to grow. This communication leads to friendship with God.

11

Listening Prayer Is Friendship with God

> ... I have called you friends, for everything that I learned from my Father I have made known to you (Jesus, John 15:15).

> Is any pleasure on earth as great as a circle of Christian friends by a fire? (C. S. Lewis)[1]

*B*ecause the Lord's disciples were in conversation with Jesus and heard Him tell what He learned from the Father, they became more than servants, they became friends. And so it is with us. As we listen, we awesomely enter into that blessed state of friendship with God.

The Treasure of Friendship

We see this state in the lives of the saints down through the ages. It is written of Moses that the Lord spoke to him "as a man speaks with his friend" (Exodus 33:11). When Miriam and Aaron in envy slandered their brother, the Lord spoke to them, saying: "With him I speak face to face. ... Why then were you not afraid to speak against my servant Moses?" (Numbers 12:8) Abraham talked with God; he listened well and

> "believed God, and it was credited to him as righteousness," and he was called God's friend (James 2:23).

Friendship with God entails language—the kind of communication, spoken and unspoken, that comes out of loving the same things, the same truths.

And so it is with earthly friendship. "Friendship is the greatest of worldly goods. Certainly to me it is the chief happiness of life,"[2] wrote C. S. Lewis to his boyhood friend, Arthur Greeves. Lewis himself had a great capacity for friendship. Understanding what it *is*, he saw the blindnesses peculiar to moderns—those which hinder their understanding of friendship and constitute strong obstacles to achieving it. Friends are treasures. Like rare and finely faceted jewels, they are not easily nor plentifully found.

Comparatively speaking, then, "Friendship is rare on earth"[3] as Oswald Chambers, C. S. Lewis, and the truly great minds and hearts remind us. This is in contrast to the shallow thinkers and lovers who write the silly, untrue things about intimacy and friendship. But it takes us mortals a long time to realize the rarity of friendship; we tend to deny it.

We are wise to study what friendship *is*—as well as the other major forms of love. C. S. Lewis's book, *The Four Loves,* is the best place to start. Such a meditation can deliver us from a great deal of sentimentality surrounding the subject. Friendship arises out of, but is something *other than,* companionship. It entails loving an objective good outside the self, thereby gaining common interests and joys.

> We picture lovers face to face but Friends side by side; their eyes look ahead. That is why those pathetic people who simply 'want friends' can never make any. The very condition of having Friends is that we should want something else besides Friends. Where the truthful answer to the question *Do you see the same truth?* would be 'I see nothing and I don't care about the truth; I only want a Friend,' no Friendship can arise.[4]

We do not gain friends by focusing on them as persons, though we may gain their affection and companionship while giving ours for awhile. Friendship comes out of having common interests and focusing on the same hobby, truth, or beauty.[5] This good "outside the self," so much more exciting when someone else shares our love for it, gives us endless food for thought and good conversation. Rather than looking at one another in the hope of gaining affection, companionship, or the affirmation we have somehow lacked in our earlier lives, we look up and out of the self. We take hands together and come into a wonderful unity of thought and spirit as we admire or enjoy a particular thing in common with another.

Eros, the love between man and woman, is a face-to-face kind of love. It quickly interferes with friendship if only one of the friends experiences it. That lovers are also friends, of course, greatly enhances eros.

Both friendship and eros are quickly interrupted when unmet infantile and childhood needs in the areas of *storge* love intervene. This basic love, which C. S. Lewis terms affection, refers especially to the warm, nurturing, nuzzling, intimate, human affection parents give to their children. But it is not confined to that. About this humble love, Lewis writes: "I do not for a moment question that Affection is responsible for nine-tenths of whatever solid and durable happiness there is in our natural lives."[6]

Those who pray for the healing of emotional illnesses know that C. S. Lewis certainly was right. Properly met, this need, coupled with our need to come out of puberty *affirmed* by either our earthly fathers or father substitutes in our gender identity and as persons, frees us into the kind of self-forgetfulness necessary to lasting friendship. When we have been deprived of the need for affection and affirmation we need healing prayer and wisdom from God[7] in order to heal and mature as people. This is especially true when the deprivations have been severe enough that we find ourselves stuck in earlier developmental stages, failing to bond aright, especially with parents.

We can know true friendship only as we link hands with others in a common interest and in love of something outside ourselves. *Subjective egoism*—that which is common to unmet or inappropriately met needs in the areas of affection, appreciation, and affirmation—gets in the way of friendship and nearly always spoils it. The needy ego demands a face-to-face relationship that brings in a dimension of *uneasy idolatry.* It is idolatrous because we are bent toward the creature, demanding the identity and affirmation we did not receive through natural stages of bonding and growth in stable home environments and through parents capable of affection. This idolatry is *uneasy* because it is fraught with ambivalence. We are emotionally dependent, a distinctly unpleasant place to be, and therefore we seek fulfillment in another. We blame others when we find that we are still empty and dependent. We demand that another person tell us who we are when ultimately only God can. We can only come out of this state through absolute dependence on God, through hearing His words. As we forgive all offenses against us, we are led into healing and freedom.

This is a description of the fallen predicament we have all known to one extent or another. We are creatures of self-interest, and we want to find our subjective needs met in the communication, love, and admiration flowing toward us from another creature such as ourselves. We are then, however, far afield from friendship—that which is predicated on common interests and goals outside the needy self.

Friendship with God, as with our brothers and sisters, entails "identity in thought and spirit."[8] Then, like Abraham, Samuel, Moses, and the saints throughout the ages, we are interested and compelled by that which God has planned, that which He has in mind. We carry forward the kingdom in His name. When Jesus calls us friends, He speaks of this oneness. "The whole discipline of life is to enable us to enter into this closest relationship with Christ."[9]

Only when we obey Christ can He take us to the Father; only then can we begin to hear His "well done" spoken over our lives. We, the adopted children by grace, are *in* the one who is the Son by divine nature. To remain in Him is necessarily to participate in His obedience, His "identity in thought and spirit" with the

Father. The outcome is friendship: "You are my friends if you do what I command" (John 15:14).

A New Self Is Born in the Presence

There is great beauty in the movement of the soul as it forsakes its alienation and inability to hear, know, and be friends with God, and comes into a position of listening, illumination, and union with Him. There is a splendid simplicity to it.

On entering the presence, no matter how twisted or bent the soul has been toward its idols, it receives the grace to renounce the bentness. As a person's *will* is thoroughly converted and made one with God's, he or she has a new backbone, upright and strong, with which to stand erect in the vertical, receiving position with the Father. The soul sees, *hears*, and comes into holy converse. It can communicate with God on the level of friendship.

The soul finds that God's love is truly, in C. S. Lewis's words, "something more stern and splendid than mere kindness." This love divides the darkness from the light, the old self from the new self. It finds that "everything, when once the light has shown it up, is illumined, and everything thus illumined is all light" (Ephesians 5:13, NEB).

A new self is born, with one's face turned up to God, seeing and hearing with singleness of heart. Christ, the Word, comes to birth and is formed within that soul. He or she now has the capacity to communicate with the Father. We have been brought into Christ, and Christ into us. There is *completion*. There is a profound beauty and simplicity in this way of *getting a self*, of finding healing and wholeness.

In all of this, our capacity to speak, hear, comprehend (our use of language) is profound and mysterious. Only humanity, of all God's creation, talks—that is, *symbolizes*—continually. In this we are made in the image of God, for God speaks. So it is that God and humans *talk*. Christ, the Word, spoke the world into existence and created us. He breathed the spark of life into Adam and called him into communication with Himself.

Language is primordial; its roots are safely hidden from our scientific urges to know all. Language has to do with the very nature of human beings who are made in the image of God and are called into conversation with Him. Apart from conversation with God we are lonely; we know a primal, and even primordial, kind of loneliness. Fallen people are born in that condition.[10]

Converting the Desert of Loneliness into a Garden of Solitude

Loneliness—the primal loneliness of separation from God's voice—was the chief challenge I had to work through on my return to God. As an exile, far from Him, I heard Him call me. As an exile I heard His word to me through Jeremiah:

> "For I know the plans I have for you," declares the Lord, "plans to prosper you and not to harm you, plans to give you a hope and a future. Then you will call upon me and come and pray to me, and I will listen to you. You will seek me and find me when you seek me with all your heart. I will be found by you," declares the Lord, "and will bring you back from captivity" (Jeremiah 29:11–13).

He had to cleanse and heal me to the point that I *could* be His friend. Only I knew what a job that was. And I knew that only in absolute obedience to Him could He bring me to this point. Thus His words, "You are my friend if you do what I command," sunk to the depths of my being. I had to listen to His every command, His every whisper, in order to die to the old self. I had to die to the old Leanne who would demand that the creature be god to her—who would insist that friendship with the creature alleviate her loneliness. Only after this could I know lasting friendship. Only after this could I be a real friend to God or another soul.

We all have to work through this. I have noted this with all who are commencing their walk in the Spirit, their listening friendship with God. Those who have known affection and affirmation in their childhoods have an easier time, for through this God prepares us to know and love Him as the heavenly Father. But because of our bentness and fallenness we are so slow to realize the rarity of true friendship. We continue struggling to find other people who can speak to this primal loneliness. The easing of this emptiness, even meaninglessness, is what we so often look for in friendship.

We can spare no one the pain of working through this. The unhealed, facing this loneliness, seek friends who can take the pain away. They bend in need-love toward another, hoping that he or she will be the friend, spouse, son, or daughter who will or can fill the void. But, as Oswald Chambers warns us, "If you become a necessity to a soul, you are out of God's order."[11] He warns us about what we today call codependency—the way we try to prevent others from feeling the pain of their condition, enable them to stay in it, and thereby keep them from coming to Christ.

Our pastoral task is to help all needy individuals face their inner loneliness, and there begin to hear God and their own true self. Every one of us—not just those who are the most visibly wounded by the darkness in humanity and the world—has to face the inner loneliness and separation from God. We all need to begin the rigorous but sternly magnificent work of converting the "desert of loneliness" within into the spaciously beautiful "garden of solitude" where the true self comes forward and flourishes. This is the self capable of friendship and Christian fellowship. Its identity is no longer in the creature. It no longer demands that the creature be god to it.

The butterfly moth provides a wonderful picture of the struggle that each soul must go through in its birthing. It is painful to see the moth struggle inside its cocoon in its effort to emerge. But if we take scissors and snip off the top of the cocoon, the moth will never fly. In this struggle against its outer shell or self its wings develop and become strong. At times before it emerges its struggle ceases for a while. We wonder if it has given up its painful work or even if it has died within its woven shell. But from a lowly worm that gorges itself all day and drags its tummy on a tree limb, it metamorphoses into a gorgeous creature that flies, its wings bearing the colors and designs of an omnipotent hand.

So it is with those for whom we pray—there will be times when the work seems to stop. But this is the very point where we can be harmful, and even destroy, a soul. It will want to bend toward us. "Meet my loneliness" it will say; "Be my mother, the mother, father, spouse, friend, I never had. . . ." And if we try to be that we will ease or remove the very pain that alone will bring the soul into listening relationship to God. Instead we are to help that person seek the presence of God, listen to Him, and to get on in his or her *becoming*. He or she has simply momentarily ceased to struggle into the vertical, listening, free position, and has bent back toward the creature.

Blocks to Friendship with God

Besides the difficulty that an "experience orientation" presents—that of wanting to apprehend God with one's sensory being—other blocks keep us from listening prayer and the friendship with God that derives from it. Remember that when we truly come present to God, we come present to our own heart as well. Christ enters in as the light of the world, a lamp that shines brightly into the dark crannies of our hearts. The following shows what can happen when one's heart has repressed and denied pain.

I recently prayed with a lovely young woman who suffered an unusually severe block to prayer. She could pray when on the run, so to speak. But whenever she drew aside into the quiet to pray, and prayed for any length of time, she came in touch with excruciating emotional pain. The pain would be so intense that she had to stop in order to keep from screaming. "Why would God do this to me," she asked, "Why do I have to stop praying in order to avoid that kind of pain?" To make matters worse, she was in need of guidance from the Lord but was afraid to enter the quiet and listen because of the pain she knew would well up.

While she anguished over this difficulty she was equally grieving over another one—a *lack of friends*. She was starved for friendship, for good conversation with good friends. She was planning to move to another area where the possibilities of making Christian friends could be better. These two problems, seemingly unrelated, wove in and out of her conversation as she shared her grief and utter frustration. She was bordering on despair.

Under these circumstances, I was a little surprised to receive, immediately as we started to pray, a picture of her heart as a lovely garden. Although this garden was not tropical, the flowers in it were so profuse that it grew like one. The picture was one of extraordinary fruitfulness and serenity.

Almost instantly I saw another garden, an arid desert. It was entirely separate from and underlying the fragrant, fertile, living garden. I knew instantly what the real problem was, which we will return to after briefly looking at her life.

This woman's early circumstances were extremely difficult, for she was born to a father who deeply despised women. He was the classic misogynist, of the Mediterranean variety, born of a long line of men trained by their fathers to hate and abuse women. He hated her simply because she was born a girl. He had verbally abused her, together with sexual innuendo, as a child, and still did when he got the chance.

A misogyny victim of the first order, she had found Christ when broken by this, and received much healing. She immediately began to help others and obeyed God with all her might. All of this was reflected in the picture the Lord gave to me of her heart as a lovely, fertile garden. Now, however, frustrated over her experiences in prayer and her need for friends, she was hurting terribly, even rent apart.

This deep loneliness is removed only through the listening prayer that leads to friendship with God, and from there into the knowledge of our being God's adopted children. She knew this, yet could not enter deeply into prayer. The pain she encountered seemed too deep, and even life-threatening. Here she faced primal loneliness with a strong complication. A significant and terrible part of that loneliness was the fact of her father's evil. This evil was so entwined with the *loneliness* that together with the evil it was repressed and denied. She had placed strong boundaries around it. Yet it lived inside of her as that blistering, utterly arid and unlovely desert underlying the fruitful one.

In order to survive she had set up boundaries between herself and this evil—even to the point of *denial* of the evil. This denial went to the extreme, even of *dissociation* from it. The memories and the fact of its existence was all in her heart, forming a terrible adjunct to the loneliness, but in a sense it was sealed off. The stench of it could not rise up and overtake her. But to come into the presence of God and remain there for any length of time was to come in touch with that from which she had *dissociated*. She would then have to come out of denial, name the evil, and "exorcise" it from her heart.

When a parent is evil, one cannot move toward spiritual maturity without coming out of all denial of that fact. Yet this is one of the most difficult things a son or daughter of such a parent will ever have to acknowledge in this life. It is therefore one of the last obstacles from which he or she is finally freed.[12] Listening prayer helps us to come out of this denial gradually. What was happening when this young woman entered into the quiet to listen?

She experienced the underlying garden where primal loneliness was mixed with her father's active hatred and disaffirmation of her as a person and a woman. She needed God's healing intervention. As long as denial was in force, two gardens would exist in her life. One reflected her wonderful walk in the Spirit, listening to God and the fruit that came from that. But underlying it was another. The pain of this garden was what she came present to when she knelt quietly before the Lord.

Her need? To come out of denial. She had to name the effects of evil and even name her father as evil as well. Rather than ignore him, she was to "excommunicate" him.[13] The pain that left her literally screaming resulted from touching a reservoir of reaction to evil that had generational connections. She felt the pain of her grandmothers along with her own pain—all that had been passed down to her as an evil inheritance through the generations in her family. This pain had to be named as coming from her earthly father's evil; it was not something sent from her heavenly Father to hinder her prayer.

To experience the denied pain—that from which she had dissociated—was to be left screaming as though in a fiery hell of hatred. At one or another level of consciousness, she was continually in this fiery hell. She would remain there until evil was named evil, and thereby acknowledged, objectified, and lifted from her. Without fully acknowledging the evil, *it could not be excised from her soul*. She herself is a temple of God, but the hell of being a continual target of a father's evil—as long as it was even partially denied—was yet with her. Internalized, she could not objectify it; when denied as coming from her dad, she could only (when in prayer) project it off onto God, blaming Him for it. "Why does God do this to me? Why does He allow it?"

One more point to make: A part of her would be stuck in immaturity until she came out of denial, fully acknowledged the evil, and separated herself from it. Like children at a certain age, she was stuck in a particular form of black-and-white thinking. She is a woman with a fine intelligence, but so long as she was stuck in denial a part of her cognitive development would be arrested. She would be trapped in the black-and-white thinking that characterizes a child's reactions and thinking at a certain age.

Christ, Our Brother, Takes Us to the Father

> For you did not receive a spirit that makes you a slave again to fear, but you received the Spirit of sonship. And by him we cry, "*Abba*, Father." The Spirit himself testifies with our spirit that we are God's children (Romans 8:15–16).

In listening friendship we find affirmation of our highest identity: our sonship. (See chapter 8 for more on this.) We are affirmed not only as people but as sons and daughters of God. From immaturity and servanthood, we move into the assurance of who we are in God's love.

When as a young girl I was so deeply moved by Holman Hunt's painting of Christ knocking at our heart's closed door, I longed to know that He had or would come in. I longed for assurance of my adoption into the love of the heavenly Father. Christ alone gives us this assurance. That is why the church, if it is orthodox, is Christocentric. By His coming into our humanity, Christ took upon Himself human form and became both Son of God and Son of Man. He became our *brother*. By virtue of His humanity, He enables us to call God Father.

My need as that young girl going into adolescence was complicated by the fact that my earthly father had died when I was an infant and there was no father-substitute. I was struggling with the effects of being fatherless and strongly needed to hear a father's voice. I needed a father's affirmation of who I was and who I was becoming. I needed to hear a father say: "You are precious to me, a young lady of promise, and someday you will blossom into a *real* and lovely woman." Although I did not then understand the effects of being fatherless, I know now I could hardly imagine a father's voice and love. I had no experience of either. This, no doubt, is partly why I was subject to the *experience orientation* I wrote of earlier.

Our earthly fathers symbolize our heavenly Father. They are ordained by God as the instruments whereby we are ushered into a secure sense of our manhood, our womanhood. Ideally their affirmation prepares us and moves us toward God's affirmation, and our full identity in Him. On the earthly plane, the affirmation of our earthly fathers enables us to come out of puberty ready to accept ourselves, in our gender identity and as people. When this affirmation is missing, it is more difficult to open our hearts to the heavenly Father. We then struggle with the type of emotional insecurity that can make puberty and adolescence the "Dark Ages" that Lewis termed it.

Healthy fathering,[14] preceded by healthy mothering, is the prescription for easing the transition. It can even make it a rewarding if tumultuous part of life's journey. We need a healthy separation from our mothers, being no longer overly dependent on her and the more nurturing, protecting concerns that come through her voice. Mothers need this separation as well. Fathers are to come between their wives and their children, helping both in this important step. At puberty, then, we need and listen for the strong, wise masculine voice that not only affirms us as persons in our own right, but points us toward the greater world outside the family circle.

Manifestly bad fathering, as in the example of the lady whose father hated her from birth, presents an even greater barrier to our becoming. The very one who is given to symbolize the ultimate masculine, God the Father, places a severe emotional roadblock in the way to the young one's reception of God's voice and love. By the same token, however, by pressing through the suffering and hearing God's voice, we find the needed healing. And it comes in no other way.

We see strong glimpses of Joseph's protection of Jesus and His mother, Mary, from His infancy on. Joseph was undoubtedly an earthly father that God used greatly to bless and affirm Jesus and point Him in the right direction. He would be the kind of father that could lovingly come between his children and their mother, at the proper time, for their benefit as well as the mother's. This type of father assures the young people that their infancy and childhood are now safely behind them, and that a responsible adulthood lies ahead.

The time came when Jesus would need to come fully present to the voice of His heavenly Father in order to mature fully. In Luke 2:49 we hear Jesus, age twelve, say to His anxious parents: "Why were you searching for me? Didn't you know I had to be in my Father's house?" We thereby see that He has successfully and decisively passed His initiation into manhood. He has passed, in a manner of speaking, from Joseph's house to the Father's house. And so must we if we are to walk in the Spirit and realize our full identity as heirs of God. It is one thing to be reasonably secure on an earthly plane; it is another to be affirmed and secure as children of the living God.

> Knowledge of God's fatherhood implies knowledge of our own sonship. When we become confident about who he is, we also become confident about who we are. . . . As Calvin pointed out in the first paragraph of the Institutes, knowledge of God is always at its deepest level knowledge of self also.[15]

Many come to Christ and never realize the meaning of being God's sons and daughters. The painting of Christ knocking on the closed door of the heart portrays this. As we listen and open the door to the divine Son, we know friendship and sonship. God the Father willed that, through Christ's obedience even unto death, we should know Him not only as Redeemer but as the Brother who takes us to the Father. He brings us into conversation with the ultimate masculine voice, which to hear and obey is to choose life.

12

How God Speaks
to His Children

[T]he Father, God in glory in heaven, the Son,
God incarnate as man, the Spirit, God
indwelling and empowering the Church and the
believer, are not three gods side by side in
uneasy competition with one another. In the
New Testament there is no going back on the
basic insight of Old Testament faith, "Hear, O
Israel: the Lord our God is one Lord" (Deuteronomy 6:4). But this one God lives his life in three
different ways. This is indeed mystery beyond
our understanding, but . . . it is authentic mystery. . . . (Thomas A. Smail)[1]

God speaks as Father, as Son, and as Holy Spirit, and we
usually know who of the Trinity is speaking. For example, when God spoke to Peter through a vision, he knew
right away the voice was his Lord's and addressed Him as such
(Acts 10:14). Soon thereafter, as the men that Cornelius sent are
at Peter's gate asking admittance, Peter heard the Spirit speaking
to him. He was no longer in the vision, the so-called "trance." This

time the Holy Spirit spoke, telling him of the three men who were looking for him. He was not to hesitate to go with them (Acts 10:19).

As in the Scriptures, so it is with those who listen today. When the word comes through the Holy Spirit, sometimes it comes with a peculiar nudging. Here is a recent example. A priest, a fine lecturer, was speaking; his lectures were set out very well in terms of substance and structure. We were ministering together and I had already had the challenging experience of God changing what I was to speak on. This man, however, was British and a bit more set in his ways. But try as he might to resist, he had to digress from what he had arranged to speak on and instead speak on what the Spirit was saying! The results were quite wonderful. Later, as he apologized and tried to explain his divergence from what was planned, he described this nudging wonderfully. Making physical motions, he demonstrated how he was poked and then almost pummeled by the Spirit at one point—until he got the message.

As in the example from Acts, we receive God's word by and through several different means. Often God has to speak the same word in several of these ways in order for us to understand. The following is a brief consideration of some differing forms through which God's message comes to us.

1. The Bible

We have already considered the extraordinarily unique place the Bible has in our listening to God. It is so unique and powerful an instrument of God's voice that many today make the mistake of saying that God *only* speaks to us through the Scriptures. The fact that this is not true lessens in no way the importance of God's written revelation to us. It is the most important way of knowing and hearing God. The written revelation, together with the way the Holy Spirit quickens particular portions as a direct word in a present circumstance, makes of it the greatest treasure trove we will have this side of glory.

2. Audible Voice

We have already seen how God speaks through an audible voice in the young Samuel's life. Recorded instances of this down through history are many. I have read St. Patrick's account of God's audible voice speaking in *The Confession of St. Patrick*, calling him out of slavery and back to his home country. This was the beginning of his great vocation of proclaiming the gospel. The saints have noted and recorded the audible voice especially because it occurs rarely in comparison to the other ways God communicates with us.

Only once have I heard the audible voice. It awakened me from a very deep sleep. I "saw" nothing—it was not a dream—and the only experience was that of hearing what I took to be God the Father speaking. He spoke only six words, St. Paul's, "to me to live is Christ." In prayer I had repeatedly asked to know the meaning of this passage. As the Father's voice poured out these words on me in a great booming voice, I felt baptized in them. The meaning washed over and through me. That day before retiring God had given me one of my early great lessons in "incarnational reality."[2] The context in which God spoke this to me was unusual. For the first time in my life I knew what it was to have a real enemy. The meaning of Paul's words in this situation meant allowing Christ to live in me and love even my worst enemy through me.

3. Experience with an Audible or Inaudible Message

God also speaks to us through an experience, such as a vision, dream, or theophany (a visible manifestation of God), with a message that is either audible or not. Christ's baptism is a wonderful example of an experience with an audible voice.

This occurred *as Jesus was praying*. We do not know what Jesus asked of the Father but we know what the Father spoke:

When all the people were being baptized, Jesus was baptized too. And as he was praying, heaven was opened and the Holy Spirit descended on him in bodily form like a dove. And a voice came from heaven: "You are my Son, whom I love; with you I am well pleased" (Luke 3:21–22).

Jesus was about thirty years old at this time. With this baptism came the empowering for ministry from the Father, and Jesus began his public ministry. "You are my Son"—you are the Messiah. The Father affirmed Him fully and publicly in His true paternity, and therefore in His full and true identity.

The evangelist Mark speaks of what Christ saw as well as heard: "As Jesus was coming up out of the water, he saw heaven being torn open and the Spirit descending on him like a dove" (Mark 1:10). John the Baptizer both saw and heard what Christ did. In addition, God the Father spoke a direct word to him:

> Then John gave this testimony: "I saw the Spirit come down from heaven as a dove and remain on him. I would not have known him, except that the one who sent me to baptize with water told me, 'The man on whom you see the Spirit come down and remain is he who will baptize with the Holy Spirit.' I have seen and I testify that this is the Son of God" (John 1:32–34).

The next time we read of the Father's voice being audibly heard was on the occasion when Jesus took Peter, John, and James up onto a mountain to pray. Here again the Father spoke in response *as Jesus was praying*. This time He spoke from a cloud. Jesus was transfigured before them, "the appearance of his face changed, and his clothes became as bright as a flash of lightning," Luke tells us. Jesus is then joined by Moses and Elijah, themselves transfigured in the glory of God:

> Two men, Moses and Elijah, appeared in glorious splendor, talking with Jesus. They spoke about his departure, which he was about to bring to fulfillment at Jerusalem (Luke 9:29–31).

It is not surprising that Peter, John, and James "were very sleepy"—earthlings do not easily function under the weight of so much glory. But they saw Christ's glory and heard the Father speaking, once again affirming the Son: "This is my Son, whom I have chosen; listen to him" (Luke 9:35b).

We do not want nor should we seek too many experiences of hearing God and seeing His glory such as Peter, John, and James had. It is too hard on the physical frame. The glory of God, the manifestation of His Presence upon and in us, has to be mediated if we are to bear it and live. To Moses God said, "You cannot see my face and live." Moses, we are told, talked to God face to face, but as a mortal he could not have seen God and lived to tell it. God manifests Himself and His will to us in varying degrees of intensity. Some are more easily undergone than others.

Other times we hear God through an experience together with an *inaudible* message. The words or pictures are "seen" or impressed on our thoughts in what we may refer to as "the still, small voice" or when it is the Holy Spirit, the gentle but insistent "nudge."

4. Experience without an Audible or Inaudible Voice

The personal example of an experience without an audible or inaudible voice that comes to mind is that of being baptized in the Holy Spirit. When Jesus baptized me in the Spirit, He spoke Himself into me in as strong and powerful a way as I will ever know this side of glory. Yet no words were spoken that I remember. There may have been inaudible words that the experience overshadowed because I was a child, but I would have remembered hearing an audible voice. God's overwhelming presence poured down from heaven upon me, entered into me, filled my entire being, and then rose up through me as a mighty shout of thanksgiving and praise to God. God could hardly speak to a person more forcefully. Christ, the I AM, spoke, and I knew that I AM was with me (Exodus 3:12). This is the gospel message, which I received at every level of my being.

5. Angels

God sends His word via angels. The Scriptures and the saints down through the ages recount many examples of this. Here again, sometimes the word is audible; other times it is inaudible. An angel once brought a message to me, and his exceedingly masculine presence so overwhelmed me that it took days and perhaps even weeks to get over it.[3] The angel was suddenly with me when I was praying most earnestly about direction about where I was to go. He spoke not a word. I was flat on my face over his presence, hugeness, and what I did see of him; I could not even look up and see his face. But as his presence faded, the message was clear in my mind. From knowing no one or nothing of the situation in the place I was to go, I knew exactly where to go, what to do, and who to see first when I got there. A powerful move of God's Spirit came out of that going, which brought leaders into the kingdom. I realized the answer had been brought by the angel only after a while.

Here again the degree of such manifestations of angels differs from time to time. I have discerned angels in our meetings and in private and group prayer, but the degree to which I consciously intuited them or "came present to them" was not so overwhelming as in this memorable instance.

6. God's Still, Small Voice

God deeply impresses His inaudible word on our thoughts through His "still, small voice." We know these are not our thoughts but those from God. This way of God's speaking can be every whit as powerful in its effects as the seemingly more dramatic way of hearing an audible voice, receiving an angelic visitor, or receiving through a phenomenal experience. Our prayer journals chronicle our experiences of listening for and obeying the still, small voice of God.

As a rule I do not cry, but I remember crying for days after one of these "speakings." While at the organ leading the congregation in a hymn, God merely impressed on me the knowledge that I was to choose and then set a goal with Him. For three days following, I had a spirit of prayer that only God could have inspired and enabled. And He would not choose for me; I had to choose, and then, as an act of the will, set the goal with Him. I had misconceptions about what I could and could not do, which God dealt with during this time. My point in sharing this is the degree to which we are impacted by the Lord's word is not determined by the mode in which He speaks to us.

7. Other People

God can and often does speak a very direct word to us through another person. King David expresses this: "The Spirit of the LORD spoke through me; his word was on my tongue" (2 Samuel 23:2). "Men spoke from God as they were carried along by the Holy Spirit," as Peter said (2 Peter 1:21b). This differs from the more ordinary ways God uses others to teach us. We become aware that God has spoken to us in a special way as by His Spirit He has moved upon and through that person. This happens under anointed preaching and teaching. It happens through the gifts of the Holy Spirit. God can speak a direct word to us through events and through His other creatures as well. When Baalam's ears were so full of the wax of his desire to please a pagan king, his ass spoke the word, getting God's message across.

8. Dreams and Visions

"Do not interpretations belong to God? Tell me your dreams"
(Genesis 40:8).

God has communicated things to me through dreams that I scarce could have grasped in any other way. Things too panoramic in scope and too great for words can flow to us through imagery and symbol. And too, they remain in us more easily. As the picture-message is hidden away in our hearts, our understanding of it grows. For example, images from certain key dreams stand out in my mind and mean even more to me now than when I first received them.

These dreams seem to come at crucial times of change—times when my conception of what God wants me to do or expects of me are more in line with what I could conceive others, and not myself, doing. This may have been the case with Joseph, as recounted in Genesis. As a young lad he was favored by his father and thereby put in jeopardy with his half-brothers. In the midst of this, he had two dreams that clearly foretold the place of leadership in his family, which God intended for him. Joseph put himself in the way of his brothers' deadly envy by telling them the dreams, for his family understood the symbolic message of his dreams.

An irony here, of course, is that the brothers believed the message in Joseph's dreams even if he scarcely could. Though the Scriptures do not record the personal impact of these dreams on Joseph, we can be sure it was incalculably great. God's message to Joseph through these dreams no doubt sustained him through not only his years in prison but in his role in saving nations during a great famine.

Only recently several members of our ministry team, including Mario Bergner, were on a difficult mission. It was to an influential church body that had come under great spiritual deception, a fact of which we had no foreknowledge. On arrival there and before any ministry was accomplished, the Lord sent Mario a dream. We were shown symbolically the problem we would face along with its genesis and extension throughout its hundreds of years of history. Only in a dream could this have been done.

It was absolutely phenomenal the way God used that dream not only to help us understand the monumental problem we faced, but to help the people ensnared in the deception understand it. They must have marveled at the wisdom God gave us. I can only say that in no other way could God have imparted to us the full nature of the problem and the naming of the key sins that needed to be confessed to begin breaking the deception over the lives of the people in that church body.

The emotional and spiritual blocks to wholeness that many suffer represent wounds to the personality that are complicated and deep. Through understanding dreams, God helps us to help hurting people as they share their dreams. The person's dreams can give us the clues needed that pertain to those otherwise unfathomable depths of the personality. As we prayerfully ask for the interpretation of the dreams and follow through in prayer for the soul's need and deprivations (and in repentance and forgiveness of others), we see that soul come to great healing. We can safely say that in many cases, apart from the message in the dream, this healing would not take place. It is a wonderful thing to watch these people grow once God has placed His finger on their hidden wounds and named them, while granting them the grace to forgive and be forgiven.[4]

Distinguishing Dreams from a Word of Knowledge

Sometimes a word of knowledge comes to us as we sleep. For example, a mother suddenly knows that her child is drowning and leaps from a nap to rescue the child. This is different from dreams, even though elements of a dream may have been in it, such as dream images as one emerges from sleep. But the message is not a symbolic one to be interpreted; it is a direct word to be acted on quickly.

The Vision

Some say that a vision is merely a waking dream. It seems to me, however, that a vision can come as we sleep or as we are fully awake. It brings a heightened consciousness of another realm, which sets it apart from the dream. A realm that is ordinarily unseen is extraordinarily present to the senses. The angelic appearance I described earlier was actually a vision that came while I was praying. In Acts 10 we read of two visions: one in which an angelic messenger came to Cornelius with the information, "Your prayers and gifts to the poor have come up as a memorial offering before God" and with definite instructions: "Now send men to Joppa to bring back a man named Simon who is called Peter. He is staying with Simon the tanner, whose house is by the sea" (4b–6). Cornelius followed through immediately.

In the meantime Simon Peter, who had been praying on his rooftop in Joppa, "fell into a trance" (this state of heightened consciousness). He heard the Lord command him three times to call nothing impure or unclean that God had made pure and clean. He was immediately called to act on this direct word contained in the vision.

From the Scriptures we can easily enough see the difference between dreams and visions. Both contain symbolic elements and need interpretation. Both require discernment as well, because words from the world, the flesh, and the devil can come through dreams and visions just as in waking life. We must remember that interpretations belong to God. Even as Peter, we "ponder the meaning of the vision"—we lay it before God with those gifted in dream interpretation, we think it through with Him, and we receive His wisdom.

Problems with Dream Interpretation

People can be so cut off from the heart's more intuitive ways of knowing that they pay no attention to dreams or to visions. Men, in particular, may even say they never dream. They do; they have simply been trained to ignore anything of this nature. Once both men and women begin to listen to God and become aware of the motions of the soul, however, they may find the dream to be an indispensable way to hear God's word.

Here, however, is where our real problem will surface. Men and women alike do not understand the symbolic language of the dream. They need godly training in which a wholly and only Judeo-Christian symbolic system is restored to them before they can receive accurate and full interpretations of dreams from God. This is also true of the symbolic elements that are sometimes, but not always, part of a vision as well.

A great hazard Christians face in dream interpretation today concerns those who have paid the most scientific and other attention to the symbolic language of the deep mind, and who therefore most value the dream. These people are either neognostic (mostly Jungian) by persuasion or biased in that direction by their training. Their dream interpretation will necessarily fit with the psychological reductionism of the day. People can and do get into serious spiritual trouble as they adopt the point of view presented by these interpretations.

In contrast, Christians who read their dreams literally rather than symbolically can be quite dangerous to others in a way a well-trained Jungian therapist who interprets the dream symbolically would not be. For example some Christians dream of another person and take the dream as a literal message about that particular person. This not only misses the meaning of the dream, which is most likely telling the dreamer something about himself or herself, but it is to believe amiss and view another person superstitiously. Paranoid people make this mistake continually, as do pagan witch doctors.

Dreams are important. We need to understand the symbolic language with which they speak. I once knew a Baptist minister who was fond of saying that if we cannot hear the "still small voice"—the way God most often speaks to us—then God will send a dream; if we pay no attention to the dream, we will learn on a sick bed. This may be somewhat an oversimplification in that God may persevere in ways other than the dream to get our attention; also, the sickbed is not the only way to learn a needed lesson. But there truly is a persevering quality to the dream. It is often repeated, presenting the same message in different ways.

9. God's Creation

God can and does speak very succinctly and directly through His creation at times. I have already alluded to this in the sixth point, but not as it pertains to the beauty and majesty of God's creation. Charles Pierce, the American philosopher whose religious beliefs are just now coming before the public, writes of the universe of God's creation as God's poem: it speaks to us. "The heavens are telling" as the Psalmist puts it. St. Paul has a succinct word to this very effect in Romans 1:19–20. By and large these are general statements of truth. At times, however, great beauty in nature or in a moral truth can be a vehicle for a direct word and impact by the Spirit of God.

10. The Gifts of the Holy Spirit

God speaks to us through the operation of the gifts of the Holy Spirit. In fact, listening to God and moving in the *spirituals* (translated from the Greek as "gifts" of the Holy Spirit) are closely interrelated. To receive a word from God is to receive a "word of wisdom" or "knowledge," a charism of supernatural "faith" or "discerning of spirits," one of the other charisms of "healings" or of supernatural speech ("tongues," "interpretation of tongues," and "prophecy"), and so on.

To allow the gifts to operate is to listen and receive from God. When the gifts are operational in our lives they facilitate listening. This is uniquely so with the gift of a prayer language—as it bypasses the more rational or conscious mind it edifies the intuitive, feeling, or so-called unconscious mind (see 1 Corinthians 14:4). When we are free to move in the *spirituals*, then, we are free to listen to God and receive the word He is speaking.

One of the chief and most common ways that God speaks to us as a prayer cell and as a ministry team is through the operation of the *spirituals*. The charisms as mentioned above operate through us simply as we are moved by the Holy Spirit, and we are all edified. First we invoke the presence of God and then praise and give thanks to Him. We share Scriptures. As we pray to Him, we receive the word of wisdom, knowledge, discernment (granting the guidance we seek or expanding our hearts to take in the greater will of the Lord), and so on.

> When you come together, everyone has a hymn, or a word of instruction, a revelation, a tongue or an interpretation (1 Corinthians 14:26).

This same thing occurs on a lesser scale—as a rule—as we pray individually.

We cannot remove the wax from our ears and listen nor move in the *spirituals* unless we "fan into flame the gift of God" (2 Timothy 1:6). And the gifts are not given, even as the NIV note on this verse states, "in full bloom; they need to be developed through use." They need to be exercised. When they operate in the corporate group not only is their efficacy multiplied through the differing strengths and gifts, but the word the Lord sends in this way is tested by all present. There is no better way to learn.

The reality underlying the gifts is Jesus Christ Himself, *the Gift*, who indwells us. The *spirituals* and all of the *fruits* of the Spirit reside in God and have to do with His presence with and within us. Another lives in us, and we acknowledge His presence. He has the Spirit without measure. With Him are all the gifts and fruits of the Holy Spirit. Because Jesus, *the Gift*, lives in the Christian, the gifts and fruits are present in our lives. They can radiate through us to a needy world.

The Lord Our Guide

> God's impressions within and His Word without are always corroborated by His Providence around, and we should quietly wait until these three focus into one point.[5]

Years ago I found a small paperback by F. B. Meyer entitled *The Secret of Guidance*. I gave them away as quickly as I bought them. That book and his *Meet For the Master's Use* greatly impacted my life, coming as they did at a crucial, formative time in my life in Christ.[6] As a young adult, I had come back to the life of faith and was asking "How can I know God's will for my life?" "How can I be led of Him?" Rev. Meyer gave me the start I needed with *The Secret of Guidance*. As the book is out of print and his wisdom is so vital for us today, an excerpt appears in Appendix B.

Of the pages excerpted there, Dallas Willard has said: "If I could keep only one bit of writing on divine guidance outside of the Bible itself, it would be hard to pass over" these. He points out, however, that Christians who have not learned to recognize the inner voice of God need more help.[7] He is right.

I believe the "something more" is the freedom that comes to us as we have our Eli's—those who have long known the voice of God, following Him in freedom. From childhood, I had recognized the voice of God. Armed with Meyer's "three lights" for determining God's will, I fared passingly well. But I lacked confidence until I had my Eli. He turned out to be a humble Episcopal priest by the name of Richard Winkler. Through a prayer for release of the Holy Spirit in my life and by his example, he taught me and many others to move in much greater freedom in this respect.

This was back in the early sixties, a time when renewal began to sweep through parts of the Episcopal Church. Fr. Winkler prayed for hundreds of priests to be baptized in the Holy Spirit, and they in turn ministered to others. One of the priests was the

Rev. Dennis Bennett who took the ministry forward in a wonderful way—especially with his book *Nine O'Clock in the Morning* and his ministry to Episcopal priests.

Fr. Winkler's group would meet weekly for prayer and then
minister to the many visitors who came from all over the world.
These ranged from prostitutes off the streets of Chicago to such
people as Catherine Marshall and others now well-known. To say
that we saw incredible emotional and physical healings is an
understatement.

But a simple point needs to be made: in order to see these
people healed, we only needed to come into freedom in listening prayer. That was the "secret" of this powerful healing ministry. We prayed for whatever was needed. Was it salvation, healing, baptism in the Spirit, guidance? We prayed for it.

Many Christians in those days did not look kindly on these
kinds of healing ministries. This is something I have never understood. There was a saying about Fr. Winkler that if he could only
reach the hospital in time to see a newborn who was dying, the
baby would invariably live. The infant would be healed as Fr. Winkler baptized it. He had absolute faith in God's desire to heal. In
listening to God and praying as he was led, his gift of healing was
truly a great one. The worldly pride in the church was such that
many people, knowing all of this, yet despised him for doing so.
Many people in his own congregation were like this. Needless to
say, they formed no part of the prayer group. In many ways we
were "under cover." We were always too many for whatever room
was available, so chairs had to go and most stood or sat on the
floor.

We were as quiet as possible about our meetings so as not to
provoke the hostility of those who hated healing prayer and ministry to the sick. We came together, quite simply and informally,
to pray for people, many of whom themselves had come secretly,
especially church or school officials. With great joy we would sing,
laugh, give testimony, and read the Scripture. Then there came
the moment when what chairs we had were formed into a circle.
The "regulars" sat down there and "agreed" in prayer. We would
pray right around the circle, each speaking out: in a tongue, an

interpretation, a prophecy, a Scripture, a song. This is just like in the Scriptures.

By the time we went around the circle, the Lord had given us the very wisdom we needed for the healing prayer to follow. We would know the "theme"—most wonderfully given, the special faith for whatever was needed. We would then seat those who needed prayer, and after ascertaining what the need or request was, five or six of us would pray for the needy one. Every gift of the Holy Spirit operated; not a one was missing. I once saw a demon-possessed prostitute, who was so horrifying to look at that I could barely stay in the room, utterly transformed. The next day I literally did not recognize her—and neither did the others who prayed with us.

We were blessed with our "Anna" who exhorted us, always praying in the church. Her name was Helen Galloway, an elderly woman who received the baptism in the Holy Spirit when she was dying in a hospital. Her husband, a pharmacist, came to Fr. Winkler saying that his wife was dying. He told him that something else was going on with her as well, and asked Fr. Winkler to accompany him to the hospital. As Fr. Winkler leaned over the dying woman and heard her low speaking, he realized that she was praying in a prayer language—and that the Holy Spirit was wonderfully upon her. He prayed for her, and she was miraculously healed.

After that, nothing could stop the elderly Helen Galloway. She had more strength and energy than anyone of her age I have ever known. She went from hospital to hospital, praying for the sick. She was all things to all people in the best Pauline sense: she met evangelical Protestants, Catholics, Jews, and those without Christ right where they were, bringing in the healing Christ. She was a great power in prayer behind Fr. Winkler as well as a great discipler of those anxious to pray aright for all who need and seek God.

How this all fits in with learning to hear God is truly unique and amazing. What happened was that in that circle we entered into *listening prayer*. Fr. Winkler invoked the special healing presence of the Lord, we began to pray in the Spirit, and our conscious minds were enlightened. Most of what was called tongues and interpretations or prophetic words—in the best sense, that which divided the dark from the light, naming sin and calling for repentance—was really the *listening* that comes after our minds have been enlightened through prayer in the Spirit. Those gifts were in operation as well, but the "messages" in tongues were not so much messages as they were the prayer language of the Holy Spirit. Our spirit was helped to commune with God for what it needed but could not verbalize. Participating in this group brought me into a freedom in listening prayer and in the gifts of the Holy Spirit that I have since endeavored to pass on.

Fr. Winkler and Helen Galloway knew how to exhort, and they exhorted fearlessly. If someone was out of order, or not quite on target, they were told. This is extremely important in learning; we all need it. Eli and Samuel were "up front" with one another. And in this extraordinarily important exercise, we have to be too. The following is an example. When I first came into the group and we sat in the circle to pray, I did not dare open my mouth. On the third time when I was "passed" over and did not participate, Helen Galloway reached over, shook my knee with her wonderful old hand, and said, "Next time, you speak, or you don't come back!" I was not about to be left out of that group, so the next time I prayed. I prayed with all my might, and the people were blessed with the prayer the Holy Spirit gave me to pray. It was not long before I was moving in the gifts of the Holy Spirit as well.

People love an exhorter such as Helen. On another occasion, a young Pentecostal man came in who had prayed for the baptism in the Spirit all his life but had never been able to receive. He started wailing and doing all the things he had seen people do in hopes of receiving—fleshly actions that had everything to do with emotionalism and nothing to do with receiving from God. I shall never forget what Helen did, matter-of-factly and quite objectively. She reached over, gave the young man a shake, and said quite firmly: "Stop that behavior, young man! It is not necessary!" In utter astonishment he stopped his shaking and crying. She then quietly prayed for him and he received.

The unity in this group was phenomenal. We were as diverse as a group could possibly be—different denominations and races. It was here that I learned the Jesus Prayer—"Lord Jesus Christ,

Son of the living God, have mercy on me a sinner." When having a difference with someone, which was so rare I can only remember a few times, we were taught never to sin against that person with our tongues but rather say the Jesus Prayer for them. Rather than think ill or speak a word against another, we would say, "Lord Jesus Christ, have mercy on so and so." We would do this until that person straightened out or until we knew what to say to the person in order to help. In this way no one sinned against another and the unity of the Holy Spirit was kept. Out of that unity flowed incredible healing power from God.

In summary, God speaks to us in a number of ways. The mode, however, is not important. What counts is that we have our hearts and minds open to receive the word that the Lord is always speaking to us, His children.

13

The Need for Exhortation and Testing in Listening Prayer

> We actually are, at present, creatures whose
> character must be, in some respects, a horror to
> God, as it is, when we see it, a horror to our-
> selves. This I believe to be a fact: and I notice
> that the holier a man is, the more fully he is
> aware of that fact. (C. S. Lewis)[1]

I can write on *how to* put together a prayer journal, but I cannot write on *how to* hear God. I can give the principles for listening prayer, but how we hear depends finally on our character and state of being. In Dallas Willard's fine book, *In Search of Guidance*, he speaks of receiving guidance. This applies to all listening prayer:

> Here as elsewhere we must take with utmost seriousness Jesus' words: "No one knows the Father except the Son and those to whom the Son chooses to reveal him" (Matthew 11:27, JB). And this means, above all else, that the conscious seeking of divine guidance is safe and sensible only within that life of experiential union with God in his Kingdom that Jesus Christ brought to

light. . . . Only our communion with God provides the appropriate context of communications between us and him.[2]

Earlier, in writing on friendship with God, I told of the lady who mistook the effects of her father's evil as something from God. She was *mishearing* because of her need for more healing. But through prayer with knowledgeable and trusted others, and in seeking their discernment, she was spared from charging God amiss. Had she continued, however, she would have ended in seriously mishearing God.

God Uses Others to Correct Us

It is not difficult for us fallen, needy ones to slander God—and many of us do. For example, we can slander God by saying carelessly, "God told me" in that what we report is not only untrue but is not in line with God's character. We can also use the Lord's name in vain in this way. A better way is to say modestly, "It seems to me that God is guiding in this way" or "it seems He is saying this to me," and so on.

We need to repent earnestly if we have slandered God or misused His name. Truth, and love of truth, is essential. We revere it, cultivate it, champion it. We must be extremely careful to speak it. Apart from *weighing carefully* what we hear, we will at one time or another take the name of the Lord our God in vain; we will slander Him.

Throughout our lives, then, we need to weigh with others the ways we perceive God's speaking and leading. We cannot thrive apart from the body, separated from the fellowship and community of the Holy Spirit. From time to time we all need correction. This side of heaven we all need ongoing healing and forgiveness. And we all have our blind spots. The apostles did, and they took correction from each other.

As I write, several Christian leaders are in serious spiritual trouble through mishearing God—and none will accept exhortation, even from those they have most loved and respected in the past. In all these cases, an overweening spiritual pride is all too evident. It can so quickly come in; none of us is immune.

This is what happened with the author Hannah Hurnard. After her courageous work in missions and her influential book *Hinds Feet on High Places,* which blessed so many, she fell into seeking a "higher wisdom." It was, in fact, a much lower one. The seeds of her later fall—subtle theological confusions and a need for emotional balance and healing—can be seen by the discerning eye very early in Miss Hurnard's life and writing. Going uncorrected, however, these blossomed later into dark fruit. A recent biography on Miss Hurnard's life by Isabel Anders deals admirably with her early work and with her departure from orthodoxy in certain areas. The fact is, her "hearing heart" tuned into a channel that was not the vertical one of listening to God. It led her straight into error.

Her later works now sell in New Age bookstores. They contain the pagan gnosticisms congenial to an age that prefers its own subjective wisdom to the Objective Real—God's truth—that eludes the unaided and deceived mind. Miss Hurnard was adversely affected by certain metaphysical philosophies espoused by false teachers in her lifetime. These new forms of gnosticism infiltrated the church's ministry of healing and prayer in her day much as they are spreading throughout the church and the world today under the guise of Jungian-Feminist psychology and spirituality. Miss Hurnard was genuinely loved and admired by Christian leaders who exhorted her; she, however, would not take correction. She continued to operate essentially as a loner.

I have two valued prayer cells. Both are made up of Christian leaders who listen to God together and seek the testing of the Lord on all we are and do. The gift these dear ones are to me is beyond my power to express. The guidance, wisdom, and understanding we receive as we listen to God together is priceless. I do not walk in the Spirit—in the kingdom of God—apart from others who love and seek correction.

The Scriptures warn us many times never to put the Lord our God to the test, which is important to remember in regard to listening prayer. But we are strongly exhorted to test just about everything else—and most especially our own minds and hearts together with the revelation that we receive. This is because how we hear depends finally on our state of being—our character. And although we are not to test the Lord, we should be thankful that He continually tests our hearts (Proverbs 17:3; 1 Thessalonians 2:4) and uses others to help us discern them. Exhortation is one of the wonderful gifts of the Holy Spirit. We are to seek the exercise of that gift—both on our own behalf and that of others. We are to *weigh carefully* (1 Corinthians 14:29) what is spoken by ourselves and others. We ask trusted others to discern with us.

We, the immature, are taught to listen so that we might grow. This is safe as long as we are part of a worshipping body of Christians that includes those who are capable of and free to discern spirits and move in the gift of exhortation.

Though I have long taught on listening prayer in our seminars, I have waited to publish this book (I started it about twelve years ago) because these groups are not easy to find. Now I know, more strongly than ever, that it is *more* dangerous to not teach Christians listening prayer. The Bible, after all, is the textbook on listening prayer; we need no other. God has already taken the chance on our mishearing—just as He has on our failures to reason aright.

What we need is a restoration of the worldview from which the Scriptures were written. With that restored we will know our souls capable of communing and communicating with God. Learners who do not have access to the gifts of exhortation and discerning of spirits must simply pray that those Christians who do will come to the fore. Would-be disciples are to pray for those who can disciple them, and then organize prayer and fellowship groups where the gifts of the Holy Spirit can operate.

Important Points to Bear in Mind

In writing down what we hear the Lord say, we should keep several important points in mind. We do not exempt what we hear from proper testing. We know we are not composing Divine Writ—words to be added to the canon of Scriptures. Looking straight into the heart of this fact leaves us ever more appreciative of the uniqueness of Holy Scripture.

Thomas à Kempis's *The Imitation of Christ* is a classic example of how God speaks to His disciples and they in turn record what they hear the "voice of the Beloved One" say. Though his book is one of the top best-selling Christian books of all times, he would have never claimed that it was on the same level as Scripture. Furthermore, we can see imperfections in some of his thought; he was a creature of his culture and time even as we are. At the same time we bless him for the great wisdom he received and passed on to us through his faithful listening to God. In every age, we need those such as Thomas à Kempis who listen carefully, speaking anew the same age-old truths but in a way our culture-laden ears can hear afresh.

1. Darkness and Silence As a Warning from God

Although the wisdom of God is ours on a daily basis as we seek it ("give us this day our daily bread"), "at times God puts us through the discipline of darkness to teach us to heed Him."[3] We need to be very careful not to slander God during these times. We need to wait and listen only to Him rather than complaining or running to others for consolation or guidance. We cannot get a better exhortation than Oswald Chambers gives:

> Remain quiet. If you open your mouth in the dark, you will talk in the wrong mood: darkness is the time to listen. Don't talk to other people about it; don't read books to find out the reason of the darkness, but listen and heed. If you talk to other people, you cannot hear what God is saying. When you are in the dark, listen, and God will give you a very precious message for someone else when you get into the light.[4]

As we wait on God we will perhaps see something we have been unable to see before.

I remember a moment when this lesson was borne in on me. The Lord's blessing on the ministry was such that I saw quick answers to prayer for healing in the lives of others. Then, unexpectedly, I had to *wait* on God for some answers. In other words, I had to sit with no answers, with nothing from God in the way of how to pray, with no guidance other than the great good of reason He has given us all—and with little or no comfort from Him! I was listening but God was not saying anything. As I waited in prayer, I realized I had undergone a subtle shift *in the focus* of my trust—from trust in God to trust in His ministry gifts to us. I repented with all of my heart, saying, "Lord, if You never move in power in my life again in those ways of communicating Your will to me, I will yet trust You. I will yet pray in faith for others!"

This "discipline of darkness" ended in a wonderful, nurturing prayer experience—one of waiting on Him for what seemed like immediate needs as well as long-term ones. Nothing can ever replace the basic prayer stance that reflects utter trust in God when He is silent toward us. He showed me that I was close to misusing spiritual power; I was close to replacing trust in Him with the use of spiritual gifts.

What a wonderful warning from God! We are to move in the power and the strength He gives to preach, teach, and heal. But in doing this, we have to be all the more careful of these subtle shifts—from focus on God and His presence to the gifts He gives. We exist to glorify God and enjoy Him forever. That is our chief responsibility and end. Everything else runs a far distant second after this, our primary goal. After that comes all else, including our good and that of our neighbors and all work of ministry. The gifts, the glory, the power—all are His to give, but none take us to that place where we no longer live by faith. We will always see "as through a glass darkly," yet must fully trust in Him.

> Song birds are taught to sing in the dark, as we are put into the shadow of God's hand until we learn to hear Him. "What I tell you in darkness" (Matthew 10:27)—watch where God puts you into darkness, and when you are there, keep your mouth shut. . . .[5]

During these times when we cannot hear, when we know not which way to turn or go, nothing but prayer in the Holy Spirit and the "Jesus Prayer" will do. Through this we hold the divine name not only in mind and heart but on the tongue.

When we do not know how to pray—or even for what to pray—and help seems far away, we remember that the holy name and the presence are one, and that

> . . . the Spirit helps us in our weakness. We do not know what we ought to pray for, but the Spirit himself intercedes for us with groans that words cannot express. And he who searches our hearts knows the mind of the Spirit, because the Spirit intercedes for the saints in accordance with God's will (Romans 8:26–27).

Far beyond what most Christians begin to fathom, there is power in the name, healing in the name, hope in the name, strength in the name of Jesus. When the darkness is so thick that no ray of light can penetrate we must continually breathe the name. In this way we remain in the presence; faithful in the name.

> Spread your protection over them
>> that those who love your name may rejoice in you (Psalm 5:11b).

> Those who know your name will trust in you,
>> for you, LORD, have never forsaken those who seek you (Psalm 9:10).

The name of the Lord is a strong tower; the righteous runs into it and is safe." Pr. 18:10

An expansion of the divine name, "I AM WHO I AM" (Exodus 3:14), is also *I AM WHO WILL BE WITH YOU* (vv. 12, 15). In a most poignant moment, Jesus applies THE NAME to Himself (John 8:58–59). He does not say, "I was," but *I AM*. Jesus is the eternal, timeless one.

The discipline of darkness grants us the space to grow patient in suffering. We discover hope and learn how to persevere, praying always the name and in the name of Jesus.

This discipline is painful. But it always unearths some of the brightest spiritual treasures, humility being one of the larger ones. Continuing to pray in the Holy Spirit, we do indeed build ourselves up in the most holy faith (Jude 20, Ephesians 6:18). When finally the rays of God's wisdom and understanding shine through to us and the darkness lifts, we then marvel at how long it took us to hear.

2. Our Need for Forgiveness

Daily forgiveness, such as we pray for in the Lord's Prayer, is necessary to ongoing fellowship and conversation with God. Like wisdom from God, it comes daily as we ask for it; we thrive on both.

When we fail to acknowledge sin as sin, our listening to God will become tainted as a result. Holiness and sanctification of our thoughts as well as our actions is essential to right listening. Deliberate sin erects a barrier between God and ourselves, breaking communication with Him.

Sin hardens the heart and it becomes deceitful. Such a heart will always hear amiss. When sin is not recognized for what it is (as in today's psychological reductionism, the calling of sin by some other name), it always grows and destroys the capacity to hear God aright. Carnal "wisdom" is the result.

3. Our Need for Unity among Believers

Where there is no unity among Christians, there is no trustworthy corporate listening to God.

"I have given them the glory that you gave me, that they may be one as We are one: I in them and you in me. May they be brought to complete unity to let the world know that you sent me and have loved them even as you have loved me" [Jesus, John 17:22–23]. The unity that Christ prays for us is essential to our listening to God together. Our individualism militates against all things divine and human; it militates against those very things that bring us into intimate communion with God or with others. It is a substitute for both personal freedom and personhood—Our Lord never spoke in terms of individuality, of a man's . . . isolated position, but in terms of personality—"that they may be one, even as We are one."[6]

St. Paul walked in incredible freedom, yet he was one with the body of Christ and worked hard to preserve their unity. Today, a counterfeit to this true unity is preserved through the failure to discern between good and evil that militates against listening prayer altogether. The unity God gives, in contrast, comes through being one in His truth and love. St. Paul knew how to love, and even loved his enemies. At the same time he never compromised the truth. We only have unity in the truth. *The only possible way to have unity is in truth!*

Our listening, our moving in the gifts of the Holy Spirit, is anemic, thin, and sickly apart from listening with like-minded prayer partners. We need to hold each other accountable and love each other enough to speak the truth, exhort, correct, and even chastise and excommunicate when and where necessary.

We have no idea of the power of prayer until we know this unity. I am amazed at how few have these prayer partners, even Christian leaders. If we are in that position, we must pray daily until we have such prayer partners. In every geographical move I have made, I have trained Christians to pray in order to form that group. I say this to emphasize the fact that if partners are not "ready made" so to speak, they are waiting everywhere to be trained.

This unity is never achieved, as I alluded to above, where there is a reconciliation of good and evil, light and darkness.

4. Our Great Need for Humility

> . . . Through God's mercy we have this ministry. . . . But we have this treasure in jars of clay to show that this all-surpassing power is from God and not from us (2 Corinthians 4:1, 7).

It is crucial to know that we are fallible and do not always hear perfectly. As "jars of clay" we are too fragile to hold completely *the Treasure* that is the Word Himself. We cannot understand fully the word of life He continually speaks. Therefore we should delight in the gift of time. We need to lift important words of instruction and guidance before the Lord, thanking Him in advance for the discernment needed.

We also need to be very careful with how we say, "God told me. . . ." Rather, we not only say, "It *seems* that God is saying," but in important matters we ask trusted others, "Would you pray with me as we lay this before the Lord for discernment?" When others correct or exhort us in regard to this discernment, we should look at our reaction closely. Is it a subjective one, where we fly to our own defense immediately? This is always a clue that something is wrong.

When others correct and exhort us amiss our response should not be subjectively defensive. If our identity is at all in our "giftedness" in hearing, it will be. And if we are receiving carnal wisdom it also will be. But when our reaction is humble, because we know that we can simply hold this word before the Lord for further understanding, the truth will eventually come forward. Our motives and the state of our heart will nearly always be revealed by the way we take correction. Our receiving in prayer is right and good only when our hearts and motives are right and pure before the Lord.

When spiritual pride sets in we arrogate to ourselves the wisdom God alone gives, the success He alone has given. "I have done it" then replaces—if ever so subtly—the celebration of "Another lives in me." The dreadful vice of conceit does not usually erupt full-blown in a life. Pride seems to seep in slowly, on little cat's paws, as little by little we claim for ourselves what can only be attributed to God:

> If anyone thinks he is something when he is nothing, he deceives himself (Galatians 6:3).

> For by the grace given me I say to every one of you: Do not think of yourself more highly than you ought, but rather think of yourself with sober judgment, in accordance with the measure of faith God has given you (Romans 12:3).

Listening and receiving God's wisdom, knowledge, holiness, and the power of the Holy Spirit for service in the kingdom all leave us no ground for conceit. "We are unworthy servants" we cry. We acknowledge that we hold these gifts, along with the Giver, in exceedingly fragile vessels. Wisdom from above is consistently characterized by humility.

> Who is wise and understanding among you? Let him show it by his good life, by deeds done in the humility that comes from wisdom. But if you harbor bitter envy and selfish ambition in your

hearts, do not boast about it or deny the truth. Such "wisdom" does not come down from heaven but is earthly, unspiritual, of the devil. For where you have envy and selfish ambition, there you find disorder and every evil practice.

But the wisdom that comes from heaven is first of all pure; then peace-loving, considerate, submissive, full of mercy and good fruit, impartial and sincere. Peacemakers who sow in peace raise a harvest of righteousness (James 3:13–18).

Worldly wisdom is characterized consistently by "bitter envy and selfish ambition." Boasting too: "Do not love the world [of sin]. . . . For everything in the world—the cravings of sinful man, the lust of his eyes and the *boasting of what he has and does*—comes not from the Father but from the world. The world and its desires pass away, but the man who does the will of God lives forever" (1 John 2:15–17, italics mine).

Worldly wisdom leaves us empty and prone to boasting and caring too much about what others think: "Refuse the honour which comes from human lips," says F. B. Meyer.[7] Thomas à Kempis says it this way:

If you will know or learn anything profitably, desire to be unknown and to be esteemed as nothing.

The deepest and the most profitable lesson is this, the true knowledge and contempt of ourselves. It is great wisdom and high perfection to esteem nothing of ourselves, and to think always well and highly of others. . . . All of us are frail, but you ought not to think anyone more frail than yourself.

. . . All perfection in this life has some imperfection bound up with it: and no knowledge of ours is without some darkness. A humble knowledge of self is a surer way to God than a deep search after learning. Yet learning is not to be blamed, nor the mere knowledge of anything whatsoever, for knowledge is good, considered in itself, and ordained by God; but a good conscience and a virtuous life are always to be preferred before it.[8]

"The words of the Lord are flawless" (Psalm 12:6). In contrast to the boastful, flattering tongues of the ungodly, they fill us to the brim.[9] Oswald Chambers speaks of "giving God the best that

He has given you. Be careful what you do with the best you have. Whenever you get a blessing from God, give it back to Him as a love gift." This will effectively replace boasting. If we are to know or learn anything profitably, we must desire to be unknown and esteemed as nothing.

> It is great wisdom and high perfection to esteem nothing of our-
> selves, and to think always well and highly of others.[10]

paradoxical

These words of Thomas à Kempis find little acceptance today. An example illustrates: The small daughter of a friend of mine is in one of the first grades of school. Her teacher is apparently deep into teaching the doctrines of self-esteem, because she told her wee little student to name some way that she was wonderful or special. The little creature objected and told her teacher, "That would be bragging." How many children would know to say that today! This was a properly affirmed child, one able to go against the prevailing custom of the classroom. To teach a child to boast falls far short of affirming and blessing him or her.

The admonition of Thomas à Kempis is at once paradoxical and wonderful: we must first accept ourselves to be able to show forth this humility. Apart from self-acceptance, such advice as his could lead souls to putting the *real self* to death, rather than the worldly wisdom (vanity and envy) that is in them. By and large, the self-esteem movement is little more than the flipside of our failure to find the great virtue of self-acceptance. This virtue comes through humility and the consequent finding of our identity in something greater than the narcissistic, envious self. In the absence of identity found in that which is greater than the self, the self is hounded from pillar to post, from vanity to self-hatred and back, over and over, without rest.

True Communion with God
Produces Incredible Fruitfulness

In the presence of the Lord there is not only dialogue but fruit: incredible fruit-bearing. We listen for the word, we are led of the Lord, we collaborate with Him; there is *LIFE*.

... I have set before you life and death, blessings and cursing. Now *choose* life, so that you and your children may live and that you may love the LORD your God, *listen to his voice*, and hold fast to him. For the LORD *is your life* (Deuteronomy 30:19–20, italics mine).

And to mix our metaphors just a little, the "tree" of life is so laden with fruit that we find we are pregnant with all good things; we are creative makers in God's image. To love and serve truth alone is to produce the fruit God calls for. It is this fruit that meets the slander, bitter envy, and vain conceit of those who would condemn us. To look back on a life governed by carnal wisdom is to look back on unbearable sterility and barrenness.

There is incredible fruitfulness where there is true communion with God. Friendship, sonship, unity, humility, holiness, fruitfulness, fullness of *being*.

You did not choose Me, but I chose you and appointed you to go and bear fruit—fruit that will last. Then the Father will give you whatever you ask in my name. This is my command: Love each other (John 15:16–17).

God's ways are higher than ours (Isaiah 55:9; Psalm 145:3); we cannot fathom them. We know only in part; we see only as through a glass darkly (1 Corinthians 13:12). Nevertheless, we have what we need for the journey, and it is so much more than most Christians experience or even deem possible.

If I have . . . all knowledge, and if I have a faith that can move mountains, but have not love, I am nothing (1 Corinthians 13:2).

The road over which we travel carrying this wisdom from above, this fruitfulness, is the royal road of love. It is here that the capacity to know—to hear God and to move in the gifts of the Spirit—will then be worth something. To walk this road "is not according to worldly wisdom but according to God's grace" (2 Corinthians 1:12). With St. Paul, we echo that this alone is our boast.

14

What to Avoid in Listening Prayer: Neognostic Listening

The deadliest Pharisaism to-day is not hypocrisy, but unconscious unreality. (Oswald Chambers)[1]

The prayer preceding all prayers is "May it be the real I who speaks. May it be the real Thou that I speak to." (C. S. Lewis)[2]

*W*hether in our own listening or in those we disciple, the main thing to watch out for is egoistic subjectivism. This is a practice of the presence of the self—the old nature—where one's feelings speak so loudly that they block out all else. Every feeling concerns itself with ego. What results is a subjectivity that not only blocks the way to listening prayer but *substitutes* for it.

In this activity our communication with God and all that is other than the self is lost. It is the isolated self communicating with itself. Herein we lose the true imagination, with its capacity to intuit the real from the realm of nature, supernature, or absolute being. Reality is blanked out; if glimpsed at all, it is reduced to what one *feels* about it.

Keeping Feelings Objective

It is tragic enough when one is consumed by egoistic subjectivism. It is doubly tragic, however, when the narcissistic mutterings of one's subjective feelings masquerade as "words from God." A very deep spiritual deception then ensues.

That the feelings should be objective and not subjective is the secret of great poetry and prose; it is the same secret we all must learn if we are to enjoy personal wholeness.

In 1904 Charlotte M. Mason, writing on feelings, put this psychological truth succinctly:

> So long as the feelings remain objective, they are, like the bloom to the peach, the last perfection of a beautiful character; but when they become subjective, when every feeling concerns itself with the *ego*, we have . . . morbid conditions set up; the person begins by being "oversensitive," hysteria supervenes, perhaps melancholia, an utterly spoilt life. George Eliot has a fine figure which aptly illustrates this subjective condition of the feelings. She tells us that a philosophic friend had pointed out to her that whereas the surface of a mirror or of a steel plate may be covered with minute scratches going in every direction, if you hold a lighted candle to the surface all these random scratches appear to arrange themselves and radiate from the central flame; just so with the person whose feelings have been permitted to minister to his egoistic consciousness: all things in heaven and earth are "felt" as they affect his own personality.[3]

The above is quoted from Charlotte Mason's excellent six-volume series on the education of children. She knew, even as C. S. Lewis understood so well, that feelings are objectifiable and therefore educable. To fail to help children in this way by not educating them in the proper objectivity of the feeling being is to leave them vulnerable to the "disease of introspection." Through this condition an *unconscious unreality* always ensues; a sickly subjective myth or story evolves—"one's personal story" told from the standpoint of an egoistic consciousness. Such a story may have some truth in it, but it will seriously lead astray.

Christians sunk in this type of "unconscious unreality" invariably begin to transfer blame for their unhappiness onto others. They will charge God and others.

And some Christians in this type of "unconscious unreality" begin to blame Satan for their plight. From there they focus on demons, principalities and powers, and so on. They add to the practice of the presence of the old self the practice of the presence of demons. They listen to them in the same way they were listening to the "wounded child"[4] or the narcissistic personality. Without exception these people end in the worst kind of spiritual deception, having concocted not just subjective myths but demonic ones as well. "Doctrines of demons," as mentioned in the Scriptures, evolve in just this way.

People trapped in their own subjectivity are difficult to be around for any length of time. A defense or strong boundary is needed against the intensity and preciosity of their feelings. They may well demand that others honor these sick feelings as heroic or even as "poetic" insight (as when dealing with the "wounded artist") by validating or participating in them somehow.

It becomes even more complicated when these people start calling the voice of these complaining feelings a "word from the Lord." "God told me this" then prefaces the expression of these sentiments, with their personal "story" evolving from there. The more intense the narcissistic personality is, the more apt he or she is to involve naive and undiscerning others in this empty world of sick feelings. Appealing to the sentimentalism and co-dependency in those surrounding them, they gain many another soul to help them "live out" their illusions and delusions—in short, their "story."

The power to feel and the capacity for "having feelings" is a wonderful gift from God. At one time or another we all need therapists and wise counselors who can reflect back to us our feelings, telling us which are appropriate and which are not and helping us to objectify them rightly.

As Charlotte Mason, writing on the feelings of children and the delicate task in training them, assures the parent:

There is only one case in which the feelings may not have free play, and that is when they reflect the consciousness of the *ego*. What are commonly called sensitive feelings—that is, susceptibility for oneself and about oneself, readiness to perceive neglect or slight, condemnation or approbation—through belonging to a fine and delicate character, are in themselves of less worthy order, and require very careful direction lest morbid conditions should be set up. . . . It appears to be an immutable law that our feelings, as our sensations, must find their occupation in things without; the moment they are turned in upon themselves harm is done.[5]

We Listen Vertically—Like Sunflowers Pointed to the Sun

> Every good and perfect gift is from above, coming down from the Father of the heavenly lights, who does not change like shifting shadows (James 1:17).

Wisdom from the Spirit of God, like every good and perfect gift, comes down to us from heaven. A part of *incarnational reality*, God's wisdom comes down to us in the pattern of the incarnation. Christ came down from above, the Holy Spirit is poured out from above, the new birth is from above: all experiences of God's presence come down to us from heaven. Our souls receive a transcendent *good* as a pure gift.

To receive from God, then, is to lift the sights of our souls from the lateral or horizontal plane of earth and self to an otherworldly, transcendent one. To do this, like sunflowers opening straight up to the sun, we lift our faces straight up to God. We are in a decidedly vertical position, listening.

That which then comes down from God *transcends* our unaided minds and imaginations, while simultaneously these created faculties of our souls are the *means* by which we receive the gift. God showers Himself upon us down from heaven—as Word and Spirit. We partake of His wisdom and his righteousness.

> We have not received the spirit of the world ["wisdom of this age"] but the Spirit who is from God, that we may understand what God has freely given us. This is what we speak, not in words taught us by human wisdom but in words taught by the Spirit, expressing

spiritual truths in spiritual words [or "interpreting spiritual truths to spiritual men"]. The man without the Spirit does not accept the things that come from the Spirit of God, for they are foolishness to him, and he cannot understand them, because they are spiritually discerned (1 Corinthians 2:12–14).

When Self Talks to the Self

Egoistic subjectivism obviously belongs to the lateral and the horizontal; it is self talking to the self. In such a context, the words of the world (worldly wisdom), the flesh (carnal desire), and finally the evil one himself predominate. Those who listen on a horizontal plane always miss wisdom from the Spirit. To develop this power of listening consciously will sooner if not later lead one into the occult and even demonic ways of "knowing." Wisdom that is generated from the fallen mind—the intellect and imagination—in isolation from God will always miss the mark. This is what the Scriptures refer to as worldly wisdom. As such it differs radically from the wisdom that comes down from above. Worldly wisdom always and finally leads to the demonic.

We are now a nation and, by and large, a church of morally and spiritually illiterate people. Our Western civilization denies God and the transcendent in nature. We have lost the moral and the spiritual good. We are therefore centered in a human self that is severely alone and diminished; we are a people sunk in materialism and therefore in narcissism.

Charlotte Mason taught Christian parents how to deal with the occasional child who would stray into and get stuck in *subjective egoism.* She instructed parents in how to help children grow in objectivity so that they could recognize that their feeling being was not their true center.

Today, however, we face an unhealed body of Christ that has a large population of adults who are narcissistically immature. Their children in turn go untrained, being raised by parents who lack the slightest inkling that the atheistic materialism and subjectivism of a dying civilization has entered deeply into their souls. Their eyes have been plastered shut so that like their blind idols they cannot see God. These parents and children now fill our counseling offices. Unfortunately, most pastors do not pray with them, helping them toward release from the words of the world, the flesh, and the devil; nor do they teach them to hear God. They are usually treated to some form of secular analysis, which is materialist in nature.

Subjectivism in Secular Psychoanalysis: The New Gnosticism

Diseased subjectivity is easily spawned through secular analysis. It could not be otherwise when the self, considered in isolation from God and all transcendent *meaning*, becomes the only god. This self speaks, gathering its wisdom from the horizontal plane.

Unresolved psychological and spiritual difficulties leave people open to counsel and spiritual direction that incorporates the subjectivism in secular psychoanalysis, particularly that of C. G. Jung's gnostic spirituality. The "Christianized" secular psychologies that are influenced by Jung have fallen into gnosticism. This entails the assigning of innocence to sin and evil. Sin and evil in a person or situation are renamed; evil is called good and good is called evil. Good and evil are thereby "synthesized"—made one and reconciled.

The results of this kind of counsel and direction are always tragic, especially for the baptized Christian. Many Christians, including ministers, writers, and teachers, have been unable or unwilling to find healing for the soul within the church and have consequently fallen into this gnosticism unwittingly. It is not easy to break with, because spiritual deception is at the heart of this soulish spirituality. Its horizontal wisdom has linked with the occult and even demonic ways of "knowing."

Those who become immersed in the therapy or so-called "Christian" counseling that incorporates the Gnostic-Jungian-Feminist mixtures inevitably experience the loss of the objective *real*, the objective *good*. The images and diseased feelings of the heart, which emanate from a needy ego, become one's "objective" word, one's holy writ. Inevitably they lead to destruction.

Those who buy into these false psychologies are given a mirror—the same mirror the tempter gives the Green Lady in C. S. Lewis's novel, *Perelandra*. One begins to see oneself walking alongside oneself, gaining a decidedly dramatic view of the self. A maddening obsession with inner voices and differentiated psychic personas ensues, such as the "wounded child," "the homosexual self," the "wounded artist," and so on.

When these needy souls can no longer live in their meaninglessness and blindness, they will take in the "spirituality" of our age by default if not given the real thing. In Jungian spirituality, these psychic persona are literally called "gods" ("archetypes"), and so an overt idolatry of self follows quickly. What they deeply need instead is a Christ-centered spirituality that apprehends the transcendent real. Lacking this, they will embrace the old paganism in one form or another.

Neognostic Spirituality

> Woe to the foolish prophets who follow their own spirit and have seen nothing. . . . Their visions are false and their divinations a lie (Ezekiel 13:3, 6).

Spirituality, as such, is common to all people and religions. Spiritualities other than the neognostic have also had their genesis only on the horizontal plane of mental and emotional cogitations. Some of these too are labeled "Christian," but are actually unholy "mixtures" that have little if anything to do with true wisdom from above.

The spirituality rampant in Western civilization today, however, is the neognostic. It always leads directly to the old Baal-Ashtoreth religion with its lustful sensuality. From its hyperintellectualism (the split between head and heart) sexual sin and orgy always follow. Neognosticism has emerged directly out of a decadent atheistic materialism that has linked hands with occult and even demonic ways of knowing. These systems synthesize good and evil. Christians of all stripes are now subject to these new spiritualities, many of which are quickly being politicized. Rather than listening to God, by and large we are sunk in egois-

tic subjectivism of one sort or another, one that assigns innocence to sin and evil.

Neognostic Listening

> They said to you, "In the last times there will be scoffers who will
> follow their own ungodly desires." These are the men who divide
> you, who follow mere natural instincts and do not have the Spirit
> (Jude 18–19).

Neognostic listening is ordinarily termed "New Age" today.
Within that movement the Objective Real has been lost entirely.
Self and its feelings are deified, constituting the only authority
recognized as worth listening to.

Only recently I was on a campus originally dedicated to Christ's
service. A professor who was seriously misleading young students
from Christian homes looked me straight in the eye and, dwelling
securely in her newfound "spirituality" that specializes in assigning innocence to sinful behavior, said to me: "The Lord told me
that it is all right for lesbians to live together; He told me that les-
bian sexual behavior is all right when two women commit themselves to one another." This, my friends, is gnostic listening.

On that campus the Objective Real has been lost. The good of
reason is flailing as lesbian-feminist-homosexual ethics and
political practices have not only flooded in but have adopted the
Mein Kampf tactics of Adolf Hitler to intimidate those who disagree with them.[6] Rank sentimentalism is rife, leaving no place
for the rational, much less the good of reason. A demonic power
was present as well, which had been summoned as part of a gnostic spirituality rooted in goddess worship and witchcraft.

I would not share this in a book on listening prayer if it were
unusual or rare. But it is proliferating today, afflicting all the major
denominations to one extent or another. I sadly watched this
neognostic spirituality penetrate and destroy the larger part of
Catholic and Anglican renewal, together with that within the
older Protestant denominations. Now it is flooding into the evangelical world. It is characterized by an absence of true learning—
the good of reason that attends wisdom from the Spirit. And it

always reconciles good and evil. It assigns innocence to sin and sinful behavior—calling it good.

Many who control church organizations today have fallen into the trap of neognosticism. They are busy not only publishing this new "gospel" to all who will listen, but because they are in authority they are enforcing their views as "politically correct"—a new "law." They are often heard or read today as "Christian" speakers, teachers, and writers. Such is the final result of our *egoistic subjectivism* and the loss of the Unseen Real.

In the face of those who follow mere instinct and yet call themselves Christian, Jude wonderfully admonishes us:

> But you, dear friends, build yourselves up in your most holy faith and pray in the Holy Spirit. Keep yourselves in God's love as you wait for the mercy of our Lord Jesus Christ to bring you to eternal life (Jude 20–21).

Cult Hunters Who Pursue "New Age" Spirituality

The greater part of Christian renewal in our day has been lost due to either an influx of neognostic spirituality or to the loss of the real spirituality (wisdom from the Spirit) through repression. This repression often comes through uninformed attempts to stamp out the gnosticism. Gnosticism is parasitic; it can only exist on a host from which it gains a tradition, ideology, or religion. It has none of its own, and always attempts to attach itself to the Christian real.

St. John had this problem with the gospel he wrote. The gnostics of his day attempted to use it and live off it as a parasite would. Our gospels were preserved by the full proclamation of the Judeo-Christian message and its transcendent way of knowing, together with its clear differences from the gnostic paganism of their day. They were not preserved by throwing the Christian supernatural out with the parasite.

Cult hunters today suffer from a severe rift between head and heart. They are therefore cut off from the good of reason and scholarship, though they often pose as scholars. And, though they will often deny it, they are also cut off from the good of the heart's way of apprehending the Unseen Real. They do not separate the parasite from its true host. Instead they destroy both together.

Professional cult hunters are as dangerous as the gnostics they so fear. They usurp the place of the true theologian-prophet who, in touch with the mind and the condition of God's people, sounds warnings and gives balanced theological answers in terms the laity can understand. The cult hunters, in contrast, turn misguided laity into ravening wolves like themselves. Without knowledge they condemn, slander, and devour the people of God along with "heresies" they think they comprehend.

The cult hunters have no positive ministry, only the negative ministry of criticizing others. They are thereby compelled to discover new heretics in order to keep their books, teachings, and television programs going. And like the neognostics they pursue, they do it in the power of an unaided intellect and imagination, their minds bereft of wisdom from above. Because they despise incarnational reality and the work of the Holy Spirit, they too are gnostics—the polar opposite from those they hunt down. This is tragic, for the only defense against the neognosticism (egoistic subjectivism) of today is a true and vibrant Christian spirituality—the Christian supernatural in all its transcendent glory.

We must always look up and out to the source of all wisdom— God, the Objective Real. When we lose this vertical focus we are open to the idolatrous and harmful practices we have discussed in this chapter. The infection we open ourselves up to will spread—as we will discuss in the next chapter.

15

When Neognostic Listening Infects the Church

To bring sin home, and to bring grace home, *we need that something else should come home which alone gives meaning to both*—the holy. . . . If our gospel be obscure, it is obscure to them in whom the slack God of the period has blinded minds, or a genial God unbraced them, and hidden the Holy One who inhabits eternity. This holiness of God is . . . the ruling interest of the Christian religion. . . .

Neither love, grace, faith, nor sin has any but a passing meaning except as they rest on the holiness of God, except as they arise from it, and return to it, except as they satisfy it, show it forth, set it up, and secure it everywhere and forever. Love is but its outgoing; sin is but its defiance; grace is but its action on sin; the Cross is but its victory; faith is but its worship. . . . What we on earth call righteousness among men, the saints in heaven call holiness in Him. (P. T. Forsyth)[1]

*W*ithin the soul of the Christian who adopts the neognostic interpretive system to any degree there will inevitably be the insinuation of the obscene into the holy—an eventual black mass of sorts within the soul itself.[2]

Many Christians have stayed overlong in apostate church organizations, trying to reform them from within. In effect they have been involved in neognostic listening through the preaching, teaching, and "healing" that comes through polluted pulpits, altars, and classrooms. Like the churches they attend, they now find themselves infected.

They resymbolize the very words of the Scriptures, redefining them to support the pagan theology inherent in neognosticism, which reconciles good and evil. Slowly they themselves are being "resymbolized." And as they continue to listen willingly their identities are being re-formed on gnostic foundations.[3]

The very altars in these places have become polluted. Those who serve the altar openly serve Baal, the god of sexual orgy; they flaunt this fact and call it good. This refers to those who are sexually promiscuous and knowingly serve the sacraments to the unrepentant. To sit at table and take hands with those who teach this idolatry is to participate in the unholy.

The true church exists; God owns it, protects it, and the gates of hell will not prevail against it. But the true church is not what many confused Christians call "church" today. The true church where "God's solid foundation stands firm" is sealed with this inscription: "The Lord knows those who are his," and, "Everyone who confesses the name of the Lord must turn away from wickedness" (2 Timothy 2:19).

This next section is especially for the precious sheep who are trapped in these infected organizations, even to the least degree. We should search our souls, asking the following questions: How am I, a creature of this century whose identity has been affected by psychological reductionism and resymbolization, to know when I overlook sin and fail to confess it as such? What steps should I take in regard to the polluting of my soul?

This is extremely important to the subject of listening prayer, for we always need to keep the walls of holiness firmly erected. When we listen to self instead of God our soul becomes infected. Not only have individuals become infected, but the institutional church as well.

Churchism

No one can serve two masters. Either he will hate the one and love the other, or he will be devoted to the one and despise the other (Matthew 6:24).

Now if once the conception of Hierarchy is fully grasped, we see that order can be destroyed in two ways: (1) by ruling or obeying natural equals, that is by Tyranny or Servility. (2) By failing to obey a natural superior or to rule a natural inferior—that is, by Rebellion or Remissness.[4]

In the name of Christian unity, some people have thrown in their lot with false shepherds. For example, in my diocese certain clergy and others disagree with the practice of ordaining unrepentant homosexuals, yet link hands with and carry out the orders of those who do. They enable the apostate hierarchy by standing with it *as if it were the church.*

These people serve a structure that is other than the real church. It becomes an idolatrous substitute for the true fellowship of the Holy Spirit. The redeemed of the Lord worldwide who follow Christ in obedience, no matter where they are in the world or of what denomination they form a part, do not obey and maintain connections to false shepherds. Above all else they guard their connection to Jesus, their head. He is the banner they raise and follow; they choose to remain in Him through loving obedience to Him. Their unity with the church universal is not only maintained but is realized beyond measure. Evangelism—the proclamation of the gospel—flows outward like a mighty, holy river. It carries *all manner of profound healing* in its wake for the spirits, souls, and bodies of fallen humankind. Instead of this incredible reality, some substitute churchism.

Churchism, as Dr. John A. Mackay states in his classic, *Christian Reality and Appearance,* is the idolatry of structure. Quoting him, "Christian reality has four distinctive but inseparably related facets." They are:

1. God's Self-Disclosure.
2. The Transforming Encounter.

3. The Community of Christ.
4. Christian Obedience.[5]

Each of the above has its imitation. It "looks like it but it is not it." In fact it is an idolatrous substitute for the reality. These look-alikes are:

1. Theologism: The Idolatry of Ideas.
2. Impressionism: The Idolatry of Feeling.
3. Churchism: The Idolatry of Structure.
4. Ethicism: The Idolatry of Prescripts.[6]

Churchism is a complex and often subtle mixture of things and ideas that is set in motion when a church organization, denomination, or sect is no longer an instrument that enables the people of God to "be the church." The organization itself has become an end. People who accept the imitation then serve this idolatrous end.

When this false end is served long enough, spiritual deception sets in. Those who serve the organization continue to do so even when it no longer looks like the church. For example, they serve it even after it raises altars to Baal, ordaining those who are unrepentant over sexual sin and practice sexual perversion. And it serves the other face of Baal, Molech, the idol god to which children are being sacrificed in abortion today. Those who serve polluted altars find themselves in the terrible position of fighting against God. They risk being given over to reprobate minds (see Romans 1), that condition where the good of all reason is lost. Confusion reigns.

John Mackay has a fine definition of what the church is:

The communal dimension of Christian reality witnessed to the fact that while to be really Christian a person must have a direct relationship to God, there is at the same time no place for pure individualism. The "new men in Christ" are members of a fellowship, a community of faith called the church, a unique association created by Christ through the Holy Spirit. This historic community was born in dramatic form at Pentecost. From its inception the church gave expression to its universal character, across all linguistic boundaries. It expressed also the reality and practical implications of loving God and one another. It was hailed by the apostles and early Christians as the "New Israel" the "Israel of God," the "fellowship of the Spirit."

Where was the church to be found? How could it be identified? In the course of the years a dictum became current, "Where Christ is, there is the church." In the contemporary era, the German-Swiss theologian Karl Barth has given expression to the Apostolic and post-Apostolic interpretation of the church as community by saying that the church is the fellowship of all those for whom Jesus Christ is Lord, the living congregation of the living Lord Jesus Christ.

While community is the core of churchly reality, the community must, for both religious and secular reasons, become organized. It must create for itself a visible organizational structure. In the course of the centuries, the Christian church has had, and continues to have, many diverse structural forms. But amid all the changes through which the church passes and whatever its organizational shape may be, across all boundaries of culture and race, of ocean, mountain and forest, there are certain changeless centralities that must be observed by all members of the community of Christ.

First, the finality of the church is changeless. It exists to bear witness to Christ and the gospel in its way of life, its forms of thought, and its course of action, taking seriously Christ's mandate to make him known to all men, to the uttermost bounds of human habitation. By so doing, the community of Christ will, in the love of God, in the love of men, and in the love of one another, give worldwide reality to a totally new type and dimension of human community.

Second, the form of organizational structure adopted by a Christian community, wherever it is located throughout the world, must be guided by this principle. Under the direction of the Holy Spirit and in loyalty to the nature and requirements of the Christian community as set forth in Holy Scripture, church organization must be such as to enable the church to "be the church," in the particular environment in which its members live and witness. That is to say, the church must not seek to absolutize a given organizational structure to such a degree that the structure becomes, in a subtle manner and with disastrous consequences, an end in itself and in this way a substitute for what the church exists to be.

The church is truly the church and can fulfill its function within its environment and in history only when it accepts itself as an instrument, a medium which God uses to "prepare the way of the Lord," that the Kingdom of God may come. The church's life and witness must be for the sake of the Kingdom. Under the lordship of Christ, the church must operate as a redemptive, reconciling reality in every facet of human life and relationships. To use the luminous words of John Calvin, the church is in essence, and must be willing to be in its existence, "the instrument of God's glory." In the life and thought of its members, individually and corporately, it must give visible expression to the character of God and his reconciling purpose for mankind.

In order that the church may be able to achieve its supreme finality and express its truly instrumental character as a community of destiny in this world and in the world to come, all its members must take their identity seriously as belonging to the body of Christ. They must therefore be educated and prepared for the fulfillment of their role as followers of Christ and members of the "household of God." For that reason, the church today must be awakened to give contemporary meaning to the injunction of the Apostle Paul in his letter to the Ephesians that the "saints," "God's men and women," in a word, Christians, be "properly equipped for their service" (4:12, Phillips' Translation). According to Paul the clergy, that is, the full-time professional leaders of the church, have it as their role to prepare the laity "for the work of the ministry" (Ephesians 4:12). It is the responsibility of each Christian to be a minister, that is, "a servant." And it is the responsibility of the church organization to see to it that each member becomes just that. Only so, can the church and its members take their calling seriously.[7]

John Mackay describes churchism—the idolatrous substitute for the church—so well that I include it here:

The Christian church, as we have observed and stressed, was born as a community of people personally committed to Jesus Christ. But naturally, like every community, the church became organized, and in order to function, assumed institutional form. As time went on, it appeared under the guise of many structures. While communal reality did not disappear, its importance in many instances diminished. At the same time, increasing significance was attached to the organization, and increasing power was vested in its leadership. The moment came when the church's leaders proclaimed that they constituted the church. They ceased to be the church's servants and became its lords. In the meantime, the church itself ceased to be God's servant and became his patron, assuming the role and rights of Deity. For many members it became more important to belong to the church and obey it than to belong to God and obey him. The church institution thus became the visible, historical expression of Christian reality and the supreme object of Christian allegiance. Reality gave place to appearance. An organization created to serve became an idol to be adored.

While this trend became most ominous in the great hierarchical churches, especially the Roman, its presence was not lacking in the church denominations of Protestantism. Following the Reformation, sectarian groups emerged who considered themselves to be the church and assumed a spirit of arrogance and complacency. Promethean institutional pride has afflicted the community of Christ through the ages and has confronted the Head of the community with many problems, both tragic and ironic. False doctrinal assumptions and sinful personal pretensions have produced ecclesiastical idols.[8]

Through repentance we must break with this idolatry and serve the true God.

Manasseh "did that which was evil in the sight of the Lord, after the abominations of the heathen, and he reared up altars for Baal" (2 Kings 21:2–3, KJV). He led his people into sexual perversion. As the face of sexual sin turned into that of Molech and the horror of ritual abuse and murder of children, this king "made his son pass through the fire." But when he humbled himself greatly, and repented, the Lord forgave him, and restored him to his kingdom (2 Chronicles 33:12–13).

The only cure for the people of God caught up in an apostate structure is a profound one. Yet it is often overlooked, perhaps because of its splendid simplicity. Our deliverance is found in corporate and individual repentance.

The prayer of repentance that the Church of the Resurrection of Illinois was led to formulate and pray as part of the divine liturgy is included in Appendix C. All pastors are encouraged to lead their congregations in this or a similar prayer.

What Is at Stake in Sexual Permissiveness

Many, strangely enough, do not understand what is at stake in condoning homosexuality and sexual sin. This is another point of infection in the body of Christ. Souls who accept this permissiveness and act it out are placed under the tyranny of sin. At stake, therefore, is the cross and its message—the very heart of the Christian faith. To opt for this tyranny is to step outside of Christ and His atonement; it is to fail to remain in Him.

> . . . Do not let sin reign in your mortal body so that you obey its evil desires. Do not offer the parts of your body to sin, as evil instruments of wickedness, but rather offer yourselves to God, as those who have been brought from death to life; and offer the parts of your body to him as instruments of righteousness. For sin shall not be your master, because you are not under the law, but under grace (Romans 6:12–14).

The following is as true today as when St. Paul wrote it. The price of apostasy is still death and immeasurable loss:

> The wages of sin is death, but the gift of God is eternal life in Christ Jesus our Lord (Romans 6:23).

To choose and obey Christ is to choose grace—the power to resist sin. The cross and the grace that issues from Christ's death and rising for us is utterly sufficient. It is more than enough! It is none other than what being Christian is all about.

Anyone can be delivered from heterosexual or homosexual sin and behavior, just as from any other sin and compulsion. But deliverance comes only with choosing to remain in God. It comes from loving Him and dying ("in the teeth of every inclination" as C. S. Lewis says) to the old wounded, narcissistic self—that which wants to be separate and on its own.

Denial of Sin and Evil

We live in a time, as Dr. Mackay declared earlier in our century, when Christian reality has almost entirely been replaced by its shadowy substitutes. These substitutions contain misconceptions that help keep blinders on people. The failure to discern and deal with sin and evil effectively is a problem that trips up many Christians, infecting the church. For one thing, the face of evil seldom looks the part:

> Few people who are evil ever appear evil, even after the evidence of their deceit, destructiveness, and hardness is exposed. The little old man who feeds birds and smiles warmly as you walk by his home might be a person who has abused a hundred children over the last fifty years. If he is caught, most will doubt the charge, or at least the extent of the harm.[9]

People who consistently choose sin usually rationalize it as somehow being okay for themselves. They then enter into denial about it. As Scott Peck wrote in *The People of the Lie*, "the central defect of evil is not the sin but the refusal to acknowledge it."

There are two chief ways in which this refusal is sustained by those who consistently do evil but deny it. One is by scapegoating others; the second is by reconciling good and evil. Dr. Peck firmly grasped the way of scapegoating of others: a psychological projection mechanism by which those who have slipped over the line

> *project* their own evil onto the world. They never see themselves as evil; . . . they consequently see much evil in others. . . . Evil people are often destructive because they are attempting to destroy evil. The problem is that they misplace the locus of the evil. Instead of destroying others they should be destroying the sickness in themselves.[10]

The second way, however, is tragically endemic to our culture. Due to the peculiar blindness of our time, few people spot the reconciling of good and evil, and have difficulty verbalizing it when they do. As an unfortunate but telling example, Dr. Peck understood so well the first way but in some of his later writing seems to have missed entirely this second way. Although we have explored this second way in chapter 14, the subject is so vitally important today that it demands further explanation.

This reconciliation of good and evil arises out of the psychological reductionism accompanying our materialism, whereby the spiritual and the moral dimensions of the human soul are not recognized and thereby remain invisible. These dimensions are in effect obliterated. Sin and evil are given other names. They are tagged with sociological and psychological labels. In this way good and evil are synthesized, made one, reconciled. The evilness of evil, and our responsibility to repent of it, is denied. It goes without saying that the goodness of God, and the way He imparts His righteousness to us, the fallen, is in no way considered.

Christians, along with their culture, have by and large reconciled good and evil—synthesizing the virtues and the vices by giving sin an exclusively psychological definition. In this way, we reconcile good and evil at the deepest level of our being—and therefore fail to confess and turn from our sins.

This is what makes the *vice of sentimentality*, so rampant in the culture today, the truly vicious sin that it is. Evil, appearing as it does within the context of a large amount of good, has already been renamed. In this vice it is simply ignored.

The Vice of Sentimentality

Inherent in the reconciliation of good and evil is the vice of sentimentality. This is a facet of another of the prime betrayers (see Mackay), the idolatry of feeling. Those in the grips of sentimentality see only the good in the favored object and screen out the evil. In effect, they deny the evil.

One example, horrifying in that it seems a caricature of this vice, is set in the context of valuing the Christian community as structure. In this case the denominational hierarchy is the favored object. An influential church leader, who goes on record as holding to the orthodox position regarding sexual permissiveness, was responding to a concerned Christian's criticism of Bishop Spong's theology, psychology, behavior, and outright heretical activity. Instead of validating the orthodox position, however, he smiled a calm, knowing, and even superior smile, and replied: "Things are not always as they seem." Those who heard his reply felt their heads spin, themselves almost mesmerized. This leader had lightly dismissed all the evil that has come upon the church due to the sin and apostasy of her ordained clergy. What a stupendous state of unreality this sentimentality turns out to be.

Sentimentality is seldom this blatant, of course. But here again, few know what to name it even when they encounter it in its exaggerated state. Subtle or plain, this vice is hideous because it denies the evilness of evil, making a nest for it. It is rampant in the church today and proudly passes itself off as love.

The best explication I have ever read is by Mark Jefferson in his essay, "What is Wrong with Sentimentality?" Agreeing that the sentimentalist misrepresents the world in order to indulge his or her feelings, Dr. Jefferson shows what is peculiar to sentimentality. He speaks of the vice as it is seen in the thrill seeker, the melodramatic person, the disdainful person, the self-righteous person, and the wondrous person. As a brief example, the "wondrous man misrepresents the world in order to feel unconditionally warm hearted about bits of it." This habit is "sustained by misrepresentation of things."

> But the nature of the misrepresentation of things differs according to the sort of indulgence desired. *Each indulgence type requires the projection upon the world of a different kind of unreality.* My contention is that sentimentality is objectionable because of the nature of its sustaining fantasy and not simply because it must employ one.[11]

"The qualities that sentimentality imposes upon its objects are the qualities of innocence." A fiction of innocence must be maintained whereby "such things as sweetness, dearness, littleness, blamelessness, etc." are imposed on the favored object. And it is here, as Jefferson points out, that we come face to face with a "direct impairment of the moral vision taken of its object."

If, as Dr. Jefferson says, one's sentimentality is focused on a poodle, and all manner of good fiction is composed and imposed on this favored pet, then perhaps our sentimentality is harmless enough. But "when its objects are people or countries," we have quite another situation altogether. He reminds his readers of E. M. Forster's *A Passage to India*, a novel that depicts the brutality that is part and parcel of this vice. Within its pages, a young British woman's virtue and veracity are sentimentalized, a tragic fiction is spun out and maintained, and an Indian man is unjustly accused and destroyed.

> To maintain the innocence one had projected upon a favored object it is often necessary to construct other, dangerous fictions about the things that object interacts with.[12]

Preaching Holiness Is Fraught with Peril

> It is a snare to imagine that God wants to make us perfect specimens of what He can do; God's purpose is to make us one with Himself.[13]

Holiness is a dangerous thing to preach when its relationship to grace and the real presence of God is not understood. The last decade or so has seen one public church figure after another, in response to flagrant sin in the church, begin to major on holiness, loudly proclaiming it over the media. Then, before the listening flock has time to put the teaching into effect, the preacher himself has fallen into sexual sin. In astonishment we ask, how can this be? It is dreadfully unholy, gross, and even, if it were not so tragic, ludicrous.

The reason, of course, is that knowing and preaching the law of God does not enable one to keep it. Only grace does that. But the preacher is supposed to know this. What is amiss here? In these cases, moralism and legalism has replaced listening to God and humbly walking with Him. Sin has entered in as a deadly infection.

God keeps us in His holiness (John 17:15) as we remain in obedient subjection to Him (Romans 6:22). We must remain in union with Christ (John 15:4–5, 17:9). But true union with Christ is hardly understood or walked out today. The abysmal rift or chasm between head and heart, acting and being, masculine and feminine,[14] leads many to think that a more or less spiritualized perfectionism is what union with Christ means. When holiness is preached apart from understanding and walking in this union—in incarnational reality—legalism is the result. Although ample lip service will have been given to grace, legalism will be there, even though in modified doses.

Where there is legalism, there is always pride. We will have that spiritualized perfectionism whereby we say, "I am by my own striving and goodness keeping the law." We forget Paul's words to the effect that when "the law revived, I died."

We can teach holiness without placing ourselves in jeopardy only so long as we realize that the godlessness of the wicked is set over and against the goodness of God and never the righteousness or holiness of the godly. Only in union with Him, listening to Him and carrying out His orders, are we holy. Any substitute for this leaves us without the knowledge of ourselves as prideful sinner as well as saint.

We are all grievously tarred with the same brush. We all have that within us that wants to remain separate, to be holy by keeping the law perfectly. In effect we want to be God. We want to carry Christ's banner—but in this age of individualism we only want to carry it if it has our name and imprint on it. We want to be in control; we want to bring others to their knees in admiration and submission. This pride is in every human heart. We tip over into evil the moment we forget to confess the tyrant within and acknowledge that our holiness is at every moment Another's: it is incarnational.

Jesus not only gives purity of heart, but Jesus is our purity of heart: "God has made Him to be our righteousness."[15]

Those who treasure holiness and produce its fruits are the poor in spirit, the humble of the earth. They are fond of the Jesus

Prayer. In one way or another they pray it over and over: "Lord Jesus Christ, Son of God, have mercy on me a sinner." They are quick to acknowledge their pride and lack of humility, repenting of it daily.

Without holiness we will not see God. That is what the Scriptures teach. Holiness is a precious commodity. It is commanded by God, it is His characteristic, and He Himself effects it in his people. To preach the gospel is to teach the way of holiness (Isaiah 35:8), and apart from holiness there is no true worship of God (Psalm 24:4). There is nothing on earth more wonderful and healing than to be in the midst of a people who truly, and with all their hearts, worship the living God.

Holiness is both a quality we are given and a way. It is the way of remaining in Christ, of walking in the presence of God. Knowledge of the law is good and necessary. But to preach the law apart from teaching the walk in the Spirit leaves the flock with what they ought to do, yet without the power to do it. Legalism is a foe of holiness because it omits incarnational reality. It can never free us to walk in the Spirit.

As we have seen, neognostic listening, churchism, sexual permissiveness, the denial of sin and evil, the vice of sentimentality, and misunderstood holiness are all infections that are spreading throughout the body of Christ. They all result from listening that is horizontal instead of vertical. To become free of these infections we must repent and look to the One who sends us wisdom from above.

Living Water

The poor and needy search for water,
   but there is none;
   their tongues are parched with thirst.
But I the LORD will answer them;
   I, the God of Israel, will not forsake them.

I will make rivers flow on barren heights,
   and springs within the valleys.
I will turn the desert into pools of water,
   and the parched ground into springs (Isaiah 41:17–18).

As a people who have prayed and ministered together over the years, my prayer partners and I have known what the Psalmist knew, praying with him:

O LORD, you preserve both man and beast. . . .
They feast on the abundance of your house;
   you give them drink from your river of delights.
For with you is the fountain of life;
   in your light we see light (Psalm 36:6b, 8–9).

Connie Boerner's wonderful hymn, "Flow, O Mighty Holy River," is one we sing often. We, who have received from the river of God's delights, pass it on. Connie was inspired to write this hymn as we on the PCM team were preparing for ministry in England. She had been interceding for England and the Christians in the Isles when, in a moment full of God's presence, she saw the Lord interceding with her. He was singing her intercessions before the throne of the Father.

Flow, O Mighty Holy River

Flow, O mighty Holy River.
Flow in measure great and strong.
Hold not back Thy generous blessing,
Flood this desert with Thy song.

Parched and arid, hear the crying
Of Thy barren broken church.
Bring revival to the dying,
Quench the aching of their thirst.

Once again, release Thy Floodgate,
Shower Heaven's fruitful touch,
Till the earth, appeased, rejoicing,
Rings the message of Thy Love.

Flow, O mighty Holy River.
Flow in measure great and strong.
Hold not back Thy generous blessing,
Flood this desert with Thy song.[1]

Needless to say, we sang this with great fervor and blessing when we were in England in 1989 and have done so ever since.

We have heard Christ say to us, even as he spoke to the Samaritan woman at the well:

> If you knew the gift of God and who it is that asks you for a drink, you would have asked him and he would have given you *living water*. . . . Everyone who drinks this water will be thirsty again, but whoever drinks the water I give him will never thirst. Indeed, the water I give him will become in him a spring of water welling up to *eternal life* (John 4:10, 13–14, emphasis mine).

And we have understood, as Elizabeth Goudge in *The Scent of Water* did, the way the terms *living water*, *eternal life*, and *Spirit* come together, one metaphor coalescing into another, in the words our Lord speaks to us. In the death scene of a Christian (see "Preparing for Death and Judgment" in chapter 5), Miss Goudge wonderfully imagines the living water as flooding the room where a dying woman lay, *eternal life* like a tide of gold, and the "light of a marvelous sunset" upon which the dying woman "sailed out on *living water.*"

After speaking deeply into the life of the Samaritan woman, Jesus spoke the same truths again to the larger crowds who followed him. The Apostle John, now with the benefit of hindsight, interprets His meaning in the light of Pentecost and the pouring out of the *Spirit* upon the faithful:

> "If anyone is thirsty let him come to me and drink. Whoever believes in me, as the Scripture has said, streams of living water will flow from within him." By this he meant the Spirit, whom those who believed in him were later to receive (John 7:37–39).

It is good to end a book on listening prayer with a brief meditation on Christ, our Lord, as the free-flowing fountain of life. In waiting on Him we receive. As those early Christians heard and followed through on Christ's commands, so have we. We have waited on Him and received the promise:

> "Do not leave Jerusalem, but wait for the gift my Father promised, which you have heard me speak about. For John baptized with water, but in a few days you will be baptized with the Holy Spirit. . . . You will receive power when the Holy Spirit comes on you; and you will be my witnesses in Jerusalem, and in all Judea and Samaria, and to the ends of the earth." After he said this, he was taken up before their very eyes, and a cloud hid him from their sight (Acts 1:4–5, 8–9).

Infinitely beyond what we can fathom or even begin to express, to live is to receive new life from Christ. We "live and move and have our being" in Him (Acts 17:28). We are empowered for the work of the kingdom. Yet, over and over again, sadly, we fallen ones forsake our own lives:

My people have committed two sins: They have forsaken me, the
spring of living water, and have dug their own cisterns, broken cisterns that cannot hold water (Jeremiah 2:13).

It is my hope that the life of prayer, as we have touched on in
this book, will encourage many to ask for and receive a mighty
baptism in Christ's Spirit as well as many a subsequent infilling
and renewing in this same Holy Spirit. I invite you to pray the following prayer, which invokes the Spirit of the Lord:

Come, Holy Spirit, come.
Pour the living water of Your presence
on the thirsty ground of my heart.

Make rivers of living water flow
on the barren heights of my soul,
and springs well up within all its valleys.

I would receive power, Lord Jesus Christ, to be your witness
at home and throughout the earth.
Be Thou in me the fountain of living water,
springing up unto everlasting life.

You have qualified me, Holy Father, to share in the inheritance
of the saints in the kingdom of light.
You have rescued me from the dominion of darkness
and brought me into the kingdom of Your dear Son
in whom I have redemption
the forgiveness of sins (Colossians 1).
You have set Your seal upon me
Your Spirit in my heart as a deposit,
guaranteeing what is to come.
In Christ, I stand firm (2 Corinthians 1:21–22).
For my adoption in You, I give you thanks.
For this I praise your holy, gracious name.

And I praise You as the One who sends forth Your Spirit
upon those who trust in Your name:
"Thou the anointing Spirit art
Who Doest thy sev'n-fold gifts impart."[2]

I ask You now for the baptism of the Holy Spirit,
and a full freedom to move in the power of your Spirit
to the glory of your Name and the advancement of Your kingdom.
I know, Lord, that the day is coming when
"the earth will be filled with the knowledge of the glory
of the LORD, as the waters cover the sea" (Hebrews 2:14).
I rejoice in this, and ask that even now, Your Spirit
will fill me, cover me, and clothe me in this way.
I ask, also, for the grace and strength to so walk before You
that Your Holy Spirit will in no way be grieved or offended,
but will remain upon me; be ever pleased to rest upon me.

Father, for this baptism of Your Spirit,
one that will continue to well up from within me
and flow out through me,
I give you thanks in advance.

It is in Jesus' holy name that I pray and receive this blessing. Amen.

We are equipped to wait upon the Lord for the healing word
He always speaks by first waiting on Him for this divine gift. Of
this experience, R. A. Torrey rightly says, ". . . It is quite possible
to have something, yes much, of the Spirit's presence and work
in the heart and yet come short of that special fullness and work
known in the Bible as the Baptism or Filling with the Holy Spirit."[3]
But there are, as the Scriptures and our own experience plainly
show, fresh infillings of the Spirit for which we are to petition: "As
new emergencies of service arise, there must be new fillings with
the Spirit."[4] "Come, Holy Spirit, come, fill me anew" surely ranks
among the most frequent petitions found in my journals, now
ranging back over a period of over thirty-six years.
I am always taken aback at the loss Christians experience
whose theological prejudices hold them back from praying
important prayers such as these. R. E. O. White, lamenting the
theological debates that give rise to these misshapen under-
standings, writes:

Differing exegesis and theological debate must not be allowed to
obscure the primary truth: that the Spirit of the living Christ seeks

to enrich, enable, empower, and use Christians in every generation. The spiritual significance of apostolic baptism and of that
prevalent in the modern church is so different that for most Christians the "fullness of the Spirit" will be an experience long subsequent to baptism. But how we describe the experience is less
important than that we open mind, heart, and will to the power
and joy which the Spirit offers to confer. The contemporary church
and the modern world sadly need Christians baptized with the
Spirit.[5]

Several of us who have been with the PCM team from its inception are growing older. We are grandparents now. As for myself,
I feel like Job in his latter days—blessed with a greatly expanded
family. Grown grandchildren, so splendid and effective in Christ,
now stand with me in ministry together with the most incredible spiritual sons and daughters I could have ever hoped for. The
ministry is passed on to them, and I see it working out in ever
widening rivers and in exciting new ways. My cup overflows.

Even though some of us are older, however, we may yet see
something of *that Day* of which the Scriptures speak. The signs
are increasing. In that "unique day, without daytime or night-
time—a day known to the LORD" (Zechariah 14:7)—the nations
will gather against Jerusalem only to find that God will make of
her an immovable rock, and that her leaders will acknowledge
the Lord (Zechariah 12). That will be the *Day* when God "will pour
out on the house of David and the inhabitants of Jerusalem a
spirit of grace and supplication. They will look on me, the one
they have pierced" (Zechariah 12:10); that day when "*a fountain
will be opened to the house of David* and the inhabitants of
Jerusalem, to cleanse them from sin and impurity (Zechariah
13:1; italics mine).

There are seeming indications that the veil is starting to lift—
from the eyes of many of God's people, Israel. When this happens, there will be a healing for the church that will surely almost
equal that of Israel's healing. I want to be part of proclaiming the
gospel in such a way that first, Christians deeply repent of their
sins against the Jews, and second, we receive such an anointing
of the Holy Spirit that we can be used of God in the lifting of the

veil. I want to be ready not only to proclaim that gospel but to stand in joy, cleansed and filled with the Spirit, when

> On that day his feet will stand on the Mount of Olives, east of Jerusalem, and the Mount of Olives will be split in two from east to west, forming a great valley, with half of the mountain moving north and half moving south. . . . Then the LORD my God will come, and all the holy ones with him (Zechariah 14:4, 5b).

> On that day living water will flow out from Jerusalem, half to the eastern sea and half to the western sea, in summer and in winter. The LORD will be king over the whole earth. On that day there will be one LORD, and his name the only name (Zechariah 14:8–9).

> On that day HOLY TO THE LORD will be inscribed on the bells of the horses. . . . And on that day there will no longer be a Canaanite [representing the immoral and unclean] in the house of the LORD Almighty (Zechariah 14:20–21).

In one of the great hymns of this our century, Christ is celebrated by a poet fated to live behind the Iron Curtain. The suffering he must have known as a Christian under those circumstances no doubt explains the profound depth of his poetic images. Here Christ is celebrated as "The Tree of Life." Once again one metaphor coalesces into another and we celebrate the life-giving tree as the Holy Cross as well.

1. There in God's garden stands the Tree of Wisdom, whose leaves hold forth the healing of the nations: Tree of all knowledge, Tree of all compassion, Tree of all beauty.
2. Its name is Jesus, name that says, "Our Savior!" There on its branches see the scars of suff'ring: see where the tendrils of our human selfhood feed on its life blood.
3. Thorns not his own are tangled in its foliage; our greed has starved it, our despite has choked it. Yet look! it lives! its grief has not destroyed it nor fire consumed it.
4. See how its branches reach to us in welcome; hear what the Voice says, "Come to me, ye weary! Give me your sickness, give me all your sorrow, I will give blessing."

5. This is my ending, this my resurrection; into your hand, Lord, I commit my spirit. This have I searched for; now I can possess it. This ground is holy.

6. All heav'n is singing, "Thanks to Christ whose Passion offers in mercy healing, strength and pardon. Peoples and nations, take it, take it freely!" Amen! My Master![6]

Truly "God has given us eternal life, and this life is in his Son" (1 John 5:11). To those who listen, the Son says:

> He who has an ear, let him hear what the Spirit says to the churches. To him who overcomes, I will give the right to eat from the tree of life, which is in the paradise of God (Revelation 2:7).

> Then the angel showed me the river of the water of life, as clear as crystal, flowing from the throne of God and of the Lamb down the middle of the great street of the city. On each side of the river stood the tree of life, bearing twelve crops of fruit, yielding its fruit every month. And the leaves of the tree are for the healing of the nations (Revelation 22:1–2).

Scripture References to Spiritual Battle
New International Version

Our Call to Fight the Good Fight

1 Timothy 1:18–19: Timothy, my son, I give you this instruction in keeping with the prophecies once made about you, so that by following them you may fight the good fight, holding on to faith and a good conscience. Some have rejected these and so have shipwrecked their faith.

1 Timothy 6:12: Fight the good fight of the faith. Take hold of the eternal life to which you were called when you made your good confession in the presence of many witnesses.

Jude 3: Dear friends, although I was very eager to write to you about the salvation we share, I felt I had to write and urge you to contend for the faith that was once for all entrusted to the saints.

We Fight against the World

John 16:33: "I have told you these things, so that in me you may have peace. In this world you will have trouble. But take heart! I have overcome the world."

1 John 5:4–5: For everyone born of God overcomes the world. This is the victory that has overcome the world, even our faith. Who is it that overcomes the world? Only he who believes that Jesus is the Son of God.

Against the Flesh

Romans 7:23: But I see another law at work in the members of my body, waging war against the law of my mind and making me a prisoner of the law of sin at work within my members.

1 Corinthians 9:25–27: Everyone who competes in the games goes into strict training. They do it to get a crown that will not last; but we do it to get a crown that will last forever. Therefore I do not run like a man running aimlessly; I do not fight like a man beating the air. No, I beat my body and make it my slave so that after I have preached to others, I myself will not be disqualified for the prize.

2 Corinthians 12:7: To keep me from becoming conceited because of these surpassingly great revelations, there was given me a thorn in my flesh, a messenger of Satan, to torment me.

1 Peter 2:11: Dear friends, I urge you, as aliens and strangers in the world, to abstain from sinful desires, which war against your soul.

Against Our Enemies

Psalm 38:19: Many are those who are my vigorous enemies; those who hate me without reason are numerous.

Psalm 56:2–4: My slanderers pursue me all day long; many are attacking me in their pride. When I am afraid, I will trust in you. In God, whose word I praise, in God I trust; I will not be afraid. What can mortal man do to me?

Psalm 59:3: See how they lie in wait for me! Fierce men conspire against me for no offense or sin of mine, O LORD.

Against the Devil

Genesis 3:15: "And I will put enmity between you and the woman, and between your offspring and hers; he will crush your head, and you will strike his heel."

2 Corinthians 2:11: . . . in order that Satan might not outwit us. For we are not unaware of his schemes.

James 4:7–10: Submit yourselves, then, to God. Resist the devil, and he will flee from you. Come near to God and he will come near to you. Wash your hands, you sinners, and purify your hearts, you double-minded. Grieve, mourn and wail. Change your laughter to mourning and your joy to gloom. Humble yourselves before the Lord, and he will lift you up.

Ephesians 6:12: For our struggle is not against flesh and blood, but against the rulers, against the authorities, against the powers of this dark world and against the spiritual forces of evil in the heavenly realms.

1 Peter 5:8–9: Be self-controlled and alert. Your enemy the devil prowls around like a roaring lion looking for someone to devour. Resist him, standing firm in the faith, because you know that your brothers throughout the world are undergoing the same kind of sufferings.

Revelation 12:17: Then the dragon was enraged at the woman and went off to make war against the rest of her offspring—those who obey God's commandments and hold to the testimony of Jesus.

Attributes Needed for Fighting the Good Fight

1 Corinthians 16:13: Be on your guard; stand firm in the faith; be men of courage; be strong.

Hebrews 10:23: Let us hold unswervingly to the hope we profess, for he who promised is faithful.

1 Corinthians 16:13–14: Be on your guard; stand firm in the faith; be men of courage; be strong. Do everything in love.

1 Thessalonians 5:6–8: So then, let us not be like others, who are asleep, but let us be alert and self-controlled. For those who sleep, sleep at night, and those who get drunk, get drunk at night. But since we belong to the day, let us be self-controlled, putting on faith and love as a breastplate, and the hope of salvation as a helmet.

2 Timothy 2:3, 10: Endure hardship with us like a good soldier of Christ Jesus. . . . Therefore I endure everything for the sake of the elect, that they too may obtain the salvation that is in Christ Jesus, with eternal glory.

1 Corinthians 9:25–27: Everyone who competes in the games goes into strict training. They do it to get a crown that will not last; but we do it to get a crown that will last forever. Therefore I do not run like a man running aimlessly; I do not fight like a man beating the air. No, I beat my body and make it my slave so that after I have preached to others, I myself will not be disqualified for the prize.

Psalm 27:1–3: The LORD is my light and my salvation—whom shall I fear? The LORD is the stronghold of my life—of whom shall I be afraid? When evil men advance against me to devour my flesh, when my enemies and my foes attack me, they will stumble and fall. Though an army besiege me, my heart will not fear; though war break out against me, even then will I be confident.

Psalm 35:1–3: Contend, O LORD, with those who contend with me; fight against those who fight against me. Take up shield and buckler; arise and come to my aid. Brandish spear and javelin against those who pursue me. Say to my soul, "I am your salvation."

God's Promises of Protection and Deliverance

Psalm 140:7: O Sovereign LORD, my strong deliverer, who shields my head in the day of battle. . .

2 Timothy 4:18: The Lord will rescue me from every evil attack and will bring me safely to his heavenly kingdom. To him be glory forever and ever. Amen.

Psalm 118:13: I was pushed back and about to fall, but the L<small>ORD</small> helped me.

Isaiah 41:13–14: "For I am the L<small>ORD</small>, your God, who takes hold of your right hand and says to you, Do not fear; I will help you. Do not be afraid, O worm Jacob, O little Israel, for I myself will help you," declares the L<small>ORD</small>, your Redeemer, the Holy One of Israel.

2 Corinthians 7:5–7: For when we came into Macedonia, this body of ours had no rest, but we were harassed at every turn—conflicts on the outside, fears within. But God, who comforts the downcast, comforted us by the coming of Titus, and not only by his coming but also by the comfort you had given him. He told us about your longing for me, your deep sorrow, your ardent concern for me, so that my joy was greater than ever.

Isaiah 41:11–12: "All who rage against you will surely be ashamed and disgraced; those who oppose you will be as nothing and perish. Though you search for your enemies, you will not find them. Those who wage war against you will be as nothing at all."

Isaiah 51:12: "I, even I, am he who comforts you. Who are you that you fear mortal men, the sons of men, who are but grass."

1 John 4:4: You, dear children, are from God and have overcome them, because the one who is in you is greater than the one who is in the world.

Psalm 20:2: May he send you help from the sanctuary and grant you support from Zion.

Psalm 27:14: Wait for the L<small>ORD</small>; be strong and take heart and wait for the L<small>ORD</small>.

Isaiah 41:10: So do not fear, for I am with you; do not be dismayed, for I am your God. I will strengthen you and help you; I will uphold you with my righteous right hand.

2 Corinthians 12:9: But he said to me, "My grace is sufficient for you, for my power is made perfect in weakness." Therefore I will boast all the more gladly about my weaknesses, so that Christ's power may rest on me.

2 Timothy 4:17: But the Lord stood at my side and gave me strength, so that through me the message might be fully proclaimed and all the Gentiles might hear it. And I was delivered from the lion's mouth.

Excerpts from
The Secret of Guidance
F. B. Meyer

ay we give a few suggestions as to knowing the way in which our Father would have us walk, and the work He would have us do? The importance of the subject cannot be exaggerated; so much of our power and peace consist in knowing this.

The manna only falls where the cloudy pillar broods. If we are precisely where our heavenly Father would have us be, we are perfectly sure that He will provide food and raiment, and everything beside. When He sends His servants to Cherith, He will make even the ravens to bring them food.

How much of our Christian work has been abortive because we have persisted in initiating it for ourselves, instead of ascertaining what God was doing, and where He would have us be. We dream bright dreams of success; we try to command it, and call to our aid all kinds of expedients and at last we turn back, disheartened and ashamed. None of this would have come about if only we had been, from the first, under God's unerring guidance. He might test us, but He could not allow us to make mistakes.

Naturally, the child of God, longing to know his Father's will, turns to the Sacred Book and refreshes his confidence by noticing how in all ages God has guided those who dared to trust Him up to the very hilt, but who at times must have been as perplexed as we often are. We know how Abraham left kindred and country, and started with no other guide than God across the trackless desert to a land which he knew not. We know how for forty years the Israelites were led through the Peninsula of Sinai, with its labyrinths of red sandstone and its wastes of sand. Joshua too, in entering the Land of Promise, was able to cope with the difficulties of an unknown region, and to overcome great and warlike nations, because he looked to the Captain of the Lord's hosts, who ever leads to victory. In the early Church the Apostles were able to thread their way through the most difficult questions and to solve the most perplexing problems, laying down principles which will guide the Church to the end of time; and this because it was revealed to them as to what they should do and say by the Holy Spirit.

The Promises for Guidance Are Unmistakable

Ps. 32:8. "I will instruct thee and teach thee in the way which thou shalt go." This is God's distinct assurance to those whose transgressions are forgiven, and whose sins are covered, and who are more quick to notice the symptoms of His will than horse or mule to feel the bit.

Prov. 3:6. "In all thy ways acknowledge him, and he shall direct (or make plain) thy paths." A sure word, on which we may rest, if only we fulfil the previous conditions of trusting with all our heart, and of not leaning to our own understanding.

Isa. 58:11. "The Lord shall guide thee continually." It is impossible to think that He could guide us at all if He did not guide us always.

John 8:12. "I am the light of the world: he that followeth me shall not walk in darkness, but shall have the light of life." The Master promises to be to all faithful souls, in their pilgrimage to the City of God, what the cloudy pillar was to the Children of Israel on their march to the Land of Promise.

These are but specimens. And yet it may appear to some tested heart, as if everyone mentioned in the Word of God was helped, but they themselves. They seem to have stood before some perplexing problem, face to face with life's mysteries, eagerly longing to know what to do, but no angel has come to tell them, and no iron gate has opened to them in the prison house of circumstances.

Some lay the blame on their own stupidity. They feel they cannot catch God's meaning, which would be clear to others. They are so nervous of doing wrong that they cannot learn clearly what is right. "Who is blind, but my servant? or deaf, as my messenger that I sent?" You, who are weary and perplexed, believe in the great love of God, and cast yourselves upon it, sure that He will come down to your ignorance, and suit Himself to your needs.

There are certain practical directions which we must heed in order that we may be led into the mind of the Lord.

1. Our Motives Must Be Pure

"When thine eye is single, thy whole body also is full of light." Luke 11:34. If we have been in darkness lately, perhaps this passage will point the reason. Your eye has not been single. There has been some obliquity of vision—a spiritual squint; and this has hindered from discerning indications of God's will, which otherwise had been as clear as noonday.

When by the grace of God we have been delivered from the grosser forms of sin, we are still liable to the subtle forms of self even in our holiest hours. It poisons our motives. It turns the spirit from its holy purpose.

So long as there is some thought of personal advantage, some idea of acquiring the praise of men, some aim at self-aggrandisement, it will be impossible to find out God's purpose concerning us. The door must be shut against all these if we would hear the Still Small Voice. Ask the Holy Spirit to give you the single eye, and to inspire in your heart one aim alone: that which animated our Lord and enabled Him to cry as He reviewed His life, "I have glorified thee on the earth." Then our "whole body shall be full of light, having no part dark, as when the bright shining of a candle doth give light."

2. Our Will Must Be Surrendered

"My judgment is just; because I seek not mine own will, but the will of the Father which hath sent me." John 5:30. This is the secret which Jesus not only practised but taught. In one form or another He was constantly insisting on a surrendered will as the key to perfect knowledge. "If any man will do his will, he shall know."

There is all the difference between a will which is extinguished and one which is surrendered. God does not demand that our wills should be crushed out like the sinews of a fakir's unused arms; He only asks that we should say "Yes" to Him. Pliant to Him as the willow twig in the practised hand.

It is for lack of this that we so often miss the guidance that we seek. There is a secret controversy between our will and God's. And we shall never be right till we let Him take, and break and make us. If you are not willing, confess that you are willing to be made willing. Hand yourself over to Him to work in you to will and to do of His own good pleasure.

3. We Must Seek Information for Our Mind

This is certainly the next step. God has given us these wonderful faculties of brain power, and He will not ignore them. In grace He will not cancel the action of any of His marvellous bestowments, but He uses them for the communication of His purposes and thoughts. We have no need to run hither and thither to ask our friends what we ought to do, but there is no harm in taking pains to gather all reliable information on which the flame of holy thought and consecrated purpose may feed and grow strong, it is for us ultimately to decide as God shall teach us, but His voice may come to us through the voice of sanctified common sense, acting on the materials we have collected. But for the most part God will speak in the results of deliberate consideration, weighing and balancing the *pros* and *cons*.

When Peter was shut up in prison, and could not possibly extricate himself, an angel was sent to do for him what he could not do for himself; but when they had passed through a street or two of the city, the angel left him to consider the matter for himself. Thus God treats us still. He will dictate a miraculous course by miraculous methods, but when the ordinary light of reason is adequate to the task, He will leave us to act as occasion may serve.

4. We Must Be Much in Prayer for Guidance

The Psalms are full of earnest pleadings for clear direction: "Show me thy way, O Lord, lead me in a plain path, because of mine enemies." It is the law of God's house that His children should ask for what they want. "If any of you lack wisdom, let him ask of God, that giveth to all men liberally, and upbraideth not."

In a time of change and crisis, we need to be much in prayer, not only on our knees, but in that form of inward prayer, in which the spirit is constantly offering itself up to God, asking to be shown His will. Wrapt in prayer like this the trustful believer may tread the deck of the ocean steamer night after night, sure that He who points the stars in their courses will not fail to direct the soul which has no other aim than to do His will.

5. We Must Wait the Gradual Unfolding of God's Plan in Providence

God's impressions within and His Word without are always corroborated by His Providence around, and we should quietly wait until these three focus into one point. Sometimes it looks as if we are bound to act. Everyone says we must do something; and indeed things seem to have reached so desperate a pitch that we must. Behind are the Egyptians; right and left are inaccessible precipices; before is the sea. It is not easy at such times to stand still and see the salvation of God; but we must. When Saul compelled himself and offered sacrifice, because he thought Samuel was too late in coming, he made the great mistake of his life.

God may delay to come in the guise of His providence. There was delay ere Sennacherib's host lay like withered leaves around the Holy City. There was delay ere Jesus came walking on the sea in the early dawn, or hastened to raise Lazarus. He stays long enough to test the patience of faith, but not a moment behind the extreme hour of need. It is very remarkable how God guides us by circumstances. At one moment the way may seem utterly blocked, and then shortly afterwards some trivial incident occurs, which might not seem much to others, but which to encourage our soul to wait only upon God till it is given. Let us cultivate the meekness which He will guide in judgment, and seek to be quick of understanding that we may see the least sign of His will. Let us stand with girded loins and burning lamps, that we may be prompt to obey. Those servants are blessed and they shall be led by a right way to the golden city of the saints.

APPENDIX *C*

Prayer of Repentance to Break with Churchism
The Church of the Resurrection of Illinois

Leader:	Lord Jesus Christ, we come before you in praise and thanksgiving. Come Holy Spirit, and hear the prayers of your people. Gracious Father, we pray for your church. Fill it with all truth. Where it is corrupt, purify it; where it is in error, direct it; where in any thing it is amiss, reform it; where it is in want, provide for it; where it is divided, reunite it; where it is right, strengthen it; for the sake of Jesus Christ Your Son, our Savior. Amen.
Leader:	We confess to you the sins of our world, our culture, and the church:
People:	Open our hearts, O God, so we may truly and humbly confess our sins.
Leader:	For our arrogance and rebellion in turning away from You;
People:	Lord, we confess this as sin and we ask for Your mercy.
Leader:	For our disregard for Your grace revealed in Jesus Christ, Your Son;
People:	Lord, we confess this as sin and we ask for Your mercy.
Leader:	For our failure to proclaim Your Word in power and to carry Your gospel to the ends of the earth;
People:	Lord, we confess this as sin and we ask for Your mercy.
Leader:	For our prideful rejection of the truths revealed to us in Scripture;
People:	Lord, we confess this as sin and we ask for Your mercy.
Leader:	For our oppression of the weak and our failure to love our neighbors as ourselves;

People:	Lord, we confess this as sin and we ask for Your mercy.
Leader:	For our failure to protect the lives of the poor, the innocent, and the unborn;
People:	Lord, we confess this as sin and we ask for Your mercy.
Leader:	For our abuse and exploitation of Your creation;
People:	Lord, we confess this as sin and we ask for Your mercy.
Leader:	For our materialistic worship of the creature, rather than the Creator;
People:	Lord, we confess this as sin and we ask for Your mercy.
Leader:	For our idolatrous efforts to satisfy our needs through addiction, entertainment, and self-indulgence;
People:	Lord, we confess this as sin and we ask for Your mercy.
Leader:	For our attempts to justify our sin by mingling the worship of a Holy God with unholy idols;
People:	Lord, we confess this as sin and we ask for Your mercy.
Leader:	For our tolerance of sexual promiscuity, adultery, and homosexual behavior;
People:	Lord, we confess this as sin and we ask for Your mercy.
Leader:	For our lack of faith and our weakness in proclaiming Your goodness, mercy, and healing power;
People:	Lord, we confess this as sin and we ask for Your mercy.
Leader:	For our failure to forgive others as we have been forgiven;
People:	Lord, we confess this as sin and we ask for Your mercy.
Leader: (silence)	We pray to you for the forgiveness of our sins.
People:	We humble ourselves before You, owning our sin and our responsibility. For the sake of the shed blood of Jesus Christ Your Son, pour out on us Your grace and forgiveness; that we may delight in Your will, and walk in Your ways, to the glory of Your name. Amen.
Celebrant:	Almighty God, have mercy on you, forgive you all your sins through our Lord Jesus Christ, cleanse you by His grace, empower you to obey Him, and by the indwelling of His Holy Spirit, keep you in eternal life. Amen.
Leader:	We pray for the church of Jesus Christ here and around the world: For a renewed vision of the holiness of God;
People:	That Your church may be found pure and spotless at the last day.
Leader:	For the unity of Your body;
People:	That Your love may be manifest to the world.
Leader:	For the raising up of courageous men and women as humble servants of Jesus Christ;
People:	That Your Kingdom may extend throughout the earth.
Leader:	For the power to proclaim the absolute sufficiency of Christ's cross;
People:	That all nations may be reconciled to God.
Leader:	For the conversion of Your enemies, O God;

People: May those who hate You fall in adoration before Your throne.
Leader: We pray that the fruit of Your Holy Spirit be made manifest in this
            congregation;
People: Form in us the body of Christ.
Leader: We will exalt You, O God, our King;
People: And praise Your name forever and ever.

Notes

Introduction

1. For more on the deep rift between the more rational ways of knowing and the more intuitive, see my book *The Healing Presence* (Wheaton, Ill.: Crossway, 1989), especially chapters 10 and 11.

Chapter 1: The Simple How-to's

1. Mother Basilea Schlink, *More Precious Than Gold* (Carol Stream, Ill.: Creation House, 1978), p. 221, December 29.

2. Available from Barbour and Co, Inc., 164 Mill Street, Westwood, NJ 07675.

Chapter 2: The Word

1. There is an important place for Bible study per se, a time when we bring our best intellectual efforts to bear on what the Scriptures teach. In this activity, we are not "praying" the Scriptures. Rather we are engaged in the important activity of learning sound doctrine, which helps us discern the difference between Judeo-Christian reality and the current materialistic and gnostic (pagan) worldviews that are in opposition to it. The more learned we are in sound doctrine, the greater our understanding of the Scriptures will be, and hence, of our listening to God through them.

2. John Gaynor Banks, *The Master and the Disciple* (St. Paul, Minn.: Macalaster Park Publishing, 1954), p. 94, July 15.

3. Ibid., p. 149, December 9.

Chapter 3: Praise and Thanksgiving

1. F. B. Meyer, *Our Daily Walk* (Grand Rapids, Mich.: Zondervan, 1961), p. 381.

2. Samuel J. Mikolaski, ed., *The Creative Theology of P. T. Forsyth* (Grand Rapids, Mich.: Eerdmans, 1969), pp. 55–56.

3. C. S. Lewis, *Miracles* (London: Collins, 1963), p. 112.

4. John Gaynor Banks, *The Master and the Disciple* (St. Paul, Minn.: Macalaster Park Publishing, 1954), p. 22.

5. Lewis, *Miracles*, p. 115.

6. See my book *Real Presence: The Christian Worldview of C. S. Lewis as Incarnational Reality* (Wheaton, Ill.: Crossway, 1988).

7. "Praise My Soul the King of Heaven," *The Hymnal 1940* (New York: The Church Pension Fund, 1940), p. 282.

8. Dallas Willard, "Be Imitators of Christ," Institute of Clinical Theology, 29–30 May 1992, Regent University, Virginia Beach, Va.

9. Ibid.

10. See Zechariah 12:10, Romans 8:15, and Galatians 4:6.

11. This is one more example of the fact that every occult manifestation of the supernatural is merely a coarse demonic imitation of a true one.

12. See Isaiah 61:3, 10.

13. For more on this see *The Healing Presence*, pp. 94 ff; *Real Presence*, chapter 8.

14. Elizabeth Goudge, *The Bird and the Tree* (London: Gerald Duckworth, 1954), pp. 226–27.

15. C. S. Lewis, *Mere Christianity* (New York: Macmillan, 1960), p. 116.

16. According to the *Evangelical Dictionary of Theology*, Walter L. Elwell, ed. (Grand Rapids, Mich.: Baker, 1984), pp. 57–58, the word "antinomianism" comes from the Greek *anti* (against) and *nomos* (law) and refers to the doctrine that it is not necessary for Christians to preach and/or obey the moral law of the Old Testament. The New Testament writers were concerned with various gnostic forms of these heretical teachings.

17. John A. Mackay, *Christian Reality and Appearance* (Richmond, Va.: John Knox Press, 1969), p. 13.

18. Quoted in *The Character Dimension of Leadership* (Burke, Va.: The Trinity Forum, 1993), p. vii.

Chapter 4: Intercession

1. Donald G. Bloesch in Walter A. Elwell, ed., *The Evangelical Dictionary of Theology* (Grand Rapids, Mich.: Baker, 1986), p. 867.

2. Agnes Sanford was a great woman of prayer, and her books are filled with the principles of prayer. Chapters 14 and 15 of her book, *The Healing Light* (St. Paul, Minn.: Macalaster Park Publishing, 1964) are splendid on the matter of global intercession.

3. *The Best of A. W. Tozer*, (Grand Rapids, Mich.: Baker, 1978), p. 37.

4. For more on this, read *The Healing Presence*, chapter 12, "Introspection versus True Imagination" and *Real Presence: The Christian Worldview of C. S. Lewis as Incarnational Reality*, pp. 66–74.

5. See Dallas Willard, *The Spirit of the Disciplines* (San Francisco: HarperSanFrancisco, 1988).

6. For an excellent overview of the place and need for ascetics in the Christian life, as well as the understanding of how we lost these important concepts to begin with, see chapter 7 of Dr. Willard's book.

7. For more on this, see *The Healing Presence*, pp. 184–192.

8. For more information on the practice of substitution, see "Incarnational Reality: The Key to Carrying the Cross," chapter 13 of *The Healing Presence*. Pages 184–192 are specifically on the matter of wrongful substitution. The teaching on it is placed in the context of Christ's substitution for us, and of what Christian suffering really is.

9. *New International Version Study Bible* (Grand Rapids, Mich.: Zondervan, 1985), p. 12.

10. Even when there is a demonic infestation, the demons are most often not dislodged through this manner of "prayer," or they will return because the sin or wound has not been adequately dealt with. We must learn how to discern (move in the authentic gift of discerning of spirits) the presence of the demonic and learn to bring the finger of God to bear on it. The demonic entity cannot stand the light and has to flee at our command. God in His mercy answers all kinds of "misinformed" prayer, but we as Christians are called to wisdom and to understand the human soul.

11. C. S. Lewis, *Screwtape Letters* (New York: Macmillan, 1962), p. 3.

12. A theology derived from E. W. Kenyon.

13. I know and have ministered to people who have come up with entire mythologies of evil powers, and these are spun out of listening to the demons whose presence they learned to practice. They were, therefore, filled with every evil superstition and fear. Some, so deceived, eventually were into a form of "Christianized" witchcraft. Everyone and everything they could not control was eventually named demonic and as "witchcraft," and a demonic myth was then spun around the unfortunate persons who fell prey to them. Deluded persons such as these can become amateur cult hunters, branding true servants of God as acting in the power of demons. Their slander of the servants of God is always of the most destructive kind.

14. Donald Coggin, *The Prayers of the New Testament* (London: Hodder and Stoughton, 1967), p. 19.

15. F. B. Meyer, *Our Daily Walk* (Grand Rapids, Mich.: Zondervan, 1961), October 1, p. 296. See also Ephesians 3:17–19.

Chapter 5: Petition

1. Donald G. Bloesch in Walter A. Elwell, ed., *The Evangelical Dictionary of Theology* (Grand Rapids, Mich.: Baker, 1986), p. 867.

2. Ibid.

3. Ibid.

4. John Gaynor Banks, *The Master and the Disciple* (St. Paul, Minn.: Macalaster Park Publishing, 1954), p. 5.

5. F. B. Meyer, *Our Daily Walk* (Grand Rapids, Mich.: Zondervan, 1961), May 28.

6. Ibid., May 16.

7. I call it *defect* as well as sin because this penchant showed up in me very early. By nine months of age my father had to build a screen over my crib (which had the usual high sides) to keep me from climbing out, and at age eighteen months I managed to escape from an office manager (in charge of me while my Mother paid our insurance), and immediately climbed out the fifth story window of that building and onto a fire-escape ladder. This odd kind of precociousness that outran natural caution at each stage of my development therefore seemed not only sin but something to which I was inherently vulnerable. My father had suffered these same characteristics, and we can trace this sort of thing back to the generation preceding him.

8. F. B. Meyer, *The Secret of Guidance* (Minneapolis, Minn.: Bethany Fellowship, 1978), p. 15. See Appendix B for a fuller excerpt.

9. Elizabeth Goudge, *The Scent of Water* (New York: Pyramid Books, 1975), pp. 7–8.

10. This is so important that I have devoted an entire chapter—chapter 9—of *Restoring the Christian Soul Through Healing Prayer* (Wheaton, Ill.: Crossway, 1991) to it.

11. Recommended Reading: F. B. Meyer, *Meet for the Master's Use*, chapters 5 and 6 on receiving from God.

12. See "Creative Power," chapter 5 of *The Healing Presence* (Wheaton, Ill.: Crossway, 1989).

13. Those who have misused their imaginations in the past through occult activities, or who have experienced severe abuse by others that has resulted in an imagination subject to fears and an eruption of repressed and distorted imagery, need healing and often deliverance of the picture-making faculty of the mind. They need this before they can pray aright and receive the true imagination from the Lord. The answer is not to repress and deny this capacity of both the intuitive and conscious (intellectual) faculties of the mind, but to purify it in order that that which is from God may be received, and thereby that which is amiss (the carnal or even demonic) be discerned.

Chapter 6: Forgiveness

1. "Temptation," in Walter L. Elwell, ed. *The Evangelical Dictionary of Theology* (Grand Rapids, Mich.: Baker, 1986), p. 1072; emphasis mine.

2. Oswald Chambers, *My Utmost for His Highest* (New York: Dodd, Mead, 1935), April 19, p. 110.

3. See *The Healing Presence*, Chapter 13, "Incarnational Reality: The Key to Carrying the Cross," "What it Means to Carry the Cross," pp. 167, 177.

4. *New International Version Study Bible* (Grand Rapids, Mich.: Zondervan, 1985) note on 1 Peter 1:5.

5. Dan B. Allender and Tremper Longman, *Bold Love* (Colorado Springs, Colo: NavPress, 1992), p. 243.

6. For examples of forgiving the "unforgivable," see *Restoring the Christian Soul*, pp. 84–93.

7. For more on this see *Restoring the Christian Soul*, chapter 7 (especially pages 92–93) and chapter 10, pages 153–54.

8. Allender and Longman, *Bold Love*, p. 243.

9. From M. Scott Peck, *The People of the Lie: The Hope for Healing Human Evil* (New York: Simon and Schuster, 1983), pp. 76–77: "Since the primary motive of the evil is disguise. . . . evil people tend to gravitate toward piety for the disguise and concealment it can offer them."

10. Ibid., p. 62.

11. Ibid., p. 69, her capitalization.

12. Ibid., p. 71.

13. Ibid., p. 72.

14. Ibid., p. 60.

15. Ibid., p. 73.

16. Ibid., p. 73.

17. Ibid., p. 74.

18. Ibid., p. 179.

19. See Mario Bergner, *Setting Love in Order* (Grand Rapids, Mich.: Baker, 1995). I also recommend chapter 10, "Loving an Evil Person" from *Bold Love* by Allender and Longman, and Peck's *The People of the Lie*.

20. Chambers, *My Utmost for His Highest*, p. 196.

21. Donald Bloesch, *Crumbling Foundations* (Grand Rapids, Mich.: Zondervan, 1984), p. 125.

22. Ibid.

23. C. S. Lewis, *The Problem of Pain* (New York: Macmillan, 1966), p. 28.

24. William Barclay, *The Gospel of Matthew* (Louisville, Ky.: Westminster John Knox, 1975), p. 318.

Chapter 8: Listening to God

1. See "Creative Power," Chapter 5 in *The Healing Presence*.
2. Thomas A. Smail, *The Forgotten Father* (London: Hodder and Stoughton, 1980), p. 28.
3. Ibid.
4. Oswald Chambers, *My Utmost for His Highest* (New York: Dodd, Mead, 1935), p. 358, December 23.
5. Smail, *The Forgotten Father*, p. 131.
6. C. S. Lewis, *Mere Christianity* (New York: Macmillan, 1960), p. 152.
7. C. S. Lewis, *The Problem of Pain* (New York: Macmillan, 1966), p. 139.
8. See my books *The Broken Image* (Wheaton, Ill.: Crossway, 1981) and *The Healing Presence*.
9. C. S. Lewis, *God in the Dock: Essays on Theology and Ethics* (Grand Rapids, Mich.: Eerdmans, 1970), pp. 159–60.
10. Lewis, *The Problem of Pain*, p. 89.
11. Smail, *The Forgotten Father*, p. 104, italics mine.
12. Ibid.
13. Ibid.

Chapter 9: Hindrances to Listening Prayer

1. For more on this, see my book *The Healing Presence* in its entirety, but especially Chapters 7 and 10, "The Terrible Schism in the Heart of Man." For a clear understanding of Descartes, and his dualism that ended by separating mind from soul and body, see William Barrett's book, *Death of the Soul: From Descartes to the Computer* (Garden City, N.Y.: Anchor, 1987).
2. Mr. Hunt painted two originals. One stands in St. Paul's Cathedral, London, and the other is at Keble College, Oxford.
3. The condition of being split, of looking at oneself analytically.
4. C. S. Lewis, *Surprised By Joy: The Shape of My Early Life* (New York: Harcourt, Brace and World, 1955), p. 71.
5. Ibid.
6. Ibid., p. 78.
7. Note how this differs from Jung's "active imagination."
8. We always ask the person what is being shown; we never suggest what, through the Holy Spirit, is happening in another's heart.
9. Oswald Chambers, *My Utmost for His Highest* (New York: Dodd, Mead, 1935), May 5.
10. R. A. Torrey, *The Baptism in the Holy Spirit* (Minneapolis, Minn.: Bethany House, 1972), a small but fine book, is recommended.
11. For more on this, see Romans 6:4–7, and chapter 10 of *Restoring the Christian Soul Through Healing Prayer*. See especially pp. 154–155.
12. Chambers, *My Utmost for His Highest*, p. 18.
13. Quoted in *Oswald Chambers: The Best from All His Books*, vol. 1 (Nashville: Oliver Nelson, 1987), p. 382.
14. Ibid., p. 381

15. C. S. Lewis, "First and Second Things" in *God in the Dock: Essays on Theology and Ethics* (Grand Rapids, Mich.: Eerdmans, 1970), p. 280.

16. P. T. Forsyth, *The Justification of God* (London: Independent Press, 1948), p. 117.

17. Chambers, *My Utmost for His Highest*, August 7.

18. Oswald Chambers, *Prayer: A Holy Occupation* (Grand Rapids, Mich.: Discovery House, 1992), p. 11.

19. Chambers, *My Utmost for His Highest*, August 7.

Chapter 10: Becoming Spiritually Mature through Listening to God

1. Henri M. Nouwen, "Silence, the Portable Cell," *Sojourners*, July 1980, p. 22.

2. For an excellent overview of the *spirituals*, See "Spiritual Gifts" in Walter A. Elwell, ed., *The Evangelical Dictionary of Theology* (Grand Rapids, Mich.: Baker, 1986).

3. William Barclay, *The Letters to the Galatians and the Ephesians*, The Daily Study Bible Series (Philadelphia, Penn.: Westminster, 1976), p. 127.

4. C. S. Lewis, *A Grief Observed* (New York: Bantam, 1976), p. 81.

5. See Dallas Willard, *In Search of Guidance* (San Francisco: HarperSan Francisco/Zondervan, 1993), pp. 51–52.

6. C. S. Lewis, *Letters to Malcolm: Chiefly on Prayer* (New York: Harcourt, Brace and World, 1963), p. 51.

7. Quoted in Dallas Willard, pp. 16–17; from *Victorious Living*, for Sunday of Week 41, (Nashville, Tenn.: Abingdon, 1983), p. 281.

8. Lewis, *Letters from Malcolm: Chiefly on Prayer*, p 50.

9. Willard, *In Search of Guidance*, p. 2.

10. Ibid., p. 3.

11. Leanne Payne, *Real Presence: The Christian Worldview of C. S. Lewis as Incarnational Reality*, pp. 131–132, quoting *The Oxford English Dictionary*, compact edition, s. v. "imagination."

12. See C. S. Lewis, "Dogma and the Universe," *God in the Dock: Essays on Theology and Ethics* (Grand Rapids, Mich.: Eerdmans, 1970).

13. Oswald Chambers, *My Utmost for His Highest* (New York: Dodd, Mead, 1935), February 11.

13. Ibid., February 10.

Chapter 11: Listening Prayer Is Friendship with God

1. Walter Hooper, ed., *Letters of C. S. Lewis to Arthur Greeves, (1914–1963)* (New York: Collier, 1979), December 21, 1941, p. 197.

2. Ibid., December 19, 1935, p. 477.

3. Oswald Chambers, *My Utmost for His Highest* (New York: Dodd, Mead, 1935), January 7.

4. C. S. Lewis, *The Four Loves* (San Diego: Harcourt Brace Jovanovich, 1960), p. 98.

5. There are, of course, immoral friendships, those based on common interests that are less than noble, good, beautiful, or holy.

6. Lewis, *The Four Loves*, p. 80.

7. See my book *Restoring the Christian Soul Through Healing Prayer* for much more on this.

8. Chambers, *My Utmost for His Highest*, January 7.

9. Ibid.

10. For more on this see chapter 4 of *The Healing Presence* (Wheaton, Ill.: Crossway, 1989), "Separation from the Presence: The Fall from God-consciousness into Self-consciousness."

11. Chambers, *My Utmost for His Highest*, March 24.

12. See the sections on denial of the evil in one's parents in Mario Bergner, *Setting Love in Order* (Grand Rapids, Mich.: Baker, 1995); see also chapter 10 in Dan B. Allender and Tremper Longman, *Bold Love* (Colorado Springs, Colo: NavPress, 1992).

13. For more on this see chapter 10 of *Bold Love*, "Loving an Evil Person."

14. This is extremely difficult to accomplish in an age and culture that has no place nor recognition for the strong, good, fathering man of integrity. Therefore there is no means of strengthening and affirming men in their duties as husbands and fathers.

15. Thomas A. Smail, *The Forgotten Father* (London: Hodder and Stoughton, 1980), p. 40.

Chapter 12: How God Speaks to His Children

1. Thomas A. Smail, *The Forgotten Father* (London: Hodder and Stoughton, 1980), p. 22.

2. For more on this, see *The Healing Presence*, pp. 87–94.

3. It was so awesome that I told very few people, knowing back then that it would be wrong for several reasons: it would not have been believed or understood, and therefore would bring no glory to God; it would have diminished my joy—I needed to hold this in my heart before God—in preparation for what He was about to do.

4. Dr. Jeffrey Satinover's book on dreams is forthcoming from Hamewith Books, an imprint of Baker Book House, Grand Rapids, Michigan. See also the appendix, "Listening to Our Dreams," in *The Broken Image*.

5. F. B. Meyer, *The Secret of Guidance* (Minneapolis, Minn.: Bethany Fellowship, 1978), p. 15.

6. Regarding the prayer of faith, I think Rev. Dr. Meyer's influence was second only to that of my mother who, as a teacher of the Word, was also a model of the joyful, believing Christian at prayer in the midst of any and all circumstances.

7. See Dallas Willard's excellent discussion of F. B. Meyer's "Three Lights" for determining what God wants us to do in *In Search of Guidance* (San Francisco: HarperSan Francisco/Zondervan, 1993), pp. 182 ff.

Chapter 13: The Need for Exhortation and Testing in Listening Prayer

1. C. S. Lewis, *The Problem of Pain* (New York: Macmillan, 1966), p. 67.

2. Dallas Willard, *In Search of Guidance* (San Francisco: HarperSan Francisco/Zondervan, 1993), p. 24.

3. Oswald Chambers, *My Utmost for His Highest* (New York: Dodd, Mead, 1935), February 14.

4. Ibid.

5. Ibid.

6. Chambers, *My Utmost for His Highest*, December 12.

7. F. B. Meyer, *Our Daily Walk* (Grand Rapids, Mich.: Zondervan, 1961), January 2.

8. Thomas à Kempis, *The Imitation of Christ* (Chicago: Moody, 1958), pp. 14, 16.

9. Chambers, *My Utmost for His Highest*, January 6.

10. Kempis, *The Imitation of Christ*, p. 14.

Chapter 14: What to Avoid in Listening Prayer: Neognostic Listening

1. Oswald Chambers, *My Utmost for His Highest* (New York: Dodd, Mead, 1935), March 16.

2. C. S. Lewis, *Letters to Malcolm: Chiefly on Prayer* (New York: Harcourt, Brace and World, 1963), p. 82.

3. Charlotte M. Mason, *Parents and Children*, vol. 2 (Wheaton, Ill.: Tyndale, 1989), p. 194.

4. Often heard today as the complaining and neglected female, "artist," "homosexual," or "race."

5. Mason, *Parents and Children*, p. 202.

6. See Eric Pollard's account of the fascist activities of the prominent homosexual organization ACT-UP in "Time to Give up Fascist Tactics," *Washington Blade,* 31 January 1992, p. 39.

Chapter 15: When Neognostic Listening Infects the Church

1. Samuel J. Mikolaski, ed., *The Creative Theology of P. T. Forsyth* (Grand Rapids, Mich.: Eerdmans, 1969), pp. 55–56.

2. For more on this see chapter 14 of *The Healing Presence*, "Renouncing False Gods and Appropriating the Holy."

3. For much more on this, read Dr. Jeffrey Satinover's fine lecture on gnosticism, now available as *The Empty Self: The Gnostic Foundations of Modern Identity* (Boone, N.C.: Hamewith Books, 1994).

4. C. S. Lewis, *A Preface to Paradise Lost* (London: Oxford, 1969).

5. John A. Mackay, *Christian Reality and Appearance* (Richmond, Va.: John Knox Press, 1969), p. 23.

6. Ibid.

7. Ibid., pp. 26–28.

8. Ibid., pp. 31–32.

9. Dan B. Allender and Tremper Longman, *Bold Love* (Colorado Springs, Colo: NavPress, 1992), p. 233.

10. M. Scott Peck, *The People of the Lie: The Hope for Healing Human Evil* (New York: Simon and Schuster, 1983), p. 74. This description is especially apt of the cult hunters described previously.

11. Mark Jefferson, "What is Wrong with Sentimentality?" in Robert B. Kruschwitz and Robert C. Roberts, eds., *The Virtues: Contemporary Essays on Moral Character* (Belmont, Calif.: Wadsworth, 1987), pp. 189–190, italics mine.

12. Ibid., p. 193.

13. Oswald Chambers, *My Utmost for His Highest* (New York: Dodd, Mead, 1935), p. 337.

14. A masculinized church such as we have today, one separated from the true feminine (that which can intuit the real, bow before it, and say with Mary "Be it unto me according to thy will") is a church that will invariably move forward through abstraction and activism. This means it will tend toward control and legalism on the one hand, or toward the hedonistic and heretical "wisdom" and knowledge of this world on the other. This is in contrast to becoming pregnant with God and thereby His characteristics: truth, goodness, holiness, and so on. The true masculine (the power to initiate, to act) must be on a continuum with the true feminine (power to respond to God immediately and obediently) in which case *being* itself is affirmed—we find the power to be. Then our doing

emerges out of our being, a being that is fraught with meaning because it is in listening obedience—union with God.

15. Peter Kreeft, *Back to Virtue* (San Francisco: Ignatius, 1992), p. 172.

Conclusion: *Living Water*

1. Recorded with Integrity-Hosanna on "Firm Foundation." © 1989 Connie Boerner Music, Jabez Productions. All rights reserved. Reprinted by permission.

2. From the hymn, *Veni Creator.*

3. See R. A. Torrey, *The Baptism in the Holy Spirit* (Minneapolis, Minn.: Bethany House, 1972).

4. Ibid., pp. 52–53.

5. Walter A. Elwell, ed., *The Evangelical Dictionary of Theology* (Grand Rapids, Mich.: Baker, 1986), p. 122. Besides Torrey's book, *Baptism in the Holy Spirit*, Thomas A. Smail's book, *Reflected Glory* (Grand Rapids, Mich.: Eerdmans, 1976) is recommended.

6. "The Tree of Life" by Pécselyi Kiràly Imre von, 1961, paraphrased by Erik Routley, 1974. Text paraphrase © 1976 by Hinshaw Music, Inc. Reprinted by permission.